Performing Antira
in Rhetoric, Writi ... cation

Across the Disciplines Books

Series Editor, Michael A. Pemberton

The Across the Disciplines Books series is closely tied to published themed issues of the online, open-access, peer-reviewed journal *Across the Disciplines.* In keeping with the editorial mission of *Across the Disciplines*, books in the series are devoted to language, learning, academic writing, and writing pedagogy in all their intellectual, political, social, and technological complexity.

The WAC Clearinghouse, Colorado State University Open Press, and University Press of Colorado are collaborating so that these books will be widely available through free digital distribution and low-cost print editions. The publishers and the series editors are committed to the principle that knowledge should freely circulate. We see the opportunities that new technologies have for further democratizing knowledge. And we see that to share the power of writing is to share the means for all to articulate their needs, interest, and learning into the great experiment of literacy.

Performing Antiracist Pedagogy in Rhetoric, Writing, and Communication

Edited by Frankie Condon and Vershawn Ashanti Young

The WAC Clearinghouse
wac.colostate.edu
Fort Collins, Colorado

University Press of Colorado
www.upcolorado.com
Boulder, Colorado

The WAC Clearinghouse, Fort Collins, Colorado 80523-1040
University Press of Colorado, Boulder, Colorado 80303

Printed in the United States of America

Library of Congress Cataloging-in-Publication Data

Names: Condon, Frankie, editor. | Young, Vershawn Ashanti, editor.
Title: Performing antiracist pedagogy in rhetoric, writing, and communication / edited by Frankie Condon and Vershawn Ashanti Young.
Description: Fort Collins, Colorado : The WAC Clearinghouse ; Boulder, Colorado : University Press of Colorado, [2016] | Series: Across the disciplines books | Includes bibliographical references.
Identifiers: LCCN 2016045186| ISBN 9781607326496 (pbk.) | ISBN 9781607326502 (ebook)
Subjects: LCSH: English language—Rhetoric—Study and teaching (Higher)—Social aspects—United States. | Report writing—Study and teaching (Higher)—Social aspects—United States. | Mass media—Study and teaching (Higher)—Social aspects—United States. | Anti-racism—Study and teaching (Higher)—United States.
Classification: LCC PE1405.U6 P385 2016 | DDC 808/.042089—dc23
LC record available at https://lccn.loc.gov/2016045186

Copyeditor: Brandy Bippes
Series Design: Tara Reeser
Book Design: Tara Reeser
Cover Art and Design: Malcolm Childers
Series Editor: Michael A. Pemberton

This book is printed on acid-free paper.

The WAC Clearinghouse supports teachers of writing across the disciplines. Hosted by Colorado State University, and supported by the Colorado State Univeristy Open Press, it brings together scholarly journals and book series as well as resources for teachers who use writing in their courses. This book is available in digital formats for free download at wac.colostate.edu.

Founded in 1965, the University Press of Colorado is a nonprofit cooperative publishing enterprise supported, in part, by Adams State University, Colorado State University, Fort Lewis College, Metropolitan State University of Denver, Regis University, University of Colorado, University of Northern Colorado, Utah State University, and Western State Colorado University. For more information, visit www.upcolorado.com.

This book is dedicated to R. Suzanne Van Meter
February 18, 1935–May 31, 2013
Mother, Teacher, Warrior

Contents

Acknowledgments

The work of antiracism is hard, especially when you're often witness to the oppression of others, and even more especially when you're not only witness but subject to racist practices. But what makes this all the more worse is when you have status and power in institutions with continuing legacies of oppressions, like schools. This is why I wish to acknowledge and thank each and every one of the contributors to this volume. They, like Frankie and me, are individuals who recognize that the work we do in academic institutions either will perpetuate the status quo built on legacies of racism, sexism, homophobia, and class domination (to name some obvious few), or intervene. I believe they have, as have Frankie and I, chosen to intervene in theoretical and practical ways.

I also wish to thank my friend, Frankie, who writes about our transracial connections stemming back to 2008 in her book *I Hope I Join the Band* (2012). She writes:

> It is a mark of the authenticity of the care that animates all sorts of relationships when this work feels joyful even in the hardest moments. In the case of transracial friendships, I think, that joy may develop more slowly, as we learn how to believe that we can lean toward one another without leaning unduly on one another: that together we can resist the power racism possesses to distort, subvert, and ultimately destroy relationships that transgress established racial order. (146)

Too many white people, I think, resist forging even casual friendships, let along deep ones, with people of color who challenge their established ways of thinking and being. And when some do forge relationships, they sometimes take a paternal or maternal stance toward their friends, even when those people of color are more accomplished or older than they are. It's a real trip. So I thank Frankie for sticking with the friendship for the sake of antiracist work, and for being willing to call out and also be called out, as we all should be.

Lastly, I wish to thank my lovely wife, Yulanda Young, who allows me to make time for work, as long as I make time for her. And I want to send out through these pages kisses and hopes to my youngest daughter, Ari Zhah Young, toward whom I hope the world will learn to be kind.

—Vershawn Ashanti Young

So far as I can tell, there is no finish line for the work of antiracism. There's no point at which anyone—at least not anyone I know—can legitimately claim to have conquered racism in their own lives or to have made a sufficient contribution to racial justice locally or globally to be legitimately done with the work. Because our ability to see ourselves and our relations, to know ourselves and the effects of our actions on others is always limited, always partial, we need one another. We need companions, guides, and friends who will both challenge us and stay with us as we labor to learn together the nature of the work before us in the most everyday as well as the most extraordinary moments of our lives.

I am exceedingly grateful to those who have graced my life and work with their presence, their patience, their dedication, and their joy. I am grateful to the writers whose work composes this volume, to our editor, Michael Pemberton, who really has stayed with us, and to our reviewers, whose kindness and critical acumen has made the work so much better. Sherita Roundtree, while a graduate student at the University of Nebraska-Lincoln, and Greg Campbell, a graduate student at the University of Waterloo, both provided invaluable assistance at different stages in the development of this book. I am grateful to the host of colleagues and friends who cajoled and encouraged me when I grew tired, mourned with and lifted me when the death of my mother challenged my will to keep on keeping on with the project.

I am thankful for Vershawn, whose friendship is one of my greatest pleasures, whose collegiality has sustained me in moments when I am most frustrated or inclined toward despair, and whose willingness to challenge and be challenged keeps me on my toes, keeps me thinking hard, and keeps me laughing, too. I am more effective in the work that matters most to me because of Vay's support. I am a better ally for his critical engagement with me and with my work. I am more joyful for the presence, the spirit he brings to our co-labors as well as our co-journeys.

Always and forever I am grateful to my family—to my children: Dan, Lucy, and Grace, who ask terrific questions, tell great jokes, and model courage as they intervene and disrupt the racism to which they also bear witness. And most of all, I am grateful to my husband, Mike, who stands with me, thinks with me, pushes me, and who stays, thank God, no matter what new chaos I insert into our lives. I could not be who I am, do what I do, sustain my hope without Mike's kind and generous presence in my life.

—Frankie Condon

Foreword: On Antiracist Agendas

Asao B. Inoue | University of Washington Tacoma

It was the second grade, Mrs. Whitmore's class, North Las Vegas, Nevada. It is one of the earliest memories I have of the classroom, perhaps the earliest I can recall in full detail. It is a memory of racism and language. Another student and I were working on something at the chalkboard, writing. The class was busy with their work at their desks. A few were at the small work area in the back of the room where the book shelves sat. Mrs. Whitmore, a white lady, probably in her 40s at the time, with a thick head of long hair coiled up in a bun, sat at her desk several feet from the chalkboard. I don't remember the boy's name, my collaborator, only that he was Black (I'll call him Shawn) and about my size and stature. I was very short and skinny in school. At one point in our work, in a half-joking manner through a smile, Shawn called me a "honkey." I thought nothing of it, had heard the term many times here and there. He said it casually, no threat in his voice.

Slurs like that were common in the neighborhood where we lived not far from the school. We lived in government-subsidized apartments on Stats Street. They were small, made of painted cinderblock, and infested with roaches. Each group of eight apartments formed a grassy courtyard with two trees in the middle, four apartments on each side. Our doors faced each other. All my neighbors were Black. I was brown, but in that context, I was considered white. Race was Black and white, binary, even to seven- and eight-year-olds. It was the first and last time in my life I was considered white. Poverty was the equalizer, something everyone knew. We breathed it. I still remember how it ached in my bones and stomach because we had so little, but I had no way of connecting the having-so-little to larger structures of inequality. I had no way of seeing the difference between my poverty and my escape from it years later, and my Black friends on Stats and their fewer chances of escaping it. All I or any of my friends on Stats could do is live with the ache, maybe blame ourselves in quiet moments. But the classroom was a heterogeneous, liminal space, a space where poverty might be put on hold, but race? It seemed to matter more, or mean more. I was coming to racial consciousness, but it was nascent.

Mrs. Whitmore immediately called us both over to her desk in a loud tone. "You two, come here!" The class stopped in their tracks. I could feel their eyes on us. She was clearly upset. Neither of us understood what was happening. She stood over us, turned to Shawn, and asked, "Do you know what that word means?" I can still recall the feeling of my skin burning from the tacit accusation of something. I thought I was in trouble too. It was confusing for a seven-year-old. Her tone was sharp and accusatory. She was making an example of us in front of the class. "Do either of you know what that word means?" We both just looked blankly at each other, speechless, afraid to say another word. "How would you feel if he called you the N-word?" Mrs. Whitmore continued to stare down at Shawn and gestured my way. I knew that word very well. Things became clearer: *oh, he's in trouble, not me.* Still I was confused. What's the problem? It's just a word. No harm done.

This was my introduction to the whitely ways of many teachers to come, teachers similar to Mrs. Whitmore with her good intentions, careful rules to be followed, and determination to treat everyone the same, even treat the racial epithets we used the same. Shawn and I were just too young to understand what words like "honky" or "nigger" meant, how one of them had heavier historical baggage than the other, how one really wasn't on par with the other, how honky just can't hurt me the way nigger could hurt Shawn. They are both ugly words for sure, but one is more magical than the other, used historically by whites to degrade and dehumanize Blacks. Nigger. It's uncomfortable to even read, to hear in your mind's ear. Isn't it? That's its magic, a residual effect of a long history of inequality, meanness, inhumanity.

To Mrs. Whitmore, I think, the words were simply versions of the same kind of racism. Her heart was in the right place, but her ears couldn't hear what was happening between us, or what had happened before that classroom. She couldn't hear the word and weigh it against the word she was comparing it to. She could not see that she was reenacting a familiar racist paradigm, a white authority harshly punishing verbally (and often physically) a Black body, reenacting the ritual of a white body in authority, a white body demanding answers when answering would seem unwise to those being accused. She was a white body in control of the bodies of color around her, a white body using words to shame the racialized others around her and claim authority over them, even in matters of racism. Her attempt to be antiracist in her classroom practice ended up being racist through the strict enforcement of a rule about racial slurs with no regard to who said what to whom or what racial slur was used, and no regard to our linguistic privacy.

I'm not defending the use of the term honkey as a slur. I am saying that Mrs. Whitmore, in her rush (and it was a rush) to stamp out racism in her classroom, didn't or couldn't—or didn't want to—see that those two racial epithets were simply not the same thing because of the racist history and structures that we live in, because of who said what to whom and how Shawn and I came to live differently in the same poverty-stricken area of North Las Vegas. She never bothered to ask other questions that might have been more profitable to both Shawn and me. How did we use that word at home, on the playground, or in the neighborhood? We used both words and many others. Everyone did. We mimicked the language we heard around us. That's how language acquisition works, immersion and mimicry. She could have asked Shawn about how he felt when using it, why he might feel the need to use it, and how I felt to be called it, and why I might be okay with it or not. But she didn't. She could have talked with us about her own constraints as a teacher, or pressure by her principal or by parents to punish such language in our classroom. She might have talked to us about how she had to be a representative of many different, even conflicting, ideas about what kind of language is appropriate in our classroom. How would our parents feel about such language? But she didn't. She assumed it was simply a universally offensive word, that if she was offended then I must be, or that her sense of propriety was the measure of racism in her classroom. If such a word was used it was used in malice. It was uniformly and always wrong. She may have thought that perhaps when a Black mouth says that word it's always out of malice. A few years later, I'd chalk up such behavior by whites around me as simply being white, shaking my head and saying under my breath, "hmm, white people."

I know, this is all unfair to Mrs. Whitmore and whites generally. She's not here to explain herself. Any teacher who may behave in such ways, who may enforce rules of propriety that are meant to enact antiracist practices in the classroom are looking for rules that promote fairness, equality, and safety. The impulse is the right impulse. It's the method that messes up things, and how and by whom the method is enforced. What gets focused on is the word, which becomes a signifier of intention, an intention placed on the word by a white authority. The intention gets punished by the white authority. The impulse, I think, is that if we are all equal we should be treated equally, which means we should be punished equally for the same class of crimes in the classroom. The problem is, treating everyone equally doesn't make us equal. Furthermore, we can pretend to be equals, but we don't live in a world that sets up Shawn as remotely equal to Mrs. Whitmore or me. So when a teacher treats race as if it is a system of politically equal categories that people fit or place themselves into and see racism as when people associated to one category are slighted or treated differently than those in another, then the method is unfair. That's not how racism works. It works by hierarchical categories, not equal ones. It works by vertically uneven relations to power, not laterally even ones. These things affect rewards and punishments, and in the academy, rewards and punishments mean assessment and grading, opportunities and chances, policies and their methods.

Am I saying that Mrs. Whitmore or white teachers should stay out of the antiracist activism business in classrooms? No. On the contrary, they should be first in line to do this work. What I'm saying is that white teachers must tread differently than teachers of color. One might think of it as cooking in someone else's kitchen.

You don't know where all the spices are. You don't know what they're saving for next week's dinner. You don't know what set of plates or silverware to use. You don't know that their oven runs a little hot. You don't really know what to bring and cook in their kitchen. I'm reminded of the exchange between Condon and Young in Condon's *I Hope I Join the Band* (2012, pp. 164–176). They discuss the territory of trust and suspicion when whites engage in antiracist work or words. Trust is a paradox. We can give it as a gift, free without someone else's need to earn it, but it is still really hard to give, maybe harder to cultivate over time, as Condon and Young agree must happen, because we all have different relations to the kitchen.

Now, Shawn and I were only seven. There's only so much critical examination a teacher can expect at that age. But we were also old enough to use those words in ways that approached the nuanced ways adults around us used the words. So we were assessing language in similar ways, then deploying that language for particular rhetorical ends. If Shawn wasn't using the word as an insult, and I wasn't offended, was it okay? Should our white teacher have simply minded her own business? Should she have realized that she was not entitled to comment or preside over our exchange, even if she was the teacher? Should she have stayed out of our kitchen, at least this time?

I think many good-hearted, college teachers are like Mrs. Whitmore in how they treat race and racism in their classrooms, especially writing, rhetoric, and communications classrooms. They have their rules about what is appropriate and what is offensive, and implement them top-down, with some discussion, of course. They implicitly tell their students, shame on you for thinking that, or doing this thing, or using that word, with little if any regard for the histories of their students, without understanding the relations those students have to other racial formations and languages in the classroom, without asking students to investigate their racialized histories with words, with others, as others, as whites, as students, as the dominated or the dominating. Students don't get to negotiate the grounds of racist actions or their consequences. They miss the necessary negotiation and dialogue in healthy and fairer methods for antiracist action. They miss the chances to give trust and cultivate it among each other.

It's an easy misstep to make. As teachers, we often take for granted that our authority granted by the institution to teach a class, to grade students' performances, to rank students according to so-called ability gives us the right to also have authority over other aspects of students' lives, actions, behaviors, and words. Communication is literacy is subjectivity is identity. We say it is our job to help students "think critically," so when we are confronted with a student's ignorance or racism, we feel we must name it, critique it, and ask the student to rethink, restate in more acceptable ways (to the teacher), or at least avoid the discussion because it's not okay in this classroom. The ideas offend others (but more specifically, they offend the teacher-grader), so we think. But do they? Or rather, how do they hurt others? Investigating language as the racially epistemological, or the way in which we articulate, understand, create, and construct concepts of race and racism, which then affect the way real live racial formations and racism as structural occurrences in our lives happens, is important work that is the job of the literacy classroom. So I don't want to suggest that teachers who make such missteps are completely misguided. They are not.

In one sense, I'm arguing, much like many of the chapters in this collection do, that investigating language can promote explicitly an antiracist agenda: what language we use, how we use that language, who uses it, what purposes we use it for, what intended and unintended effects or consequences are there for our language, how are those effects distributed unevenly across different racialized audiences, in what historical ways has language like ours been deployed? These are some of the questions that should be inflected by race in literacy and communication classrooms, and may form the content of antiracist agendas. Because our world is structured historically and economically in racial terms, and we find racism everywhere around us, these kinds of racially epistemological questions are important rhetorical lessons for all students to struggle with?

Let me be even more specific about the kind of antiracist work and agendas I'm referring to that I think any teacher can do. No matter the kind of course, topic, teacher, or group of students, there is one common thing that all teachers must confront in any course: assessment and grading (these are not necessarily the same thing). How do we respond to the code-meshed, multilingual, heteroglossia (in writing and speech) of our students when language is not normalized, when there is no living "standard" English in practice, only Englishes performed, only the infinite varieties of *Parole* without a *Langue* (to reference Saussure's *Third Course of Lectures on General Linguistics*). This is something that many have discussed and affirmed in other ways (Canagarajah, 2009; Lippi-Green, 2012; Lu & Horner, 2013; Young, 2007; Young et al., 2014; Lu & Horner, 2013; Lippi-Green, 2012; Canagarajah, 2009; Young & Martinez, 2011). These scholars just haven't addressed the ways this knowledge about the infinite varieties of English should be the seeds of an antiracist agenda for all teachers' assessment practices. Yes, our assessment practices should be guided by an antiracist agenda. This means we also might have ideal consequences or outcomes in mind, goals we hope to see accomplished because of our antiracist agendas, but we'll need the help of our students to know this part.

Now, let me be blunt. If you grade writing by a so-called standard, let's call it Standard English, then you are engaged in an institutional and disciplinary racism, a system set up to make winners and losers by a dominant standard. Who owns the dominant standard? Where does that standard come from? What social group is it most associated with? Who benefits most from the use of the standard? How is that social group racialized in our society? Do you see where I'm going with this? To evaluate and grade student languaging by the method of comparing it to some ideal standard or norm—no matter what that norm is—will participate in racism. Is this avoidable? Maybe. Do I blame teachers for grading by a dominant standard? No, not completely. We're often forced to do so. But that's not a good enough excuse to continue doing it. If you had to break the law in order to save someone's life, wouldn't you? It's really the same principle. We know grading by a standard is harmful and unfair, even unhelpful in teaching students how to write or communicate, we know that grading itself is a bad practice for teaching students anything, but we still do it. We still use standards of language and grades. So if you know this now and agree, it should make your assessment practices in the future more troubling, more problematic in the ways Freire talked about "problematizing" existential situations of writers (Freire, 1970), only I'm saying that writing assessment as a practice should problematize teachers' existential assessment situations.

With statements like *Students' Right to Their Own Language* (Conference on College Composition and Communication, 1974) by our national professional organizations, we cannot deny the racialized aspects of students' languages used in our classrooms, nor can we deny dominant languages used as yardsticks by which to measure students' linguistic abilities, capabilities, thinking, and competencies. I don't mean to elide the important pedagogical agendas for ESL and some multilingual students and their teachers in my call for antiracist writing assessment agendas (see Atkinson et al., 2015). I'm not speaking of those agendas, which are different. I'm speaking of the majority of monolingual and multilingual students who come to the university classroom from other U.S. classrooms in high schools, who are not learning the rudiments of communication in the language, but learning a new English, learning how to "invent the university" in the ways that Bartholomae's (1985) famous phrase suggests, even though I have reservations about his argument. I'm thinking about the translingual (Horner et al., 2011; Lu & Horner, 2013) and code-meshed practices (Young, 2007; Canagarajah, 2009) that all U.S. college students engage in and that get assessed by teachers according to monolingual approaches—assessment practices that set up many students for failure.

In *Marxism and the Philosophy of Language*, Voloshinov explains that language has no "inert system of self-identified norms." Any language, such as English, is a "ceaseless generation of language norms." He goes on to say that "language presents a picture of a ceaseless flow of becoming" (1986, p. 66). This means that not only is there no authentic living standard by which we might judge student's articulations, but if we do use a standard to judge and rank, to grade, it is arbitrary and a political move made by a teacher-grader who either misunderstands how language exists in the world, or willfully ignores the way language exists in favor of a comfortable fiction because she thinks she knows what's best for her students. The second is a form of whitely ways that disturbs me more than the first, one based on ignorance. This nature of people's languaging may account for why issues of error in writing assessment are so problematic, theorized as phenomenological (Williams, 1981) and socially constructed (Anson, 2000). It also explains why grading has been understood as harmful to students' development as writers and learners (Bleich, 1997; Elbow, 1993; Kohn, 1993, 2011). Even perceived error by a teacher, when marked and counted as such, is not simply a superficial move by the teacher, but a claim about the writer's languaging and thus the writer. These claims, depending on how they are couched, and who is making them to whom, can be racist rhetorical enactments that produce unequal social formations in classrooms. They can work against other antiracist agendas and projects of the course, such as all the classroom examples given in this collection.

Failure in writing, in learning to write, in communicating—failure of languaging—in a classroom does not have to be a marker of racism, of course. I've discussed ways that one might retheorize failure in learning to write by rethinking the way one grades and thus the way one responds to students' writing and students themselves (Inoue, 2014). This kind of theorizing can lead to antiracist assessment practices by teachers, which I think is important for all teachers to do, and it should be dictated by one's context, students, courses, and institutional constraints. But teachers should be mindful of the difference between responding to one's institutional constraints, and hiding behind constraints and students in order not to engage in antiracist writing assessment practices that critique the racist structures of the academy and institutions we work in. In the end, each teacher must decide how far he or she is willing to go, what sacrifices to make, what things to focus on, exactly where he or she stands.

The book you have in your hands offers valuable ideas for writing, communications, literature, and cultural studies classrooms. The chapters offer a good mix of the theoretical, the personal, the performative, and the practical (I realize these are somewhat forced distinctions: why is theory not practical, or performative not personal?). What I value most about this collection, and why I'm truly honored to offer this forward to readers, are the various antiracist agendas that come through each chapter so clearly. For several years now in various venues, some published (Inoue, 2009; Inoue & Poe, 2012), some in professional organizations (CCCC and CWPA), I have argued for teachers, writing program administrators, and journals to have an antiracist agenda. In fact, I believe our fields' various professional organizations should have explicitly stated antiracist agendas, with clearly attainable goals and benchmarks, with a philosophy and vision of what social justice in the organization should be.

A helpful antiracist agenda offers an understanding or explanation of race, racism, and the particular racial formations that develop in and around the classroom or program in question. It defines and explains the particular realms of experience that both individuals and groups find themselves involved in at that site or classroom. This means the agenda may discuss how racism tends to be a part of the structures and mechanisms of grading in writing classrooms, in teacher feedback, in the ways that the school admits and places students into classes, in how and what it values in writing and how those values are related to larger dominant discourses. It explains the particular brands of whiteness and whiteliness that occur in the classroom and in assessments. It acknowledges the need and power in telling stories and offering narratives about antiracist struggle, counterstories and institutional ones that may more obviously participate in the hegemonic. These stories do not ignore the evolving needs of students to participate in the dominant and hegemonic, even at the cost of anti-hegemonic and antiracist action—we all have to buy our bread and put a roof over our head. Finally, antiracist agendas should, perhaps through discussions with students, reveal the difference in classrooms between feeling safe and feeling comfortable. When it comes to race, racism, and antiracist work, it is important that everyone feels safe, but equally important that many also feel uncomfortable. It's only through discomfort, perhaps pain and suffering, that we grow, develop, and change for the better.

When I think again about Mrs. Whitmore's class and Shawn's use of the word honkey, one could argue that she made us uncomfortable in order that we learn a valuable lesson about racism. And in one sense it worked. Shawn and I never said such words again, at least not around her. It worked because I can think back on it now and see how her whitely ways reinforced patterns of racism by white authorities that I do not want to mimic as a teacher of color—yes, teachers of color can embody whitely ways. But I believe she created more than discomfort through her method (i.e., stern words and accusatory questions meant to shame and blame). The incident was unsafe. Had either of us felt safe enough to engage in a conversation with her about our racist language practices, one of us would have said at least a word in response, but neither of us did. To do so would have risked our safety. And I'm not exaggerating. Earlier in the year, after having taken allergy medicine, I felt asleep in class, only to be woken up abruptly by Mrs. Whitmore shooting a squirt gun—a squirt GUN—at my face, the entire class circled around my desk laughing at me. It was a terrifying and confusing moment, one that made me feel eminently unsafe in that classroom. I never said any words to her after that.

I don't think Mrs. Whitmore was an evil or unusually mean teacher. I think she was trying her best, but wasn't trained to know what to do in a diverse class like ours. In fact, I feel compassion for her and white teachers like her, wanting to do the right thing (to invoke Spike's film title) but not having all the necessary tools in order to do that work. But then I think about the element of truth in the old adage, "the road to hell is paved with good intentions." Antiracist work in classrooms, as Mrs. Whitmore shows me, is not an easy task. We all will make mistakes.

However, the problems of racism and the linguistic hierarchies that accompany such issues in the academy will not go away if most teachers and researchers do not have explicit antiracist agendas, if teachers do not fold those agendas into their assessment practices in the classroom, if programs do not think carefully about the ways their program assessments attempt to understand and combat social inequality of all kinds. How we enact assessment, from classroom grading practices to program assessment, is vital to these social justice agendas, but the agenda is the first step. The agenda is the articulated dream, the vision, the goal. It may not articulate what the "promised land" of social equality looks like or will feel like, but it points us in the direction. How can we get to where we wish to go if we don't know in what direction to walk? This book, through various examples of classrooms and exchanges between teachers and students, shows us possible directions for antiracist agendas in higher education, showing us paths to walk. In short, if a teacher is going to be serious about antiracist struggle in her classroom, then that struggle should not just be a reading or an activity or two. It should be, as many chapters in this collection illustrate, the way the classroom breathes, the status quo of the classroom.

References

Anson, C. M. (2000). Response and the social construction of error. *Assessing Writing, 7*(1), 5–21.

Atkinson, D., Crusan, D., Matsuda, P. K., Ortmeier-Hooper, C., Ruecker, T., Simpson, S. & Tardy, C. (2015). Clarifying the relationship between L2 writing and translingual writing: An open letter to writing studies editors and organization leaders. *College English, 77*(4), 383–386.

Bartholomae, D. (1985). Inventing the university. In M. Rose (Ed.), *When a writer can't write: Studies in writer's block and other composing-process problems* (pp. 134–166). New York: Guilford Press.

Bleich, D. (1997). What can be done about grading? In L. Allison, L. Bryant & M. Hourigan (Eds.), *Grading in the post-process classroom: From theory to practice* (pp. 15–35). Portsmouth, NH: Boynton/Cook.

Canagarajah, S. (2009). Multilingual strategies of negotiating English: From conversation to writing. *JAC, 29*(1–2), 17–48.

Condon, F. (2012). *I hope I join the band.* Logan, UT: Utah State University Press.

Conference on College Composition and Communication. (1974). Students' right to their own language. *College Composition and Communication*, 25 (3), 1–18.

Elbow, P. (1993). Ranking, evaluating, and liking: Sorting out three forms of judgment. *College English, 55*(2), 187–206.

Freire, P. (2005). *Pedagogy of the oppressed* (Ramos, M. B., Trans.). New York: Continuum. (Original work published 1970)

Horner, B., Lu, M., Royster, J. J. & Trimbur, J. (2011). Language difference in writing: Toward a translingual approach. *College English, 73*(3), 303–321.

Inoue, A. B. (2014). Theorizing failure in writing assessments. *Research in the Teaching of English, 48*(3), 329–351.

Kohn, A. (1993). *Punished by rewards: The trouble with gold stars, incentive plans, a's, praise, and other bribes.* Boston, New York: Houghton Mifflin.

Kohn, A. (2011). The case against grades. *Educational Leadership,* 69(3), 28.

Lippi-Green, R. (2012). *English with an accent: Language, ideology, and discrimination in the United States* (2nd ed.). London: Routledge.

Lu, M. & Horner, B. (2013). Translingual literacy, language difference, and matters of agency. *College English, 75*(6), 582–607.

Voloshinov, V. (1986). *Marxism and the philosophy of language.* (Matejka, L. & Titunik, I. R., Trans.). Cambridge, MA: Harvard University Press. (Original work published 1929).

Williams, J. (1981). The phenomenology of error. *College Composition and Communication, 32*(2), 152–168.

Young, V. A. (2007*). Your average nigga: Performing race, literacy, and masculinity.* Detroit: Wayne State University Press.

Young, V. A. & Martinez, A. Y. (Eds.). (2011). *Code-Meshing as world English: Pedagogy, policy, performance.* Urbana, IL: National Council of Teachers of English.

Young, V. A., Barrett, R., Young-Rivera, Y. & Lovejoy K. B. (2014). *Other people's English: Code-Meshing, code-switching, and African American literacy.* New York: Teachers College Press.

Performing Antiracist Pedagogy in Rhetoric, Writing, and Communication

Introduction

Frankie Condon and Vershawn Ashanti Young

I

> *We have the somewhat inchoate idea that we are not destined to be harassed with great social questions, and that even if we are, and fail to answer them, the fault is with the question and not with us. Consequently we often congratulate ourselves more on getting rid of a problem than on solving it.*
>
> —W. E. B. DuBois

The great American racial wound is periodically hidden from our view, covered over by civil rights legislation, by the economic success of a few people of color who are held up as evidence of its suture, and by the widespread denial of its existence by white Americans. Now, as the number of Black men and boys shot down by the police or by armed white citizens mounts, as anti-immigration rhetoric increases in stridency and Band-Aid solutions by "progressives" are offered in response, as income inequality deepens, the scab is torn away. Structural inequality seems more entrenched than ever and the denial of white Americans both more inexplicable and more intractable. However, the evidence of ongoing racism seems insufficient either to convince white Americans that racism is both real and matters or to compel them to address racism in any systemic way.

For as long as we have been thinking, talking, working at antiracist activism within and beyond the bounds of the academy, we have encountered denials and scapegoating for the most blatant racist incidents, and roadblocks in pursuing antiracist discussions and pedagogies. We have been asked to justify that work—to explain to our colleagues, our students and to our readers why such work is necessary. We admit our frustration at the question. We should also admit that the answers seem obvious and commonsensical to us. We might similarly admit that the fact we are still questioned about the necessity for the work represents evidence that the work is still necessary and urgent. And we should admit that, in some regard, we feel despair because it seems that no amount of responding to the question provides a sufficient and compelling answer to those who continue to ask us to justify antiracist work. In short, understanding that racism exists and operates beyond the academy is foundational to the work many of us engage as scholars in our fields. In our experience, however, even those of us who make the study of racial injustice our life's work struggle to acknowledge and address those forms of racism in which we participate, however unintentionally, within the academy.

We sense that some part of the resistance we encounter from our colleagues centers around a collective yearning to believe and have our belief affirmed that a fully realized multi-racial American democracy is possible. We are too often struck by the refusal of our best-intentioned colleagues to recognize and acknowledge the degree to which we have not realized this vision, however: not in society at large and not in our universities, our departments, our classrooms. We have not meaningfully addressed the perniciousness and ubiquity of structural racism and the rhetorics of racism (however coded) that sustain its everyday reproduction within the academy. It's hard to look around—in our classrooms, departments and committee meetings, in residence halls and cafeterias on our campuses, in our communities, our states, our nation—and not conclude that American idealism, if that's the explanation for why we are continually asked to provide a rationale for talking about race and racism, requires a rather high degree of obtuseness.

We have been traveling to colleges and universities across the country for years to talk about race matters. And we have learned through these travels—even more than through our studies—that there are many scholars whose research interests and political commitments coincide with the work of antiracism. It is difficult, however, for even the most committed of us to perceive, name and contend with the ways in which racism winds its way to our classrooms—through unexamined curricula, careless, ill-considered or unreflective teaching practice, or talk to and about our students. We think of this phenomenon as a form of what Joyce E. King has termed "dysconscious racism." She writes, "[d]ysconscious racism is a form of racism that tacitly accepts dominant White norms and privileges. It is not the *absence* of consciousness (that is, not unconsciousness) but an *impaired* consciousness or distorted way of thinking about race." King argues that "[d]ysconsciousness is an uncritical habit of mind . . . that justifies inequity and exploitation by accepting the existing order of things as given" (1991, p. 135). Even for those of us who work against racism daily, the racism that is closest to us, that we unknowingly and without intention participate in is most difficult to perceive and resist.

We're being deliberately direct here because racism didn't die down in 1963 and resurface in the first decade of the twenty-first century. Expressions of surprise and shock each time some new example of racism in the academy comes to light grow wearisome. For instance, on October 1, 2012 *Inside Higher Ed* (IHE) published an article by Alexandra Tilsley about university blogs designed to expose racism and other forms of hate on campus by republishing student tweets and Facebook status posts. "The blogs have brought to light," Tilsley writes, "the surprising willingness of students to mock and make negative comments about various groups, especially Asian students, who have notoriously been the subject of cruel jokes and racist comments on campuses in recent years." Given not only the frequency, but the long history of American racism, we wonder why folks continue to be surprised by the exposure of racism at work among us. We wonder why each new exposure of the ubiquity of everyday forms of racism is attended by claims of innocence and ignorance ("I had no idea!"). The fact of these ongoing expressions of shock, we think, is less evidence of genuine ignorance than of the extent to which many academics labor to preserve their insulation from those quite regular conditions that compose the everyday lives of students, faculty, administrators and support staff of color on and off campus.

Commentators on Tilsley's article appear to be invested in reframing the racism exposed by the haters' blogs as something other than racism: as rudeness or insensitivity—as almost anything other than racism. The prevailing concern among the commentators is whether or not the posts from OSU and UNL are examples of hate speech. "Dan" writes,

> The comments described are discourteous to be sure, but are they really hate speech? They threaten no violence, nor even non-violence. I think they're squarely protected under the First Amendment, and no official organ of any university has any right to prosecute them. I may not agree with what you say, but I'll defend to the death your right to say it. But I do like Indian food . . .

While the comment about Indian food in this post debating whether discourteous racial comments is hate speech might seem like an obvious non sequitur, it points up precisely the kind of unintentional racism that is committed by folks who believe themselves to be non-racist. If "Dan" defends folks who publicly make discourteous racial comments, what do you think would be his reaction to someone pointing out that his own comment "But I do like Indian food" is itself discourteous, culturally reductive, and an example of what is theorized as Racism 2.0, a version that in effect says "call me on it and I'll tell you that you're the reverse racist or the hyper vigilant, hyper sensitive activist who can't see a compliment when it's given." Commentator "steverankin" writes,

> A notable use of terms in this article. Consider the impact of the word "derogatory" to describe the offensive posts. Now consider the use of "hate" or "hateful." "Hate speech" has become a staple term in public rhetoric. I hate hate speech, but I'm beginning to worry that we use the label too indiscriminately.

Another commentator counters calling the posts examples of "insensitivity" and argues that "sensitivity training" should be a required element of first-year orientation programs. "We live in a global culture," he writes, "and if these issues aren't understood BEFORE American students leave college, it's an injustice because it places them behind other global students in learning and understanding cultural differences in the workplace."

Although the debate among the commentators is neither heated nor long-winded (only nine comments appear beneath the article in question), its focus seems typical to us—in the sense of being both ordinary and frustrating. Emphasis on the legalities of hate versus discriminatory speech and what forms of speech might be protected by the First Amendment contains the dialogue about racism within the sphere of individual action and intent. The question of whether to ignore, punish, train or educate the writers of the original tweets and status posts displaces recognition and acknowledgement of the long term and cumulative effects of being the subject of and subjected to everyday racisms. Such a discussion frames racism as the product of individual actions that deviate from the *normal, non-racist* actions of *most* of *us* or from the *sensitive* practice of suppressing our racism. The injustice of conditions of racism within which students of color are forced to study go unremarked. Instead, injustice is characterized by the failure of colleges and universities to prepare (white?) students to succeed in the global marketplace by not teaching them to be sensitive in their representations of difference.

The tweets posted on OSU- and UNL-Haters are all ostensibly written by students. But on the bulletin board in Frankie's office hangs a Post-It note. Scribbled on it is this quotation, recorded during a break in an interminably long committee meeting when two colleagues were speaking rather unguardedly about their students: "So I say 'oh sure that English you're using might be just fine where you come from, but around here we speak white English.'" Frankie has kept this Post-It note for years. It has traveled with her from academic post to academic post. This is evidence, she thinks: evidence that she isn't crazy—that racism is real and right here/right now, not merely an effect of rural poor and working class miseducation and not merely the irrational outpouring of an armed survivalist, white supremacist militia or cult. Frankie knows that the utterance of the word "white" was a *slip* of the tongue. This colleague wasn't thinking, wasn't guarding her speech. But Frankie also knows, she knows, that even if her colleague has used the word "formal" or "professional" or "academic" beneath the surface of these other words would have roiled the truth: in the context of a predominantly white university and a predominantly white department (in which nearly every faculty person of color has left or struggled to achieve tenure and promotion), to an audience composed of either one or a few students of color or a white colleague—*white* is what she meant to say. But we live in a post-racial America and work in post-racial universities where we have learned (unless we slip up) to substitute words like "professional" for white so that any racism that might be revealed is semantically concealed.

At this point, we should admit that rage tempts us. Can this really be the highest caliber of conversation of which folks who are scholars are capable? But we re-center ourselves, pull ourselves back together and reach toward some more measured entrance into yet another discussion of both the problem, racism, by exposing it, and what we promote to counter it, antiracism. And we recognize in our efforts that the enabling conditions for impoverished and unproductive conversations about race and racism, antiracism, and antiracist pedagogy extend far beyond the bounds of colleges and universities and into the broad and deep mire of American public discourse on race.

If you have picked up this book, in all likelihood, you are thinking carefully and critically about race, racism, and pedagogy. We guess you understand that racism is real and already have some grasp of its impacts on the lives of people of color. We imagine that you already have some investment in action from where you are to teach for racial justice. We are thankful that you are with us and many other American educators in this struggle. We hope that you are here—at the beginning of this book—because you have already begun or are ready to begin to engage critically and reflectively with the work of antiracism not only out-there, beyond the academy, but also in-here, within our classrooms, within the logics that shape our course design, content, and pedagogical practice.

II

The writers whose work composes this collection write from a variety of perspectives about addressing the problem of racism in our institutions, our classrooms, among our colleagues, our students, ourselves. They are teachers and scholars who recognize, acknowledge, and actively engage in resistance against the material realities of structural, symbolic, and institutional racism. Chapters included in the volume are organized in sections by theme. The first section, Actionable Commitments, addresses from a variety of perspectives the relationship between the stories we tell about race, racism, and writing (and the frames shaping those stories) and our engagement with antiracism within and beyond the classroom.

In their chapter, "Making Commitments to Racial Justice Actionable," Rasha Diab, Thomas Ferrel, Beth Godbee, and Neil Simpkins move between antiracist principles and practice to articulate ways of thinking, speaking, and acting against racism/for social justice. In contrast to the shock/amnesia responses to everyday racism we critique above, these writers argue that in order to work effectively against the "ongoing micro-aggressions and micro-inequities" of institutional racism we all need to learn to engage in self-work, but not to mistake that labor for the whole of an actionable commitment to racial justice. Diab et al. examine the ways in which individual and institutional narratives about racism take the form of the confessional. Rather than dismissing the form altogether, however, the authors call upon readers to push through the confessional narrative to an articulation of actionable principles in service of creating conditions of accountability for change. Central to these principles, they suggest, is the attending practice of work within the dialectic between "self-work and work-with-others" as we allow ourselves to be disturbed by racism even as we engage reflectively, critically, and actively in everyday labor for racial justice.

In his chapter, "Teaching African American Discourse: Confessions of a Recovering Segregationist," Calvin Logue begins with the teaching of Black Rhetoric and African American Discourse at the University of Georgia during the 1970s narrating in reverse chronological order a personal and professional journey from unexamined acceptance of a segregationist racial order to active pedagogical engagement in the transformation of that order and the racist logics that inform it. In the chapter that follows, Aja Martinez discusses the application of critical race theory, in general, and the resisting practice of counterstory, in particular, to the teaching of writing. Finally, in Section One, Mya Poe explores the racial frames shaping institutional discourse about race and writing. While Poe acknowledges some use-value in common existing frames (e.g., the multicultural frame, the achievement gap frame, the post-racial frame), she argues for recognizing the ways in which race accrues meaning within our local institutions and classrooms, shaping our understanding, our expectations, and our responses to students as speakers and writers. Poe suggests re-framing received, but largely generalized and thus unhelpful accounts of race in service of teaching writing across the disciplines.

Section Two, *Identity Matters* includes chapters examining the implications of racial identifications, privilege, and disenfranchisement on teachers and learners. Like Poe, Charise Pimentel, Octavio Pimentel, and John Dean examine framing practices shaping stories we tell about race and racism. "The Myth of the Colorblind Classroom" focuses, however, on the "diversity" frame and, in particular, on the ways in which "polycultural" approaches are grounded on maintaining the myth that colorblindness is a necessary condition for racial justice. In contrast to this frame, Pimentel et al. argue for antiracist pedagogies that acknowledge the ubiquity of racialism within and beyond the classroom and critically address implicitly and explicitly forms of race privilege that accrue to white teachers. Using teacher narratives braided with theoretical analyses grounded in critical whiteness studies, the writers suggest both the necessity for and the inevitable incompleteness of antiracist pedagogy. Rather than using this incompleteness as a reason to disengage with antiracism, however, Pimentel et al. argue ultimately that the aim of antiracist work is not the achievement of non-racism in one's students or one's self, but is rather to sustain and extend antiracist engagement with and in service of student learning.

Authors Bobbi Olson and Dae-Joong Kim examine the powerful work of whiteliness—the rhetorical performance of white privilege—in the construction of teacherly authority. Writing from distinct subject positions—white, American-born, and native English speaking on one hand and Korean-born, international, and multilingual on the other—Olson and Kim narrate and theorize the ways and degrees to which each has variously engaged whiteliness in service of establishing authority. The authors narrate also their encounters with whiteliness among students who are resistant to teacherly (or linguistic) authority. Finally, Olson and Kim argue for productive engagement with dissensus in the writing classroom as a means of making rhetorical enactments of whiteliness visible and available for ongoing reflection, analysis, and critique.

In her chapter, "Why Am I So Damaged?," Deatra Sullivan has composed a narrative anthem even as she questions ideological and material conditions that create the need of an African American woman in the professoriate for an anthem. Sullivan acknowledges the pain and fear she experiences as a Black woman in the academy even as she strives for an enactment of self as teacher/scholar who no longer feels the need to strive toward a racially other identification.

The third section, *In the Classroom* includes chapters focusing on antiracist pedagogical performativity and enactment. In her chapter, "Whiteboys," Sophia Bell explores the evolving racial rhetorics and silences of two young men of color in a gateway writing course. Of particular concern to Bell is the internalized racism she reads in narratives composed by students who have navigated racial identity in predominantly white academic contexts. Bell notes the ways and degrees to which both students complicate the idea of whiteness generally as well as their own racial identifications and dis-identifications. But Bell also examines the ways in which her assignment construction (personal narrative) and expectations for that assignment reveal her own racialized frames for reading student performances of identification and dis-identification. Like many of the writers included in this volume, Bell concludes not with prescriptions, but with conviction about the necessity of carrying on with antiracist pedagogy as well as with ongoing critical reflection about the pedagogical performances of antiracism as they are enacted in assignment design, class facilitation, and in feedback.

In her chapter, "Writing and Un-writing Race: . . ." Jessica Parker discuss the use of hip-hop as a vehicle for opening and enriching discussions about race and class. Parker argues that the study of hip-hop helps students to engage deeply and critically with identity matters including the continuing prevalence of racism, practices of cultural appropriation, and the historical intertwinement of race and class in American Society. In a drama that, like Aja Martinez' work in Section One of this volume, pursues the literary tradition within critical race studies of playing with genre in service of braiding storytelling (narrative or parable, for example) with theory and critique, the co-authors of "Dangerous Play," use theatrical conventions to dramatize the complexity of identity, affiliation, and antiracist pedagogy in a graduate classroom. Chiara Bacigalupa, Susan Leigh Brooks, Timothy Lensmire, Rebecca Nathan, and Nathan Snaza describe experimentation and associated risk in a classroom setting around language, identity and the performance of and resistance to socially assigned racial roles and rules of racial standing.

The authors whose work comprises this volume have each focused their work in the dynamic interplay between theoretical analyses and grounded teaching practices. From multiple identities, the writers offer readers theoretical support and pedagogical models for acting on or making real individual and shared commitments to the advancement of racial justice through the teaching of writing. Although we might wish the truth to be otherwise, we remain convinced that so long as the material force of racism persists in the US, those of us who teach will be called upon to pursue our commitments to social justice in our classrooms.

The special issue of *Across the Disciplines* that was the source of this volume and this book, itself, have been several years in the making. During that time, we have followed innumerable stories of celebrities appearing in black-face at public and private events, the exclusion of models and designers of color in the fashion industry, the political gerrymandering of voting districts across the US to disempower voters of color, and the justification and exoneration of white gun owners in the executions of young Black men and women on the street. A professor in Minnesota has been disciplined by her institution for creating discomfort among white students during a classroom discussion of structural racism. The bar in Louisville, Kentucky where we sat talking about our work together on this project has been accused of denying service to a party of Black men. And, following the publication of the UNL Haters blog and a series of racist incidents in the fall of 2013 the University of Nebraska–Lincoln has begun an antiracism campaign they are calling "Not Here Not Now." As powerful as the collective desire of Americans may be to achieve a post-racial democracy, we have not arrived. The necessity of acknowledging and resisting the historical force of racism by teaching about racism and by developing pedagogical approaches that enact and model antiracist engagement remains pressing.

So long as racism persists in any form—from the micro-aggressions of racism 2.0 to implicit and explicit structural forms of disenfranchisement—those of us who teach and who are committed to the creation of an increasingly just society will need to choose whether and how we address racism in our classrooms. Our hope is that the chapters included in this volume will assist faculty across the disciplines in seeing the choice to engage in such addresses as both possible and pedagogically viable. We hope readers will recognize the teaching of writing across the disciplines as a vehicle for engaging students in resistance to racism in their own lives and that the chapters included here, which are theoretically informed and practical will assist readers in making their own commitments actionable.

III

> *I think that the hard work of a nonracist sensibility is the boundary crossing, from safe circle into wilderness: the testing of boundary, the consecration of sacrilege. It is the willingness to spoil a good party and break an encompassing circle, to travel from the safe to the unsafe.*
>
> —Patricia Williams

The special issue of *Across the Disciplines* on the theme "Antiracist Activism: Teaching Rhetoric and Writing" that preceded the publication of this edited collection was first conceived in the midst of and, in some ways, as a result of a contradictory and still circulating rhetorical phenomena: the widely touted pronouncements of the death of racism that surrounded and followed the historic campaign and election of the first U.S. president of African descent.

These claims were and are still uttered by two different constituencies, who, interestingly enough, rarely agree on other matters. We read and heard sentiments expressed by perhaps too-hopeful liberals, acquiescing to the hype that racism is only a problem for those who unreasonably perceive themselves to be victims of a time long gone. The other group might be called the staunch conservatives (and these are definitely not limited to political categories)—the Rush Limbaugh types—who attempted to de-trope race, to unlink remarks, policies, perceptions, and practices clearly designed to stigmatize, berate, and oppress people of color from the perpetuating legacies of white privilege. For both groups, President Barack Obama was and still is a poster child, because as Senator Harry Reid (D–Nevada) put it once, he is read by many as a non-threatening "light-skinned African American with no Negro dialect, unless he wanted to have one" (Cillizza, 2010). Thus he can be Black enough to represent the liberal agenda for minorities to reach the upper echelon of politics and American society, but not Black enough to stoke the prejudices that conservatives hold against Black cultural forms of speech and behavior. The only racial barrier might be the look of his skin, but as Reid intimates, even that's light enough not to offend.

But the notion that the US has achieved post-racial status did not begin with the election of President Obama. In a weekly radio address delivered in 1986, President Ronald Reagan, claiming affiliation with Dr. Martin Luther King, argued that the American approximation of racial equality, while not perfect, was sufficient enough that the structural address of social and economic inequality through programs like Affirmative Action was a) no longer necessary, and b) would, if pursued, have the effect of producing imbalance in the other direction—advantaging people of color who had attained an acceptable degree of equality over and against whites (http://www.presidency.ucsb.edu/ws/?pid=37302).

In other words, Reagan was saying that in a society in which *sufficient* racial equality has been achieved, systemic and institutional racism are no longer of concern. What prejudice remains accrues to and is reproduced by individual actors. According to this worldview, like the Wicked Witch of the West, those actors have no power here; in the political sense, in a post-racial America, they are unable to enforce their prejudices using structural means. Therefore, the work before the rest of us is to train them in the practices of what we now understand as civil speech in order that they, too, may profit from post-racialism. The effect of this racial "color-blindness" lauded by President Reagan doesn't eliminate the problem but creates an obstacle for those who speak of race and racism, suggesting it is they who have the regressive understanding: if you're still seeing race, still experiencing racism and still talking about race and racism, then you're the racist. But this strategy is not new.

Consider this: Co-editor Vershawn Ashanti Young used the now infamous 2011 video of former UCLA student Alexandria Wallace mocking Asians on *YouTube* and the chancellor's criticism of such parody in a lecture to illustrate how to analyze the rhetoric of a digital media controversy. After class, he was approached by one of his two African American students, both females. She said that showing the videos were a waste of class time and that race was not an appropriate topic for a rhetoric class. Because of his previous experiences discussing race, even in classes such as African American literature and African American studies, Vershawn has backed off from discussing race in general education courses. That was the case in this freshman writing class, where these videos were the only instance where race was discussed, and this time in a unit designed to examine controversies in digital media.

As a result of this and sundry other experiences, Vershawn often wonders what makes students, even students of color, so skittish about analyzing race. What makes students believe that race is something that resides outside of college? If even in ethnic studies classes some students are race shy, then in what classes and in what forms should race be considered in curricula? And what would be the result if there were no discussions of race at all? Would the campus be more peaceful? Would racism die? On the other hand, what might happen if more colleagues engaged rigorous examinations of racial politics? Would race raise from taboo to understanding, to increased racial consciousness?

DuBois' words, with which our introduction begins, seem not only apt in his time but also prescient. We may all be tired—worn past the point of exhaustion by the necessity of addressing powerfully and productively the systemic problem of

American racism. There is, in fact, no compelling evidence that as a nation we have resolved the great question of how to create and sustain a robust and just multiracial democracy. We may have gotten better at developing strategies to "git rid of the problem" by obscuring it, but we have not solved it. With the authors whose work is collected here, we have not abandoned hope, but rather, as Cornel West suggests, work to actualize an increasingly just world by continuing to engage resolutely against racism and its effects in our homes, our communities, and our workplaces.

Over the years, as we have traveled to give talks, workshops or to consult with faculty, staff and students across the US, as we have written or co-written with one another or other colleagues, and as we have talked together over coffees, lunches, and dinners, we have developed and continue to evolve a conceptual framework and vocabulary for the work we do. We don't believe that it is necessary for all of us who work at antiracism to employ either conforming conceptual frames or language in this work. We have not, therefore, attempted to police the terms writers choose in this volume. We do believe it is useful to be both conscious of and critically reflective about how well our words are working, whether our conceptual frames at any given moment help us to deepen and extend our analysis of racism in all its forms, and how aptly those frames and the terms we employ describe and help us to study and intervene in what we see. We offer the following, then, not as a key to concepts and terms we have insisted that writers in this volume adopt, but as an example of tools we continue both to use in our work and to adapt as our understandings grow. We offer them with the hope that others will find them useful, but also that others will contribute to the development of them, helping all of us to both understand the work that needs to be done more clearly and do the work more effectively. A version of this list has previously been published in the volume co-authored by Anne Ellen Geller, Michele Eodice, Frankie Condon, Meg Carroll and Elizabeth Boquet, *The Everyday Writing Center: A Community of Practice*, published by Utah State University Press.

Working Definitions and Key Concepts

Race: A social construct. A historical concept rather than a set of "natural" categories that orients around the classification and ordering of human beings in service of domination. While race is an *imaginary*, the idea of race continues to have material consequences and to condition the lived experiences of both whites and people of color.

Racial Prejudice: Dislike, distrust, or fear of others based on perceived racial differences. Individual racial prejudice is learned and, at the early stages or antiracist awareness, is often unconscious.

Racism: Racial prejudice coextensive with the unequal distribution of power within communities, institutions, and/or systems. In other words, or framed as an equation: race prejudice + power = racism.

Dysconscious Racism: tacit subscription to white supremacy, domination, and/or norms that distorts one's ability and willingness to recognize or acknowledge racism or race matters.

Institutional Racism: Visible and often invisible differential and unequal treatment of constituencies based on race. Inequalities with regard to access, power, and inclusion that are sanctioned by commission or omission by an institution.

Systemic Racism: The web of ideas, institutions, individual and collective practices that, taken together, ensure the perpetuation of social, political, and economic inequality along racial lines.

Whiteliness: Learned ways of knowing and doing—of thinking, speaking, and writing—characterized by a racialized sense of oneself as best equipped to judge, preach, and to suffer. This is a term coined by Minnie Bruce Pratt and taken up by Marilyn Frye to describe the ways that ideologies of white supremacy are taken up in thought and speech. She writes that "[w]hitely people generally consider themselves to be benevolent and goodwilled, fair, honest, and ethical . . . Whitely people have a staggering faith in their own rightness and goodness and that of other whitely people." (2001, pp. 90–91; see also Condon, 2012, p. 34) Note: whiteliness is not particular to white people, but can be learned and practiced by people of color as well.

Manifestations

Internalized Racial Superiority (IRS): The unconscious uptake, by whites, of the logics of white supremacy, such that one lives *as if* the idea of white supremacy is true.

Internalized Racial Inferiority (IRI): The unconscious uptake, by people of color, of the logics of white supremacy such that one lives *as if* the idea of white supremacy is true. Internalized Racial Inferiority may take the form of self-hatred, of cynicism or dismissiveness about one's own racial group, or of race prejudice toward other groups of people of color.

Whiteliness: Examples: the practice of representing the needs or interests of an entire racial group; refusing to hear or take seriously the concerns of people of color unless and until those concerns are represented in a particular way;

judging or adjudicating the needs and interests of people of color according to racialized, normative standards that implicitly assert the primacy of or that privilege whiteness.

Unconscious or Unintentional Racism: Learned and deeply internalized racism that we carry with us through our days. Some part of our work as antiracists is interior work: becoming conscious of our prejudices and actively working to transform ourselves. For example: feeling nervous or uncomfortable when encountering an individual or group of people from another perceived racial group.

False Attribution: The tendency to explain the actions or inactions of individuals or groups other than our own in negative terms (while excusing our own actions or inactions). For example: assuming that a child of color is struggling academically because her parents are uneducated or un caring or conversely assuming that academic excellence among children of color is anomalous (abnormal or unusual).

Triangulation: Assuming prejudices are shared among majority peoples: For example: expressing negative, derogatory, or racist views to other whites and assuming that they will all agree.

Unsolicited Nominations: Expecting or asking members of a marginalized or oppressed group to speak for that group.

Neglect: Providing unequal and inferior service, support, communication, and/or care to people of color or other members of marginalized, excluded or oppressed groups. For example: calling on, praising, or offering academic enhancement opportunities to white children in a classroom with more frequency than children of color.

Gatekeeping: Actively or implicitly preventing or obstructing people of color or other members of marginalized, excluded or oppressed groups from obtaining services, benefits, or privileges that are normally or regularly available to majority peoples. For example: regular tracking of students of color into remedial courses or programs. Or making exceptions to regular practices or procedures for whites, but not for people of color.

Individual Physical Racial Violence: Physical assault motivated by race hatred.

Symbolic Violence: Verbal assault motivated by racism, homophobia, or another form of oppression communicated and reproduced through signs and symbols. For example: the association of Black men with violence and hyper-sexuality through media representations in film, television, and print.

Group or Community Sanctioned Violence: Physical and/or symbolic assault motivated by hate and participated in or sanctioned by a group or community.

References

Cillizza, C. (January 10, 2010). Post politics. *The Washington Post.* Retrieved from http://www.washingtonpost.com/wp-dyn/content/article/2010/01/09/AR2010010902141.html.

Geller, A., Eodice, M., Condon, F., Carroll, M. & Boquet, E. (2007). *The everyday writing center: A community of practice.* Logan, UT: Utah State University Press.

King, J. (1991). Dysconscious racism: Ideology, identity, and the miseducation of teachers. *The Journal of Negro Education, 60* (2), 133–146.

Reagan, R. (1986) Weekly Radio Address. Retrieved from http://www.presidency.ucsb.edu/ws/?pid=37302.

Tilsley, A. (2012). Spotlighting hate. *Inside Higher Ed.* Retrieved from https://www.insidehighered.com/news/2012/10/01blogs-aim-bring-light-hateful-speech-online.

Section One
Actionable Commitments

Making Commitments to Racial Justice Actionable

Rasha Diab, Thomas Ferrel, and Beth Godbee,
with contributions by Neil Simpkins

In this chapter, we articulate a framework for making our commitments to racial justice actionable, a framework that moves from narrating confessional accounts to articulating our commitments and then acting on them through both self-work and work-with-others, a dialectic possibility we identify and explore. We model a method for moving beyond originary confessional narratives and engage in dialogue with "the willingness to be disturbed" (Wheatley, 2002), believing that disturbances are productive places from which we can more clearly articulate and act from our commitments. Drawing on our own experiences, we engage the political, systemic, and enduring nature of racism as we together chart an educational framework that counters the macro-logics of oppression enacted daily through micro-inequities. As we advocate for additional and ongoing considerations of the work of antiracism in educational settings, we invite others to embrace, along with us, both the willingness to be disturbed and the attention to making commitments actionable.

This chapter is inspired by the question: how can commitments to racial justice become manifest and actionable in our everyday lives? We have in different ways sought to answer this question and to find ways to embody transformative racial justice in our personal and professional lives. In doing so, we hope to initiate dialogue and to emphasize the processual nature of this work. Our work hinges on dialectic thinking, which engages the necessary tension between the critique *against* racism and the critique *for* social and racial justice. Critique is differently defined but is always considered an essential condition to making change. Like Porter et al., "[we] are not interested in simply reporting how evil institutions are; we think critique needs an action plan" (2000, p. 613). Power structures and systems of oppression are not changed *enough* by critique *alone*, but can become more entrenched by each conversation, presentation, and article that reveals oppression (Kincaid, 2003). As The New London Group (2000/2002), Porter et al. (2000), and Kincaid (2000) all argue, change requires new stories, new ways of collaborating, and new

need goals

ways of living. In other words, critique (in its many forms) should dovetail with opportunities to take action (also in its many forms).

Our work with the critique *against* and critique *for* is motivated by the desire to re-write the stories we tell and experience regarding racial oppression and racial justice. The narratives we tell (confessing our early encounters with racial oppression) hover closer to the critique *against* (and rarely move toward the critique *for*). Hence, we term such narratives confessional narratives: they confess pains and tribulation, but do not aspire toward actionable commitment. This realization made us think about their affordances and limits. Our chapter starts with this recognition. The trouble with the limits of narrative accounts catalyzed for us the move toward constructing a model for the reflective pursuit of racial justice.

In what follows, then, we first consider how "confessional narratives" often trap us into thinking of racism as primarily located outside of ourselves and solvable by completing specific tasks (along the lines of a checklist). We argue that one must (1) move from confessional narratives (2) with "a willingness to be disturbed" (Wheatley, 2002, p. 34) (3) to articulations of commitment that are (4) paired with reflective action. A great deal of self-work is required on the journey of growth from articulating a commitment to racial justice to making that commitment actionable and sustainable. In this chapter, therefore, we discuss (intrapersonal) self-work through cultivating emotional intelligence and finding time and space to work on racial justice matters. Thinking dialectically, we understand self-work is done alongside (interpersonal) work-with-others, which moves us toward institutional change. By calling for actionable commitments, we suggest the need to work in complementary *intrapersonal*, *interpersonal*, and *institutional* domains. Working with self and others in these three domains to pursue justice is a demanding project, which entails more than the long-term goal to end white privilege and oppression, while affirming the full enfranchisement of all people. Because this multi-dimensional work is processual, self-reflexive, and taxing, it hinges on a willingness to be disturbed—that is, a willingness to cultivate a tireless investment in reflection, openness, and hope for a better, more fulfilling future for us all.

Moving Beyond Confessional Narratives

Confessional accounts—efforts toward disclosing positionality, sharing an emergent recognition of oppression, and stating complicity paired with the need to counter injustice—are commonplace in antiracist, feminist, class-conscious, and other social justice discourse. Yet, we realize that these confessionals, like all genres, have affordances, limitations, and consequences. There are certainly important reasons for the continual re-emergence of confessional narratives. We, like many others, write such narratives responding to the desire to record: we feel the urge to know and to articulate the *when*, *where*, *how,* and the agonizing *why,* which together catalyze an increased recognition of oppression and dominance. This accounting transcends memory and recovery *per se*. We document to process, interpret, and testify. We also need to account for and often justify our investment in antiracism, providing an originary moment, evolutionary history, and critical genealogy for our commitment. An articulation of positionality is necessary for the ethos of the speaker/writer who chooses to address racial justice in order to understand the stake or mandate in the discourse. As such, narratives *can* ground our argument, pinpoint manifestations of racism, and renew our commitments. We also acknowledge that confessional narratives can be important indirect arguments against claims of (dis) trust as well as toward establishing alliance or solidarity. Recognizing these different functions is important, but the discourse that emerges within confessionals can also *limit* the possibility of where the originary moment might lead.

Confessional accounts can trap us between narratives of victims/saviors and of villains/heroes. The confessional can lock us into the moment of countering outright denials or reluctant dismissals of claims of injustice (e.g., that racism doesn't still exist today or that it exists outside of the self). Confessional accounts can trap us into a stasis of fact: in affirming the presence of racism through countering denials of its existence. The classical rhetorical stases are invention/interpretive tools, pinpointing crucial questions that inform, constitute, and probably constrain our racial equity discourse. Put differently, sharing confessional narratives can keep us in the realm of the known and long proven, accounting for the fact that racism does exist, thrive, and morph, for example—even though many scholars have demonstrated this (Villanueva's 2006 analysis of master tropes being one prominent case). These personal histories can only provide us with a *starting point* when exploring together our commitments to racial justice and how we make these commitments actionable.

Accounts are bound to be local and individual, and so *separately* they deflate the political dimensions of all encounters with oppression. We see value in the adage "the personal is political," but the value also comes from showing the seamless and seamed connections between these domains. The personal is not just loosely situated in a bigger political scene where power is, on the one hand, (ab)used to maintain inequities and privilege and, on the other hand, minimally contested and optimally re-configured and subverted. Rather, personal experiences of racism and interventions for antiracism also find their meaning in systems and institutions (including academic ones) that define and distribute power both in explicit and implicit ways. Such power is, in turn, affirmed in epistemological landscapes and networks of access and resources. The political nature of the personal is a constitutive dimension, for the personal occurs as we perceive it through the lens of experience (individual and collective), which is "a product of entire systems of social relations which are essentially time-bound, historically, culturally, and materially conditioned" (Leach, 1992). In other words, our individual action originates from and acts with or against systems of oppression and empowerment. While the work of composing, sharing, and circulating narratives is indeed crucial, there is nothing inherent in these narratives that leads narrators and interlocutors from narration to transformation, from conjecture to policy making, from problem-posing to solidarity-building. Confessional narratives must complement the move toward more systemic understanding of oppression with personal commitments to and action against oppression and toward justice. Only then may we better recognize the political and find ways to intervene and work with/against systems of power. Transformation, policy-making, and coalition-building are processes that are commitment-driven and demand long-term investment and frequent renewal.

Considering an Illustrative Example

As a case in point, we look to writing centers neither because they are anomalies nor the only site where we see confessional narratives. Rather, they exemplify one among many places across the curriculum and within institutions where the pattern manifests. As evidence, much writing center literature discussing race and racism appears invested in the confessional narrative—in descriptive storytelling about racism observed in the center. Often, writing center literature posits tutors and directors as white, American, and native speakers of English and then recounts a story where the inability to recognize the systemic nature of racism leads to a tutor or writer of color ending their relationship with their writing center. These narratives tend to posit justice as teaching white tutors and writing center staff how to approach tutoring writers of color.

One example is *The St. Martin's Sourcebook for Writing Tutors*, which opens with vignettes of different kinds of writing conferences in which the tutor is presented as an ostensibly white, middle-class, and American undergraduate struggling to meet a student's needs. One pair named Patrick and Sabah work on a paper for Sabah's graduate seminar. Sabah, an international student from Singapore, struggles with talking about herself positively. She states, "In my country it is considered inappropriate and too prideful to brag on oneself" (Murphy & Sherwood, 2008, p. 12). Patrick coaxes her to write confidently, but the text subtly emphasizes how his American values are more useful within the academy; the text states, "As an American, Patrick could boast of an accomplishment, or even take a justifiable pride in his achievements, but the same was not true for Sabah as a native of Singapore. Instead, her culture advocated restraint in discussing one's achievements and held that one should not claim excellence" (Murphy & Sherwood, 2008, p. 12). Sabah's inability to express pride is described purely in cultural terms and as a complication for a white American tutor to avoid when tutoring an international student. This rendering, like others we have read of writing conferences, examine a racially charged situation as a moment for a tutor to adapt, rather than to question the systemic nature of power in tutoring. The global is collapsed and dismissed into the local. One-time strategies of avoiding or downplaying racial tension in conferences trump long-term, expansive, and explicit ones.

In many staff education texts and handbooks that exist in writing center studies, the influence of tutors' identities on writers' self-disclosures is never discussed. The common characterizations of tutors and writers not only ignore the needs of tutors of color and international peer tutors, but also invest in and rely on white privilege and power. These narratives position students of color as liabilities to writing center discourse, resulting in a polarized/polarizing dynamic of liability where racial privilege emerges and is affirmed. White tutors, in turn, learn to work with writers of color and multilingual writers with a set methodology that limits the flexibility that marks good tutoring practice. Relying on the confessional narrative in our literature, conference spaces, and interpersonal relationships gives us a false sense of one-time, interventive response to racism, often fueling frustration when the "problem" of racism isn't immediately solved. These narratives do little more than reveal the presence of racism and express displeasure in its appearance at specific moments, in specific writing sites/spaces.

Narratives, in this sense, further the idea of individual (rather than systemic) racism, indicating that change can be made by focusing our attention on "the racist" out there or celebrating the "racially conscious" in here—picking up the ways we are trained to see "the racist" as the other, the few, and the obscure rather than thinking of "racism" as very much our own and embedded in all our everyday interactions. Illustrating the limits of the confessional, these narratives keep us in the realm of the (individual, local) problem, and they fail to move us toward articulations of our commitments or considerations of what ought to be. In effect, they hinder important self-work and work-with-others.

Shifting the Narrative and Its Uptake

How do we move beyond confessional accounts to truly transformative narratives? To shift our uptake of narratives, we need to recognize the political and global aspects of largely personal and local accounts. Indeed, confessional narratives share a larger purpose, as they are often written in response to two frequent critiques of antiracism work. The first dismisses manifestations of racism or other forms of oppression as relics of the distant past and as random, individual occurrence. The second argues against this work on the grounds of its relevance to composition and rhetoric studies and writing center work and scholarship. (Villanueva's piece counters the former, and the CCCC Diversity blog has sought to counter the latter.) These dismissal and jurisdictional arguments miss two key points: (1) the local is global, and (2) the personal is political. First, scholarship has well articulated the nature of racialization and racial formulation, pinpointing "that racial identities and the social meanings attached to racial groups are widespread and deeply embedded in social, educational, political and economic institutions" (St. Denis, 2007, p. 1071). Local articulations of racism can never be separated from national and international racial formulations. The decoding of the political nature of race issues evoked by individual and local narratives are crucial at this point in history where boundaries between peoples around the globe are shrinking. If we see that our goal is to teach more than reading and writing as techné and instead to invest in citizens who can participate in and enrich deliberative democracies (which is essentially a political project), we indeed need to recognize that "race issues cannot be treated as strictly local, for they are also caught up with national and international power relations" (Thompson, 1997, p. 9). Second, the political is always experienced on a personal level when people feel that their aspirations are undermined, stifled, or thwarted by political formulations that reproduce specific power articulations. Personal accounts can help us identify with the variegated nature of oppression.

Both global and political aspects of the local and personal account call for a different kind of engagement that willingly commits to listening and being disturbed (e.g., embracing a "willingness to be disturbed") by what narratives uncover as they testify to our increasing racial consciousness and commitment to racial equity. Through listening and reflective response, we can move from the realm of narrative as a personal account to narrative as collective, transpersonal, and resistive knowledge. If we choose to listen rhetorically to the narratives and recover the shadows of discourse they answer (or are perceived to answer), we might reconsider how we recount and redirect uptake. Collective interpretation of narratives—that is, testifying and processing together—is crucial to collective recognition of our problems, our commitments to counter them, and our efforts toward making commitments actionable. Only when we dare to confront racial ideologies can we fully tell a transformative story, a story that is not just confessional. Then, telling the story is an attempt at re-cording the ties we create with stories we choose to tell—toward motivating and grounding our actions.

While nothing in writing narratives inherently pursues the long process toward racial justice, we value narratives and see how they can be used toward pursuing our commitments—particularly when we choose to capitalize on their power for understanding the process (the means) toward change (particular ends). Narratives *can* be an important first step, particularly when written and told for self-reflexivity, but they do not constitute the entirety of antiracism work. Reframing the uptake (ours and others) to the narrative itself requires an *attitudinal* and *action-oriented* shift. It is this shift that can lead us to re-write our narratives as we move toward racial justice.

To make our commitments to racial justice actionable, we need to disrupt confessional narratives in order to move collaboratively toward an actionable stance. We also need to shape-shift, to re-narrate stories that capture our vision. Much like the "trickster moments" that Geller et al. (2006) urge readers to embrace and seek out, we pursue narratives that "can be generative, can nudge us to be mindful, to notice more" (p. 17). And, like The New London Group, by utilizing Design to improve Available Designs, we want to be "designers of our social futures" (2002, p. 36), focusing on rhetorical, systemic, and institutional work that makes "our working lives, our public lives (citizenship), and our personal lives (lifeworlds)" (p. 10) more racially just. Toward acting on these goals, in what follows we argue for cultivating the stance of willingness to be disturbed. We then propose three interdependent rhetorical moves that have the potential to re-design, transform, and move us closer toward racial justice. Namely, these moves are (1) embracing a willingness to be disturbed (2) articulating our commitments, and (3) making these commitments actionable. By no means are these final points of our thinking or in our long work together, but they are, we hope, valuable in proposing the types of self-work and work-with-others (e.g., intrapersonal, interpersonal, and institutional work) needed to engage in everyday/over-time, local/global, personal/political antiracism. We start with the first move: embracing a willingness to be disturbed.

Embracing a Willingness to Be Disturbed

> As we work together to restore hope to the future, we need to include a new and strange ally—our willingness to be disturbed. Our willingness to have our beliefs and ideas challenged by what others think. No one person or perspective can give us the answers we need to the problems of today. Paradoxically, we can only find those answers by admitting we don't know. We have to be willing to let go of our certainty and expect ourselves to be confused for a time. (Wheatley, 2002, p. 34)

A willingness to be disturbed underlies the work of articulating and making commitments actionable, as we are often challenged, confused, and even disturbed at times—wrestling with our personal narratives, our racialized positions in the world, and our relative power and privilege. Through choosing to be willingly disturbed, we have come to believe, as Wheatley does in *Turning to One Another*, that "[c]uriosity and good listening bring us back together" (2002, p. 36). Our willingness to be disturbed and our willingness to listen help us overcome seemingly insurmountable divides in the face of institutionalized racism enacted daily through a series of ongoing micro-aggressions and micro-inequities (Sue et al., 2007). Willingness to listen and to be disturbed makes us develop ways to resist how these micro manifestations of aggressions and inequities recycle their ever-present historical legacies.

We follow Wheatley's challenge to embrace a *willingness to be disturbed* to signify the important role self-work plays in our project. Like Wheatley, we value encountering disturbances because doing so helps us "see [our] own views more clearly," and is "a very useful way to see invisible beliefs" (2002, p. 36). Entering into the work with a willingness-to-be-disturbed stance signifies that personal epistemologies are part of systemic racism and oppression. This willingness also signals an openness to dialogue and a recognition that antiracism work is messy and ongoing. Antiracism is not a one-time deal: we are here with each other and with others to learn, to recommit ourselves, and to work toward making our commitments actionable in our lives. We strive, therefore, to confront our individual and collective fears and respons(a/i)bilities—work that we have found necessitates a willingness to be disturbed, as Wheatley calls us to. We believe that disturbances are productive places from which we can clearly articulate and act from our commitments.

Articulating Our Commitments

Just as it is important to open to a willingness to be disturbed and to move beyond confessional narratives, we see a need to articulate our commitments so that we can make them actionable. What grounds our vision and guides our process of embracing and sustaining the work of antiracism? The act of articulating (and re-articulating, regularly) our commitments is important for ensuring ongoing engagement with antiracism rather than a performance that is easy to drop in and drop out of. Further, we have found that it's not enough to engage *just* in a "critique of" or "action against" racism (or stances that make us complicit), but rather we need a positive articulation of "critique for" and "action toward" to keep our eyes on the *ought to be*, to pull from Horton (1997), Mathieu (2005), Branch (2007), and others.

Put simply, our shared commitment is to equity, to justice, to humanity. Work for antiracism is simultaneously work for racial justice and, as we understand it, work for social justice broadly, as our identities overlap and systems of power and privilege are intertwined. Equity work is always incomplete and involves always striving. It is everyday and local, while systematic and institutional. We have come to this understanding through seeing how systemic racism is enacted in small, regular, and everyday micro-inequities and micro-aggressions—bias enacted often not through conscious intent, but through the normalization of inequitable experience and seemingly small, though consequential, acts (see, e.g., Rowe, 1990; Sue et al., 2007). As we work at unlearning white supremacy and undoing this everyday racism, we engage in a process of tracing how systems of power and privilege work similarly, and yet differently, across enactments of oppression based on (assumed) group memberships. Therefore, the work of articulating commitments involves deep, iterative self-reflexivity. This involves, for example, asking questions of ourselves, such as the following:

- *Values:* What values, attitudes, and actions *can* and *must* we practice for racial justice?
- *Emotions:* How can we experience and act from joy in the pursuit of justice, and how can we mobilize joy to sustain and leverage our commitments over time?
- *Relations:* What networks best fuel—sustain, support, and nourish—our actions so that, for instance, time is spent caucusing (e.g., whites building solidarity with other whites committed to racial justice) and in building cross-racial coalitions and meaningful relationships?
- *Conditions:* What conditions enable the development of beliefs/values, attitudes, and actions consistent with antiracism? What conditions foster cross-racial relations? What conditions best sustain and motivate ongoing action and activism?

These questions cover a huge territory, but each question reflects our understanding of the multi-dimensional work of making commitments actionable, which comprises (1) intrapersonal self-work and (2) work-with-others on both the interpersonal and institutional levels. We turn next to these dimensions in which we see possibility for making commitments actionable.

Making Our Commitments Actionable

Our proposed multidimensional framework grows out of and responds to the need for *dialectical thinking*—residing in a liminal space of both/and. Drawing on Papa, Singhal, and Papa, we understand the dialectic *not* as simple dualisms, but as processes with four elements: "(1) contradiction, (2) motion, (3) totality, and (4) praxis" (2006, p. 43). Together, these elements help us understand how seemingly contradictory stances and moves are not only necessary, but mutually constitutive and supportive. Dialectic thinking is a strengths-based approach toward personal and micro-level change with the goal of influencing political, institutional, and more traditionally conceived macro-level change. The dialectic approach helps us value where we are and, at the same time, aspire toward where we'd like to be. This means appreciating what has been learned and also setting goals toward observing and intervening more frequently and in more nuanced and timely ways.

We are drawn to dialectic thinking largely because it allows us to see the productive tensions between critique and action. We can neither be so drawn to the realm of critique *against* that we miss other ways of taking action with others, nor can we be so focused on outward action that we lose critical, introspective reflection upon our methods, processes, and goals. As an approach for making our commitments actionable, the dialectic allows us to understand the importance of self-work alongside work-with-others, two ways of conceptualizing critique-and-action that we explore in what follows.

Doing Self-Work

Dialectic thinking directs our attention toward the important role of intrapersonal self-work—or individual "self study," with the goal of building self-reflexivity—and occurs alongside work with others. This self-work entails an investment in a serious, processual self-reflection and a rich dialogue with the self about how we think, how we feel, and finally how we invent time and space as lacking or available. The following sections reflect this process of self-reflection, which involves, among other considerations, the work of cultivating emotional intelligence and finding both time and place for the work. We offer these examples to begin operationalizing our commitments and understanding self-work as action-oriented and valuable.

Cultivating Emotional Intelligence

We have found that self-work often begins by being attentive to our emotions—that is, checking in about not only what we think (head) and plan to do (hands), but also how we *feel* (heart). Emotional intelligence refers to our ability to recognize and to manage effectively our emotional states, and it relates broadly to "self awareness, self management, social awareness, and the ability to manage relationships" (Goleman, 2006). We can cultivate emotional intelligence through self-reflection and deliberate attention to the nature and function of our emotions, especially anger and joyful commitment—two emotions we explore here. We reference anger and joyful commitment because they represent two different ends of the spectrum, noting how each can be a generative force that helps us work to attain racial justice.

Recognizing our own emotional responses helps us to act even through uncertainty. This reflexivity springs from a recognition of the generative potential of emotions. Reflective recognition of our emotional states helps us to take up a productive, albeit discomforting, liminal stance. From this stance, we can ask ourselves many questions: Can we reside in a place of creative possibility, while naming our range of emotional responses (e.g., *anger* because of oppression; *frustration* because we are not doing enough; *hurt* because we are misunderstood)? Can we reflect on what positive/negative emotions have to teach us? Are we *acting*, *reacting*, or both? These questions are partly informed by Lorde's (1984) essay, "The Uses of Anger: Women Responding to Racism," in which she explains how anger (even fury) is an appropriate response to racism. These questions are also informed by Buddhist monk Nhat Hanh's book *Anger* (2001), which discusses the need to *acknowledge* and *care for* one's anger the way we would care for a broken leg (and not hide, neglect, or cut it off). Both Lorde and Nhat Hanh are powerful activists who recognize the generative force that resides in our uses of anger to move ourselves and others forward. This *moving forward* is not automatic though. Because harnessing the generative potential of emotions is neither automatic, dispensable, nor easy, we must intentionally attend to connecting our head, heart, and hands, while reflectively renewing our actionable commitments.

Reflecting on the uses of anger, we seek to come to a place where we are less resigned to the presence of racism and other oppressions. Racism shifts and changes and may seem impossible to quantify or truly represent; it is false to say that "we're in a better place" now than we were fifty years ago. Many of us who work to end oppression come to places where we have little more energy than to recount the oppressions we see, to patch and piece together solutions for people wronged by our institutions, and to choose which oppressions in our life we have the time to battle. For example, while writing this, laws like Arizona's HB-87, Alabama's HB-57, and Georgia's HB-87 (copycats of Arizona's bill) legislate racial profiling and discrimination and, in effect, write into law the association of whiteness with citizenship. We must balance anger with the works of faith: our seemingly small interventions will bring tides of change in the years to come.

Antiracism is so often associated with struggle, yet acts of struggle—and especially of resistance—can be full of joy, excitement, learning, and growth. We recognize that these emotions, though at very different ends of the emotional spectrum, teach us and help us act toward a more equitable and just world. Inspired by the work of Martin Luther King Jr. and by Buddhist teachings, Hartnett (2010) writes about the need to commit ourselves to activism while caring for ourselves and others. "Joyful commitment," writes Hartnett, "asks us to pledge ourselves to work for social justice and for personal growth, to be both radical in our demands and gentle in our demeanor, both outraged by inequality and oppression and joyous in our commitments to end them" (p. 71). As such, functional, generative uses of anger and the move toward a joyful commitment nourish our spirit. Functional, generative uses of our emotions offer transformation that can both result from and sustain the pursuit of racial justice. We find that cultivating emotional intelligence is important for inspiring frequent re-commitment, for sustaining us, and for building strength for the long haul.

Finding Time and Space

For the most part, the self-work involved in cultivating emotional intelligence comes neither easily nor naturally. We often find any number of priorities claiming our attention, so it's necessary to devote time and space not only to the work of antiracism, but especially to the self-work required for actualizing our commitments. So we find that part of self-work is about dedicating the time and space for ongoing reflection—reflections on one's own positioning and power, on one's relations and ways of relating, on one's participation and leadership, and on so much more. Finding time and space for self-work is perhaps most important when it is in such limited supply and when self-care is considered a privilege in and of itself. The dialectic helps us see the value in *prioritizing time* for self-work, as this work informs and strengthens work-with-others. Similarly, the dialectic helps us to understand the *importance of holding space*.

Racial justice work often does not receive the time and attention it should because it is often seen as *in addition to* other responsibilities. Geller et al. (2007) write that many writing center directors—and, by extension, writing program administrators (WPAs)—feel they do not have time for anti-oppression and antiracism education for their tutors (and consequently for themselves) because ending racism is posited as a Sisyphean task that is overshadowed by the other pressures and mandates put on writing units at their academic institutions. Thus, we look for ways to make antiracism part of every task and to articulate the goals of antiracism as central to our writing programs, teaching, and scholarship. To do this, we need to hold time and space to get out of our normal, local, and patterned contexts to think with each other about how our commitments can become *integral to* all responsibilities. We need the time and space with allies to discuss matters and plan action that can jumpstart change. We need the time and space to help us deepen our commitments, creating really important synergies and partnerships. When in the absence of the luxury to participate in (inter)national networks, we must work harder to establish local networks.

As we work against oppression and for social justice, we complement self-work with work-with-others. The cumulative impact of cultivating emotional intelligence and finding time and space to renew our commitments can help us work with others differently and more effectively. Through the dialectic, we see that action-oriented self-work is every bit as important as working with others. The ways we do this work may align, overlap, and even diverge. At times, self-work may become the central means for articulating and pursuing our commitments, while at other times, we may be largely engaged in outward-oriented partnerships or institutional work. What is important to note is that each actionable move necessitates, informs, and strengthens the other.

Doing Work-with-Others

As a complement to and extension of self-work, we recognize the need to do interpersonal and institutional work within groups and across groups, which is crucial to systemic intervention toward racial justice. This complementary work not only differs from self-work, but also necessitates ongoing reflection on *the means* and *the ends* of collaboration, participation, and leadership. Too often in doing antiracism, we skip over the various types of work-with-others, which we here are trying to tease out and attend to with care. Working with others has many dimensions: cognitive, affective, and processual/procedural. Such work also balances dialectic possibilities like responding tactically, while planning strategically; being in-the-moment, while thinking long-term and working over-time; attending to interpersonal dynamics, while taking on institutional leadership. This multidimensional work is facilitated by two conditions: namely, creating and holding space for self and other and listening rhetorically. First, we would like to create more space for self-work with others who can help us listen more and more deeply to the "disturbances" in our accounts, to the articulations of our commitments, and to the moves toward making those commitments actionable. We need to hold space so that we can engage with others in critical, reflective, courageous dialogues (Singleton & Linton, 2006) about power—both in the sense of privilege and power *over* and in the sense of power *with* and *for*. Second, as we work with others, we need to attend to the relational and affective work involved in creating racially just institutions in which all members' rights are realized. In making institutional change, we must reflect on and recognize power relative to others, which involves deep attention to the *right to tell* and the *obligation to listen*. As we describe below, some of these moves are procedural, some interactional, some rhetorical—and all informed by the dialectic approach.

Doing Self-Work with Others

In this section, we focus on two (of what surely are many) dimensions of working with others toward social justice. These are (1) critical reflection on one's own power, privilege, and positioning and (2) taking care of the collective. These dimensions show the need for self-work with others to be reflective, dialogic, and affective, as well as ongoing. This work cannot be a one-time deal. As we care for ourselves, we care for others, and others care for us: care toward intra- and cross-racial solidarity can only be built through ongoing self-work, courageous dialogue, and the willingness to be disturbed.

Reflecting Critically on One's Own Power, Privilege, Positioning

When working with others—both through caucuses (i.e., within one's racial membership group) and through coalitions (i.e., in cross-racial collaborations), critical reflection on one's role is important for building solidarity and sustaining relations toward collaborative work over time. Recognition of power and privilege, especially our own, is difficult but doable and indispensable in work-with-others. Though it is possible to train oneself to notice how we articulate power, it is in relation to others that we tend to *make claims about* or *use* our power. Critical reflections on power—and the manifestations and implications of power *over*, *with*, and *for*—are essential to antiracism. These reflections not only teach us about the logic of oppression as a discourse—a dynamic articulation of collective power *over* and power denial—but these reflections especially show us how our own power makes solidarity possible. In other words, the very same power *over* brings to sharp relief how commitment makes solidarity (power *with*) for racial justice (power *for*) possible and necessary.

Fortunately, we often find ourselves situated to make commitments to fairness and justice actionable. This often happens when we choose to be in the generative place of being teacher/learner with our colleagues and students—for example, when we interrogate with others what it means to be a confidant and, in turn, an ally. The ally role is not a role that one should enter without giving thought to the harm as well as the good that can be done. In the case of antiracism, well-meaning white folks can do damage when acting only on what *they* see as the right thing to do in terms of racial justice without listening to folks of color. Instead, to prevent the hurt that eliminates the possibility of cross-racial solidarity, whites need to recognize that in working with others, there's a need to appreciate, to challenge, and to be willingly disturbed. When it is well used, the ally role is relationally intelligent and can open much possibility. But when it is not done well—that is, without critical reflections on one's power, privilege, and positioning—it can hurt ourselves and others and get us further mired in the mud of institutionalized racism.

Doing self-work with others involves ongoing care-full self-reflection that takes place, in part, through courageous dialogues. Institutes, retreats, and seminars can play important roles, for example, in facilitating and supporting reflective self-work, while establishing networks of colleagues who can help us look, look again, and listen more carefully than we probably would on our own, in the everyday context and rhythm of life. National and international networks can support everyday activism in local contexts and help to build disciplinary and cross-institutional change. Further, within these networks, we can *courageously* confront our own prejudiced assumptions. To do so, we need equally to learn from and listen to others (both within and across racial groups) who can help us realize these assumptions. Collaborative processing leads us to a second dimension of work-with-others: caretaking of the collective.

Taking Care of the Collective

Effective and sustained work-with-others tends to the needs and the goals of all parties involved. The absence of such attention risks foiling the condition of togetherness that enables a dialogic process in the pursuit of racial justice. This is why it is crucial to complement cognitive, critical reflection with affective and relational resources that we can use to support one another. Community organizers recognize the value of "caretaking of the collective," foregrounding our need to build intentional structures to care for ourselves and each other when engaged in antiracism work. We struggle with embodying the wisdom of this notion (the value of caretaking), and it seems that we are not alone, as is evidenced by a question posed to one of us recently: *How do we better cultivate peace within ourselves when we're engaged in peace-work?*

The work of everyday antiracism necessitates the emotional intelligence we've discussed earlier. Knowing when we need to re-fuel is important for sustaining the work, and it is equally important to recognize when others need time to refuel. This self-care can happen with others, as we process together modalities of oppression, while leaning into each other's needs and strengths. At its best, caretaking can facilitate and build a collaborative antiracism network, as partnerships and collaborative leadership are needed for making institutional change. Thinking dialectically, we see that engaging in self-work with others can strengthen work within institutions (e.g., in our classrooms and writing programs), just as working together for institutional change can allow us to do self-work with others. That said, critical reflection and caretaking come into play just as much when working for institutional change: we never leave behind self-work, but carry qualities such as reflection, dialogue, and emotional intelligence with us into more structural ways of making our commitments actionable. Likewise, we continue to find time and space for sustained and commitment-driven work-with-others *institutionally*.

Working Together for Institutional Change

In relation to institutional change, reflecting on and acting from places of power become essential. As we work with others toward institutional change, the process and result of the dialectic critique against oppression and critique for justice will vary. That said, we work within this dialectic as we articulate and act from our commitments, while also deliberating the consequences of choosing to *interrogate, relinquish,* and/or *use* power (especially when our work seems to reproduce the status quo). To this end, in these final sections focused on institutional change, we complement (1) interrogating power with (2) utilizing power. This interrogation of power *over*, however, can't be done only on a one-with-one level because it creates instances of insulated, local response to manifestations of racism. Instead, we need to make this interrogation structural so that it is independent of any person (e.g., the director of a writing program/center). Interrogating power should be part of an institution's culture, history, and vision—i.e., woven into its institutional fabric.

Interrogating Power

Our desire to interrogate power directs us to be more deliberate about questioning who, when, how, and to what end power is used in writing instruction, writing programs, and educational institutions more broadly. At times, our response may be troubled by an urge to relinquish power to resist oppression; however, we neither think relinquishing power is the only choice we have to pursue racial justice (though the urge to do so is understandable), nor is it necessarily useful or inherently altruistic. We can, alternatively, choose to use power *with* one another and *for* the pursuit of racial justice. As power *over* is relational (a relation of domination), so is power *with* relational, thriving when people together are willing to: (1) resist the urge to speak *for* others; (2) embrace the duty to listen to claims of grievance, even when un(der)vocalized; and (3) embrace respons(i/a)bility.

First, power *over* can be interrogated as we resist the urge to speak for. We invoke here Alcoff's (1991–1992) recognition of the very fine line between advocacy and totalizing (reducing and misrepresenting) the experiences of others even as we attempt to be allies. What makes us cross that line—tripping, reproducing, and preventing a discourse of testifying and solidarity? Alcoff offers a reflective process that can start by *at best* resisting and *at least* interrogating the desire to speak for others.

Second, it is almost impossible to resist the urge to speak without embracing the duty to listen. This begs the question: How can we listen better and ask others to listen better so we don't need the "proxy speaker" or the "sponsor"? Rhetorical listening has been addressed well in the literature (e.g., Glenn & Ratcliffe, 2011; Kelley, 1998; Oleksiak, 2014; Ratcliffe, 2005;), asking us to interrogate our assumptions about who has the right to tell and what accounts or interests impede us from recognizing this right. Rhetorical listening invites questions like: Who has the right to tell and to testify? How do we signal a commitment to listen when others' testify and seek to be heard? What is the impact of not telling and not listening? If the process of interrogating power starts with this model of critical examination, it goes deeper and becomes more demanding when we, as Alcoff suggests we do, examine our positions and the tacit ideological discourses that define how we know, feel, be, and—we would like to add here—listen. Alcoff (1991–1992) recommends, therefore, a serious analysis of our standpoint and context, an openness to critique and accountability, and an attentiveness to consequences of our privileges and the affordances of our positions. All enable listening.

Third, embracing responsibility and response ability is part of the dialogic, recursive nature of the work toward racial justice. There are numerous manifestations of the challenge of interrogating power *over*, which we think, when balanced by the choice to embrace joyful commitment, can result in response ability. We've seen white folks start antiracism work and then abandon it: leave articles half-written, committee charges half-met. It also prompts us to think about how white people so often get "credit" for doing antiracism work (i.e., professional credit and academic cultural currency), while people of color are expected and over-required to do "diversity work" without much, if any, credit. And even with the research and many narratives about faculty of color doing "double duty" (Gloria, 1998, p. 37)—that is, over-doing service, advising, teaching, research, and writing work—the problem is so entrenched that whites committed to antiracism continue to benefit from it. For example, white faculty who write about race and antiracism are recognized for this work and can trace professional gains from it (see, e.g., hooks, 1994). Even when recognizing the problem, whites committed to antiracism participate in and benefit from this structural inequity. Another way of saying the same thing: though whites committed to antiracism participate in and benefit from this structural inequity, relinquishing the work neither alleviates the asymmetrical distributions of responsibility to recover from racism nor does it solve the problem. Rather, it invites us to contemplate a central question: What rhetorical and leadership skills do we need to develop for the kind of solidarity and advocacy toward restructuring/countering the power of whiteness? We believe these skills come from an approach where we are willing to be disturbed and to let go when summoned to listen. The skills, practice, and responsibility of interrogating power are necessary alongside the skills, practice, and responsibility of using power for wider institutional change.

Using Power

Because racism is institutional, we believe that a significant part of making commitments actionable must happen within the institutions we occupy and shape. Institutions are big structures full of bureaucracies, and as Fox points out, "Most of us, even in rhetoric and composition, aren't prepared for working in bureaucracies" (2009, p. 15). However, institutions can be changed, and we look for ways to use institutions for greater access and equity. Consider what Porter et al. say about institutions:

> Though institutions are certainly powerful, they are not monoliths; they are rhetorically constructed human designs (whose power is reinforced by buildings, laws, traditions, and knowledge-making practices) and so are changeable. In other words, we made 'em, we can fix 'em. Institutions R Us. (2000, p. 611)

True, not everyone within an institution holds the same power, but we shouldn't allow our individual positions to determine whether we act. When we are in the shadow of power feeling small and subjugated, too often deferral—saying it's not our place to speak/act or it's someone else's struggle—presents itself as an easy move. But why not change our perspective? If we're in the shadow of power, that means we are really, really close to power, and with some creativity, we may be able to make something of the situation.

Teachers, WPAs, and writing center directors are ideally positioned to do institutional change work, forwarding equity and justice goals. And, as Porter et al. write, "for those of you who think such optimism is politically naive and hopelessly liberal and romantic, we believe that we (and you, too) have to commit to this hypothesis anyway, the alternative—political despair—being worse" (2000, p. 611). Again, though, commitments must be actionable and more than hopeful rhetoric. Within the context of understanding racism as a manifestation of institutional culture, politeness, and silence, we believe intentional efforts must be made to disrupt the status quo. Working toward more racially diverse teaching and tutoring staffs and cultivating the conditions that support racially just pedagogy and administration represent two areas well suited for activism and institutional change.

Faculty, WPAs, department chairs, deans, provosts, presidents, and chancellors occupy positions of power making them responsible for structural components of an educational space. These spaces have the potential to harm, heal, empower, and produce any number of other negative and positive consequences related to race and equity matters. "We cannot remake the world through schooling," The New London Group points out, "but we can instantiate a vision through pedagogy that creates in microcosm a transformed set of relationships and possibilities for social futures" (2002, p. 19). WPAs' conscious work (e.g., toward recruiting, hiring, and retaining a racially diverse staff as well as providing professional development opportunities) can help teachers/tutors confront racism within themselves, their classes/conferences, and writing programs/centers in general.

A specific example of an institutional shift occurs when faculty and administrators think critically about staff in regards to race and other identity memberships. The suggestion to hire more people of color at first seems tokenizing, and this suggestion is potentially motivated by tokenizing efforts. We have seen, however, remarkable shifts through conscious hiring when this hiring accompanies a move toward actively supporting tutors of color and changing the climate of the program/institution. For example, new hires draw in new students and colleagues from their networks, forward new perspectives on what the program/institution should be, and participate in shared leadership. Moving away from attempting to effect change *only* from top-down, one-time efforts and shifting instead toward all-in, long-term approaches helps us change the culture of a writing program and higher education as a whole, mitigating the disappointment accompanied with slow change.

Documents like "Continuum on Becoming an Anti-Racist Multicultural Institution" (Crossroads, n.d.) show the gradual nature of change and specify fundamental, observable markers of institutional change, but even such carefully constructed documents sometimes contain ambiguity, which represents both an entry into dialogue and potential impediment to action/goal actualization. Using power to effect change institutionally involves work-with-others in which we act based on commitments. Careful articulations—combing over word choice and phrasing—go hand-in-hand with the dialectic of interrogating and using power. These are different manifestations of power, which remind us of the role intrapersonal self-work plays when working with others, both interpersonally and institutionally. The many ways in which we make our commitments actionable—many of which are discussed here, while many more we continue to explore and find together—necessitate the *both/and* stance characteristic of dialectic thinking. And the dialectic, we find, brings us back to cultivating a willingness to be disturbed—that is, a stance of genuine openness to listening, learning, and leading on one's own and with others.

Conclusion

Together, we believe that an everyday educational process toward racial justice works against the macro-logics of oppression enacted daily through micro-inequities. A dialectic intervention focused on self-work and work-with-others might, at first, seem to have only local impact. However, if the local and personal converse with or gesture toward historical, social, economic, or otherwise material roots and implications, we believe they have the potential of addressing the larger macro-logics of inequity and oppression. We address inequity also by acknowledging how we experience, see, understand, participate in, and advocate against these macro-logics and micro-inequities differently based on our racial identities, personal histories, and intersecting positions within broader systems of power and privilege. Talking and listening across these differences has meant, for us, struggle, yet hope; vulnerability, yet possibility.

Through working together, we have come to realize the care-full, processual, reiterative, and self-reflexive nature of the work for equity and social justice in educational settings. It is this togetherness and openness to being disturbed that allows us now to think about a transformative narrative, one that moves beyond confessional accounts. Ultimately, we write toward the goal of making our commitments actionable and, in turn, creating new realities that are more racially and socially just. By continually doing self-work and work-with-others, we hope to live a recursive theory-practice-theory-practice life allowing us to never stop learning and acting with our local, national, and international communities. We hope to inspire this willingness to be disturbed in others, and we look forward to learning from and engaging with and alongside *you* on the long haul toward racial justice.

References

Alcoff, L. (1991–1992). The problem of speaking for others. *Cultural Critique, 20*, 5–32.

Barron, N. & Grimm, N. (2002). Addressing racial diversity in a writing center: Lessons and stories from two beginners. *The Writing Center Journal, 22*(2), 55–83.

Branch, K. (2007). *Eyes on the ought to be: What we teach about when we teach about literacy*. New York: Hampton Press.

Condon, F. (2007). Beyond the known: Writing centers and the work of anti-racism. *Writing Center Journal, 27*(2), 19–38.

Crossroads Anti-Racism Organizing and Training. (2007). Continuum on becoming an anti-racist multi-cultural institution. In *Teaching and training methodology documentation & evaluation report* (Appendix 5). Matteson, IL. Retrieved from http://crossroadsantiracism.org/wp-content/themes/crossroads/PDFs/Crossroads_Anti-Racism_Documentation_w-_Appendices.pdf.

De Jean, W. & Elsebree, A. R. (2008). Queer matters: Educating educators about homophobia. *Rethinking Schools, 22*(3). Retrieved from http://www.rethinkingschools.org/archive/22_03/quee223.shtml.

Denny, H. (2010). *Facing the center: Towards an identity politics of one-to-one mentoring*. Logan, UT: Utah State University Press.

Dunlap, L. (2007). *Undoing the silence: Six tools for social change writing*. Oakland, CA: New Village Press.

Freire, P. (2006). *Pedagogy of the oppressed*. New York: Continuum. (Original work published 1970)

Geller, A. E., Eodice, M., Condon, F., Carroll, M. & Boquet, E. H. (2007). *The everyday writing center: A community of practice*. Logan, UT: Utah State University Press.

Glenn, C. & Ratcliffe, K. (Eds.) (2011). *Silence and listening as rhetorical acts*. Carbondale, IL: Southern Illinois University Press.

Gloria, A. M. (1998). Searching for congruity: Reflections on an untenured woman of color. In L. H. Collins, J. C. Chrisler & K. Quina (Eds.), *Arming Athena: Career strategies for women in academe* (pp. 36–39). Thousand Oaks, CA: SAGE.

Goleman, D. (2006). *Emotional intelligence: Why it can matter more than IQ*. New York: Bantam Dell.

Hartnett, S. J. (2010). Communication, social justice, and joyful commitment. *Western Journal of Communication, 74*(1), 68–93.

Hoefer, B. K. (2008). Personal epistemology and culture. In M. S. Khine (Ed.), *Knowing, knowledge and beliefs: Epistemological studies across diverse cultures* (pp. 3–22). Dordrecht, NL: Springer.

hooks, b. (1994). Feminist scholarship: Black scholars. In b. hooks, *Teaching to transgress: Education as the practice of freedom* (pp. 119–127). New York: Routledge.

Horton, M. (With Kohl, H. & Kohl, J.). (1997). *The long haul: An autobiography.* New York: Teachers College Press.

Kelley, A. (1998). On listening. *Peace Review, 10*(4), 529–532.

Kincaid, J. R. (2003). Resist me, you sweet, resistible you. *PMLA, 118*(5), 1325–1333.

Leach, M. S. (1992). Is the personal political? Take two: Being one's self is always an acquired taste. *Philosophy of Education.* Retrieved from http://www.ed.uiuc.edu/eps/PES-Yearbook/92_docs/Leach.htm [no longer available].

Lorde, A. (1984). The uses of anger: Women responding to racism. In A. Lorde, *Sister outsider: Essays and speeches by Audre Lorde* (pp. 124–133). Berkeley, CA: The Crossing Press.

Mathieu, P. (2005). *Tactics of hope: The public turn in English composition.* Portsmouth, NH: Heinemann.

Murphy, C. & Sherwood, S. (Eds.). (2008). *The St. Martin's sourcebook for writing tutors* (3rd ed.). Boston: Bedford/St. Martin's.

New London Group, The. (2002). A pedagogy of multiliteracies: Designing social futures. In *Multiliteracies: Literacy learning and the design of social futures* (pp. 9–37). New York: Routledge. (Original work published 2000)

Nhat Hanh, T. (2001). *Anger: Wisdom for cooling the flames.* New York: Riverhead.

Oleksiak, T. (2014). *Listening language and student interaction in online writing spaces* (Unpublished doctoral dissertation). University of Minnesota, Twin Cities, Minneapolis/St. Paul.

Papa, M. J., Singhal, A. & Papa, W. H. (2006). *Organizing for social change: A dialectic journey of theory and praxis.* Thousand Oaks, CA: SAGE.

Porter, J. E., Sullivan, P., Blythe, S., Grabill, J. T. & Miles, L. (2000). Institutional critique: A rhetorical methodology for change. *College Composition and Communication, 51*(4), 610–42.

Ratcliffe, K. (2005). *Rhetorical listening: Identification, gender, whiteness.* Carbondale, IL: Southern Illinois University Press.

Rowe, M. P. (1990). Barriers to equality: The Power of subtle discrimination to maintain unequal opportunity. *Employee Responsibilities and Rights Journal, 3*(2), 153–163.

Singleton, G. E. & Linton, C. (2006). *Courageous conversations about race: A field guide for achieving equity in schools.* Thousand Oaks, CA: Corwin Press.

St. Denis, V. (2007). Aboriginal education and anti-racist education: Building alliances across cultural and racial identity. *Canadian Journal of Education, 30*(4), 1068–1092.

Sue, D. W., et al. (2007). Racial microaggressions in everyday life: Implications for clinical practice. *American Psychologist, 62*(4), 271–286.

Thompson, A. (1997). For: Anti-racist education. *Curriculum Inquiry, 27*(1), 7–44.
Villanueva, V. (2006). Blind: Talking about the new racism. *The Writing Center Journal, 26*(1), 3–19.
Wheatley, M. (2002). *Turning to one another: Simple conversations to restore hope to the future*. San Francisco: Berrett-Koehler Publishers.

Teaching African American Discourse: Lessons of a Recovering Segregationist

Calvin M. Logue[1]

In the early 1970s at the University of Georgia I developed and taught a course in "Black Rhetoric" seven times. (Later we were fortunate to engage an African American professor to adopt and further develop the class.)

The first challenge, after compiling a working prospectus, was getting the course approved. At this time there was no Black Studies program at the University of Georgia, only isolated courses in such disciplines as history, sociology, and probably literature. After submitting a proposed syllabus and extensive reading list to the Curriculum Committee of the College of Arts and Sciences, sometime later I was called before those representatives from the sciences, social sciences, fine arts, and humanities to explain why Black rhetoric should be studied at a university. A professor asked, "Are you going to teach our students to speak like Stokely Carmichael?," one of the many advocates included in the syllabus. Eventually the proposal was approved.

Looking back on that time, over forty years ago, I was probably among a number of white teachers feeling increasingly concerned and guilty about the long season of abuse experienced by African Americans in the United States in general and my southland in particular. We were presenting and hearing papers at conventions on the need for African American studies and the difficulty of accessing copies of speeches, writings, and other materials by African American activists that could be made available feasibly to students. Thinking about it now, my efforts in the classroom at the time, when contrasted with the dangers confronted by African Americans daily and when sitting-in restaurants, marching in hostile streets, confronting police dogs and fire hoses, and being jailed, were tame indeed. Hopefully some students benefited.

Because the class I taught would be something of a pioneering effort, at least at our university, and was open to all undergraduates, I wrestled with exactly what to cover, how much, and how. (Since few courses in African American studies were available, a graduate student or two audited this class, helping with assignments, doing further research, and writing papers.)

I reduced the content to four units. First we began studying Arthur L. Smith's (later Molefi Kete Asante) *Rhetoric of Black Revolution*, one of the few sources known to me at the time that students could purchase. From Asante's book we identified recurring persuasive strategies employed by Black activists that we could apply in our analyses of their discourse throughout the term.

Secondly we explored efforts to abolish slavery. Drawing upon Patrick Kennicott's dissertation, his article in the *Journal of Black Studies*, and a variety of additional sources, we investigated how Black southern and northern preachers opposed bondage in the nineteenth century. We read about "local Black agents" sponsored by anti-slavery societies. We found "fugitive agents" recalling personal experiences to dramatize abuses of slavery. We dissected arguments communicated by advocates such as Charles Lenox Remond, Fredrick Douglass, Sojourner Truth, Henry Highland Garnet, and William Wells Brown.

The third unit consisted of viewing excerpts of speeches by contemporary African American speakers on film. With funds from the department of communication studies, I purchased Technicolor films from *Time-Life* for $500.00. About four minutes long, each film provided a workable and valuable overview of the philosophy and rhetorical approach of a particular speaker. For example we observed *what* Bayard Rustin, Rap Brown, Shirley Chisholm, and Coretta Scott King advocated and *how* they persuaded audiences. Viewed in light of Professor Molefi Kete Asante's explanations of strategies, topics, and audiences, we began to better understand the motivation, role, discourse, and influence of Black spokespersons active from anti-slavery to recent times.

The fourth unit incorporated individual and group assignments: oral reports, a brief essay, and role playing. To assist with these requirements, I provided an extensive bibliography of library holdings plus numerous articles from the Bobbs-Merrill Reprint Series in Black Studies on such topics as "The Rural Negro Minister: His Work and Salary," "The Professional Fugitive in the Abolition Movement," "The Klan Revival," "Douglass' Mind in the Making," "History of the Black Man in the Great War," "The Forgotten Years of the Negro Revolution," and "The Real Benjamin Banneker." I also supplied reprints of picture-essays on Black advocates from *Life Magazine* that cost twenty-five cents each. Students were encouraged to browse on their own through old documents, including newspapers, journals, letters, and diaries on microfilm.

Informed by these various sources, each student gave a brief oral report and wrote a short essay on a particular subject of her or his own choosing. One young white woman interviewed a local Black preacher and visited his church on Sundays, certainly a new experience for her. Concerned about their own heritage, several African American students researched particular anti-slavery speakers. Others examined the discourse of contemporary leaders. One individual researched the "ghetto as audience."

We also relied upon role playing. Usually the class enrolled between sixteen and twenty students, divided somewhat equally between Blacks and whites; interesting, because few African Americans were enrolled at the University of Georgia at the time. These groups were asked to represent four factions active under slavery: politicians, scholars, preachers, and anti-slavery speakers. Portraying these roles, individuals in each of the groups addressed the class as a whole using arguments identified with their characters.

From the first day, students were informed that ideally members would consider exchanging experiences and views against the backdrop of Blacks' opposition both to slavery and current separate-but-unequal conditions and opportunities. Even on the quarter system we met two days a week for two hours, providing time for the various initiatives in class. When not viewing films, to promote discussion we often sat in a circle.

To some extent, the results of class discussions could be unpredictable. In the fall of 1973, a white student from New Jersey commented, "I simply have never been around many colored people." A young Black woman responded: "It's obvious you have never been around many Black people; in my high school if you had said 'colored,' you would have been in trouble." Participants spoke of the significance of self-identity. Some contrasted the appropriateness and inappropriateness of saying "Negro" and "Black." (At the time "African American" was not as widely spoken.) Dick Gregory had recently talked on campus, teaching us how to say "Black" and why. Others questioned or debated the relevance of such "white" celebrations as Fourth of July, referring to Frederick Douglass' assessment of that occasion. Some students discussed openly; others did not. Near the end of one term, a young Black woman read the following statement to the entire class:

> I see the pale, blank, expressionless faces of our "white" classmates who, while listening to Nikki Giovanni—STARE, fidget at their nails, and STARE. They are so conditioned to coldness that they cannot warm up and feel—feel like human beings. Their blue-green eyes sweep and survey as if trying to find some understanding. What does it take to break the ICE around your heart, your mind, your precious soul. If you are ignorant, ask to allude yourself of your ignorance. If you are afraid, VOICE your fears in order to overcome your fear.

* * *

Should I attempt to teach a course today in the history and criticism of public discourse for undergraduates, I would still have to decide what to teach, how much, and how. Some challenges would be the same, others different. First I would review the wide scope of literature published in recent years on issues of race, probably better understanding the complex forces at work in issues of race in contemporary society. Maybe the content would be equally distributed between historical and present issues, strategies, and ideologies.

I wonder what views Black and white students would bring to such a class today, in contrast to those enrolled during the 1970s. Were the public and/or private schools they attended more racially integrated today or less, and with what results? What topics and concerns would the students bring up? What subjects would they choose to research? In class would more students or fewer participate readily or withdraw? In general would whites and Blacks today be more receptive or hostile to issues that arise and to each other? Would they think that conditions and opportunities for African Americans are better or worse? In what ways?

Probably many contemporary examples of situations confronted by African Americans would be discussed, maybe good and bad. Would they consider a wealthy owner of a National Basketball Association professional team advising a friend not to accompany Blacks to his games to be representative of attitudes among whites or unique? Is racism more subtle today than during the day of rigidly segregated restaurants, buses, schools, motels, and restrooms. In what forms does one find this more subtle abuse? What strategies are being devised and deployed by African American spokespersons to meet this more cunning means of racism?

In teaching the class today one thing would not change. While attempting to serve as an informed and concerned mentor, I would plan the instruction so that students could hear, read, study, analyze, and discuss the concerns and choices of African Americans expressed in their discourse.

* * *

What led me, one socialized in rigid racial segregation, to plan, submit, defend, and teach a course in African American public address? Certainly I had enough to do teaching courses in public speaking, group discussion, social movements, and rhetorical criticism. And I had not been taught content needed for a class in African American discourse. Indeed, in my own graduate programs in speech (now communication studies), there was no course or seminar in the history and criticism of African American discourse, only the mention of the varying emphases of Booker T. Washington and W. E. DuBois.

To explain why I decided to teach African American discourse, I will describe my transformation from one separated from Blacks by law, custom, and choice to an individual seeking a better way. In planning and teaching this course, I drew, not only from the diversity of sources noted above, but also my own personal experiences growing up in Pine Apple, Greensboro, Evergreen, and Auburn, Alabama, and beyond.

* * *

Figure 1. (Photograph property of Birmingham Public Library, taken from inside the church looking outward. Courtesy of Birmingham Public Library Department of Archives and Manuscripts, Catalog Number, 85.1.22.)

On Sunday, September 15, 1963 at 10:22 a.m., dynamite set off by at least three white men at the 16th Street Baptist Church in Birmingham, Alabama killed four young African American girls who were attending Sunday school and injured numerous others. Approximately thirty minutes later, Mary Jo, Michael—our 2½-year-old son—and I were driving home from Sunday school on 17th Street, across Kelly Ingram Park from the bombed house of worship. The following photograph is of damage done to the Sixteenth Street Baptist Church, Birmingham, Alabama, by dynamite, 1963.

That morning around 9:00 a.m., we left our rented home on Arkadelphia Road across from Birmingham-Southern College and drove to Trinity Methodist Church on Oxmoor Road in Homewood, following a route through downtown that took us past Kelly Ingram Park, 16th Street Baptist Church, and over Red Mountain by the Vulcan statue.

In 1961 I finished the master's degree at Florida State University in speech and took a job the following year at Birmingham-Southern, a Methodist liberal arts college located in the city. I taught public speaking and oral interpretation and coached the debate team. I can recall that at the invitation of the local chapter of the American Association of University Professors (AAUP), Charles Morgan, Jr., a young lawyer from Birmingham, spoke at the college on racial problems confronting society and what responsible people should do to solve them. (Mr. Morgan passed away in 2009.)

When we first moved to Birmingham in 1962, we rented an apartment in Homewood. Each morning when I drove to Birmingham-Southern College to teach, because of congested traffic downtown, I skirted the city. In 1963, when an old home owned by Birmingham-Southern College just across Arkadelphia Road from the campus became available to rent, we moved there, but we continued to worship at Trinity United Methodist Church in Homewood. On that fateful Sunday morning, we arrived at Trinity United Methodist Church around 9:30 a.m. After Sunday school, about 10:55 a.m., deciding not to attend the 11:00 a.m. worship service, we got into our two-toned 1958 Ford and started home.

Anticipating that the downtown streets would be deserted on Sunday, since the stores were closed and many residents would likely be at home or in church, we decided to return home by the same route that we had come to Sunday school. From Oxmoor Road we drove down Red Mountain on 26th Street to the Vulcan statute, where 26th becomes 20th Street, the main thoroughfare through Birmingham. We drove thru Five Points South, under the railroad tracks, turning west onto 4th Avenue. We turned north onto 17th, a two lane street, and came to Kelly Ingram Park situated across from the 16th Street Baptist Church.

As we drove adjacent to Kelly Ingram Park across from the east side of the dynamited church, we came up behind cars that had stopped in the road as if there were a wreck up ahead. People scampered about as if leaving a fire. Wondering what was happening we looked out the windows of our Ford into the angry faces of young African American men lining the curb on the side of the road.

Suddenly there was a loud crash that seemed to come from inside our car. Then we saw young African American men standing at the curb with concrete coated bricks in each hand, one brick hanging down in the left hand at the ready and one

Figure 2. (Photograph property of Birmingham Public Library. Courtesy of Birmingham Public Library Department of Archives and Manuscripts, Catalog Number 85.1.9.)

drawn far back for throwing in the other. With angry shouts and all their might, they hurled bricks onto our car, striking the side and the back, their momentum causing them to lunge off the curb into the street. Nearby was an old building that had collapsed, seemingly making available an endless supply of bricks reinforced with concrete.

Mary Jo and I were frightened and curious as to what was happening. We were sitting targets, bumper-to-bumper with cars in front and behind. There was no escape. We quickly locked ourselves in the car. Sensing the heightened tension, little Michael began to cry. I urged Mary Jo to squat down in the floor with Michael. Doing so, she placed Michael beneath her as well as she could. I was holding on to the steering wheel and trying to keep the clutch of our straight-shift drive pressed down so that the car wouldn't stall. From inside the car each smash of a brick sounded like an explosion. Fearing that a brick would crash through a window, we attempted to turn away, half-duck, and shield our heads with a free arm and hand. The following picture is another photograph of the bomb scene, with the church to the right.

* * *

Some seven years earlier, in 1956, during combat training in the U. S. Marine Corps at Camp Lejeune, North Carolina, I was crawling in the dirt with back pack and M-1 rifle under barbed wire, bullets flying overhead and explosions going off all around me. In January of that year, after nearly two years enrolled at Alabama Polytechnic Institute (later Auburn University) in sociology, I had taken the train from Auburn to Montgomery to join the Army. Upon finding that the Army recruiter was away for lunch, I went next door and joined the Marine Corps for a three-year tour of duty.

Immediately the Marine recruiter in downtown Montgomery had me transported to a large hangar at Maxwell Air Force Base out from town where several hundred other men were sitting around waiting for orders. I assumed they all had joined the Marine Corps. Over the public address speaker we heard this loud command: "All men who joined the Marines step up to the desk." Only two persons stepped forward, amidst wisecrack warnings from the other recruits—Isaac Ward, a young Black man whom I had never met, and me. Later I learned that Isaac Ward was from Dothan, Alabama, where Mary Jo, my wife, grew up.

* * *

I was born in 1935, and reared in small towns in Alabama—Pine Apple, Greensboro, Evergreen, and Auburn—where schools, churches, movies, restaurants, motels, rest rooms, water fountains, and bus stations were racially segregated. Wherever one went there were written signs as well as unspoken mores separating "whites" from "coloreds." By legal and cultural definition, whites and Blacks as a rule did not mingle unless Blacks provided some service. I had only communicated with Blacks from what we whites in the South and beyond perceived as a superior social and racial status, a perception that gave rise to many of our personal and communal misconceptions and prejudices.

As a result I knew many Blacks but always on my terms. For example, when at ages five and six I played with "Tom" in Pine Apple, I assumed that he was visiting as a friend, only to learn later that this young African American was only accompanying his Mother, "Mary," our cook. Certainly we did not play at "Tom's" home. Once Mama apparently sent "Tom" home, or perhaps had "Mary" send him home, when a white boy visiting with us began taunting him. She didn't want "Tom's" feelings hurt or him to get into trouble. At this time that was probably a typical solution when it came to matters of race, sending "Tom" home rather than confront the racist ridicule practiced by young whites. "Tom," my brothers, and I rode horses barefooted in the dirt driveway made from chinaberry limbs. "Tom" told us about his father who had seen turtles in the "islands" so big one could ride on their backs. Since we had seen how big turtles at the branch behind our house actually got, not for a second did we believe him.

On occasion in Pine Apple several of we white boys walked across the pasture behind our house, careful not to wear a speck of red, because of the giant bull that guarded the grounds, crawled up behind a log, and spied on residents of "colored town" as if we were looking down upon aliens. There were many smoking pots, as a number of African American women took in washing, doing it over outdoor fires.

When Daddy left his job teaching vocational agriculture in Pine Apple to become Assistant County Extension Agent in Greensboro, Alabama (Hale County), Mama wanted "Mary" the cook to move there with us. Reportedly "Mary" wanted to go, but another employer somehow wouldn't allow it. He was likely the same clerk that Mama upset one day. The clerk was waiting on a Black person when Mama came into the store. When the clerk shifted his attention to what Mama wanted to purchase, she told him that the Black customer was there before her and should be waited on first. Mama said that the clerk was infuriated by her stand. Mama mailed Christmas clothes and other items to "Mary" for the rest of her life. Still, thinking back, I cringe at the assumption that "Mary" would be asked to leave her family and community to travel with a white family segregated from her by race to a different locale.

Mama grew up in Bay Minette, Alabama. She was graduated from Agnes Scott College in Atlanta in French and music and taught school in Luverne, Alabama, where she met Daddy. My three brothers and I were born in the house in Bay Minette where Mama was reared, in the care of her father, a physician. Our grandfather, the doctor, apparently treated African Americans and whites medically the same. Whoever came in his office first, he probably saw first. Day and night, on "house calls," he drove—first in horse and buggy and later in a Dodge—to both white and Black homes, often on rough dirt roads. In the 1930s, the "Tar Plant's" union voted to drop Granddaddy as their physician. Only two voted for him, both Blacks. Like many of us early on, however, in some ways he was captive of the nineteenth century, providing separate waiting rooms at his office.

In Greensboro "Arabella" served as "Mary's" replacement as family cook. In the fourth grade or so, when I first walked into "Arabella's" home, right across the dirt road from our own house, I was surprised to find it so orderly and well appointed, another example of the negative and inaccurate assumptions we whites learned early in life. When we left Greensboro, "Arabella" informed Mama that, because of her age, she could no longer look after her dog, Jack. He went with us to Evergreen. When Jack was dying of cancer, Mama held him in her lap and fed him aspirin water. Such good deeds occurred more often than one might think, however, at times they also enabled we whites to deny and rationalize the subservient segregated conditions under which African Americans were forced to struggle.

I never knew the family names of those African Americans whom I encountered so often in our homes and beyond in the small Alabama towns where we lived. While I was taught to address "Mary" and "Arabella" as "Ma'am," "yes Ma'am," and "no Ma'am," I was not required to address African Americans with "Mrs." or "Mr." Eventually one would have to be peculiarly insensitive or acutely socialized in racist traditions to overlook the indignity of this discriminatory practice.

We moved to Auburn in 1948 when Daddy became the 4-H Club Leader for the State of Alabama, following three years of service as County Extension Agent in Evergreen (Conecuh County). Daddy grew up in Troy, Alabama, and was graduated from Troy State, a two-year college at the time. Later he received the B.S. and M.S. degrees in agriculture from Auburn University.

Our first Sunday in Auburn, Daddy parked the Ford on Gay Street equal distance between the First Methodist and First Presbyterian churches, and announced that "each person could go to the church of his choice." My older brothers, Mickey and John, began walking toward the Methodist church, while Daddy, Mama, and young Lamar started in the opposite direction. In Pine Apple, Greensboro, and Evergreen we all were active in the Methodist Church. Earlier, however, while Daddy was enrolled in Alabama Polytechnic Institute in Auburn, he and Mama had been members of First Presbyterian. Hesitating, thinking my older brothers wouldn't want me tagging along, still I stayed with the Methodists, among whom later I would meet the Reverend Ashland Shaw. As is often true even today in many mainline churches, at that time few if any African Americans worshiped in "our white" services.

I recall, soon after arriving in Auburn, walking up to the counter in Wright's Drug Store, where an African American woman and child were already waiting to order ice cream. The server looked beyond them to me, a thirteen-year-old, and asked what flavor I wanted. I knew that it was unfair for me to take precedence, but unlike Mama, I didn't protest. If these discriminatory experiences began slowly to wear on some young whites, one can only imagine what humiliation and anger African Americans endured. The advantage of courses in African American studies such as my own is that these incidents and feelings can be fully expressed, explored, explained, and opposed.

Later on I drove from Auburn to Opelika, the Seat of Lee County, Alabama to register to vote. When the official called me back in the office of the Court House, I saw an elderly African American man sitting at a desk concentrating upon what appeared to be an official document. After I had filled-out a registration form and was leaving, I noticed that the senior African American gentleman was still working thru the document in order to "qualify" to vote. As was true when I was sold ice cream first, I knew that this treatment of the elderly citizen was wrong. But like most whites I did not question this discriminatory way of denying African Americans their civil rights, placing me in the category that Dr. Martin Luther King assessed as good people doing nothing so that evil could thrive.

One day Mama and I were in our living room at home on Brookwood Drive in Auburn. As the young Black carrier rode up on his bike to deliver our newspaper, we heard white kids say something like, "get out of here n_____r." When she heard the ugly racist remark, I noticed that Mama bit her lower lip, shook her head in shame, and shed tears, a rare protest at the time. As curious as it sounds, Mama and Daddy taught and required us always to show respect to all individuals regardless of race. Had I insulted any individual Black or white person at any time, when we returned home, I would have paid dearly. Daddy was a tough disciplinarian. But we also were required to obey the verbal and nonverbal signs that separated "whites" from "coloreds" throughout the region. From birth, in one way or another, we learned these racist attitudes and practices at home, church, school, store, street, and playground.

From 1941, when I entered the first grade in Pine Apple, through 1960, when I received the B.A. at Auburn University, no Black students, as a rule, had been allowed in "our" public educational institutions. In 1961, I wrote my master's thesis at Florida State University on "The Status of Speech Education in the White Public Schools of Alabama."

* * *

Only once, before meeting Isaac Ward at Maxwell Air Force Base in 1956, had I conversed with African Americans on an equal status. This occurred in 1955, when as a sophomore at Auburn University, motivated by Reverend Ashland Shaw, I attended the Student Volunteer Movement Quadrennial Conference in Athens, Ohio. The meeting was planned in part by Ms. Margaret Flory, one of the leaders of the ecumenical movement of the twentieth century. More than half the 4,000 students attending came from outside the United States. Upon returning home, I had my film developed of that racially integrated interaction, but I hid the pictures. Figure 3 is one of the pictures taken with my camera on our way to the Ohio conference that I hid. (I am second from the left.)

Even so, my sense of racial justice was growing more acute through participation in the Wesley Foundation at Auburn where, under the leadership of Reverend Shaw, we had begun to discuss and question the evil of the separate-but-unequal treatment imposed upon African Americans in which we were participating. While some later wrote that we were the silent generation, actually many of us then were quite vocal in small groups, if short on action. While Mama was demonstrating opposition to abuse of African Americans at home, Ashland Shaw was reforming my consciousness at the Wesley Foundation. Elsewhere African American activists such as Dr. King were being increasingly heard on television from Montgomery, Selma, and Birmingham, along with journalists such as Ralph McGill of the *Atlanta Constitution.*

When Isaac Ward and I walked up to the desk of the U. S. Marine master sergeant whose dress blues were covered with medals of service and heroism, we probably both needed a friend, but neither one of us spoke. Instinctively, even before boot camp, we both knew there were times when one should just listen and obey.

Figure 3

After my physical exam, when I covered the same weak eye twice so I could pass the test—a decision on the rifle range at Parris Island I would regret—I looked around for Isaac Ward, but he was gone. I did not see him again until the next morning when I boarded the train in Montgomery for Parris Island, South Carolina, via Atlanta, Georgia. I had stayed the previous night at a very nice hotel in Montgomery, courtesy of the U. S. Government, a new experience for me. When I naively asked Isaac Ward where he disappeared to after our physical exams, he replied matter-of-factly that he had spent the night in a part of Montgomery that I did not see, another situation to be examined in a minority studies class.

Surprisingly we were able to sit together on the train trip from Montgomery to Parris Island, a new experience for me. When we got off the train in Atlanta for a layover, I was upset by the separate waiting rooms and decided to sit with Isaac Ward in the "colored" section of the depot. I guess I assumed that Blacks would be less likely to protest my presence in their waiting room than would whites oppose Isaac Ward in theirs (ours). Certainly that was a rare experience for me. Isaac Ward didn't express an opinion. Looking back now, one can only speculate what Isaac Ward was thinking and how he was adapting, growing up in the segregated Deep South, now volunteering to serve his country in the Marine Corps, having been assigned the night before to a separate hotel in Montgomery. I suppose many who did not grow up in the South under this segregated system will have difficulty understanding all the forces at work, a condition that students could closely examine.

While waiting for the train to Parris Island in Atlanta, together Issac Ward and I walked over to the *Atlanta Constitution* building to speak to my brother, Mickey, who covered college sports for that paper. I probably assumed that a newspaper that published Ralph McGill's columns in support of equal opportunities for African Americans would likely be more receptive to racially mixed guests.

Little did I realize that day on the way to Parris Island that a few years later, while working on a doctoral dissertation at Louisiana State University, I would be sitting in Ralph McGill's office, taping an interview with him about his many speeches on human rights. Having returned to Auburn in 1958 to complete a B.A. degree in sociology and earning the M.S. in speech at Florida State, in 1967 I finished a Ph.D. at Louisiana State University in the history and criticism of public address. My dissertation was on the theory and practice of Ralph McGill's persuasive discourse.

* * *

All units in the Marines in which I served during the three years were racially integrated, also a new experience for me. I learned later, however, that there were no African American drill instructors (DIs) at Parris Island during my time there. Isaac Ward and I became relatively close during our training at Parris Island.

Just before our scheduled graduation from boot camp, I came down with pneumonia and was told to go to the base hospital. Hospitalization meant that all my buddies in Platoon 6 would graduate without me, go home for a 30-day leave, and return for combat training as a unit without me. After my leave, I would have to join a unit of strangers for combat training and deployment to a permanent duty station.

When I returned from the physician's office to pack my sea bag for the hospital, 70 fellow Marines in our platoon and the Drill Instructor looked on. For a reason known only to himself, the drill instructor yelled, "Private Ward get up here and help Private Logue pack his sea bag!" Isaac Ward and I spoke few words as we both held the sea bag open and placed my personal and military articles in it. We managed only an awkward farewell more appropriate for the drill instructor than for each other, a rare pause in the unremitting day and night training.

Some weeks later, when I returned to training from the hospital, that drill instructor met me at the bus, arranged to have me join a new platoon that—thankfully, like my original platoon—was close to graduating from Parris Island, and walked me down to a base seamstress to have PFC (private-first-class) stripes sewn on shirts and coats. In Figure 4 I'm pictured at Camp Lejeune, North Carolina, 1956, my first permanent duty assignment soon after finishing boot camp, trying to look "salty."

Figure 4

At Parris Island at that time, drill instructors employed intimidation to motivate young Marines-to-be for war. Most of the persuasive coercion was more mental than physical. Reverend Ashland Shaw had served in the Army, and when he heard that I was dropping out of Alabama Polytechnic Institute to enter the military, he somehow arranged to meet me at the depot to warn me of the psychological pressures I would experience. With my train on the way, there was no time for indirect counseling. He expressed no doubts about my managing the physical demands, but was concerned about the emotional strain.

Fortunately, Daddy's cowboy belt discipline and three years of grueling football practices under Coach R. L. Beaird at Auburn High School had braced me well for boot camp mentality. Reverend Shaw also cautioned me about the risqué side of military service, and asked if I knew the "hand method" on which to rely if necessary. Once while our small survey unit was camped in concert with an engineering company deep in the interior of Luzon Island in the Philippines, a local resident rolled a sad-appearing prostitute to the fringe of the encampment in a makeshift wheelbarrow. Figure 5 shows a photograph of Reverend Ashland Shaw.

During boot camp training, the Drill Instructor who later met me at the hospital bus and directed me to the base seamstress, yelled out to the squad bay for "Private Logue to get in here." Following the careful regimen taught to all Marine recruits, I knocked three times firmly on the wall outside his office. Upon his order, I marched into the small forbidden office and stood rigidly at attention, looking straight at the wall. He commanded me to look down by the numbers. Glancing down and back up quickly, I saw a fellow recruit lying on his back, the drill instructor astraddle his stomach and a bayonet at his throat.

The drill instructor said, 'Private Logue what should I do with this n_____r!" I was scared speechless. Once again, as often happened in the South, an African American was placed in a defensive and dangerous situation, another circumstance students would do well to explore and discuss in a Black studies program. Finally the drill instructor let the young African American recruit stand and ordered me to "fight him." At Parris Island no recruit dared disobey an order, any

Figure 5.

order; just as few whites and Blacks in the South did not risk ignoring the ever-present written and unwritten signs requiring racial discrimination and separation. Trying to appear to obey the drill instructor's command that I fight, without actually following through, I edged forward and asked meekly, "Private ____ do you want to fight me?"

There was also a practical dimension to this Parris Island dilemma. Having gotten to know and respect this private well during our rigorous training, I knew that in any fight he would beat me badly. In response to what I perceived as a military order, rather than do something that would get me maimed by my fellow recruit and further upset the drill instructor, such as telling him, "Sir this is wrong" or "Sir this is not right"—attempts at moral suasion some might have tried—I managed somehow to do nothing. Finally the drill instructor dismissed us to the squad bay, terrified but unharmed. The drill instructor was from Alabama and I believe he assumed that I, also an Alabamian, would welcome an opportunity to humiliate and frighten a Black recruit. He was damn wrong.

Once while our platoon was standing at attention in front of our racks (beds) waiting for inspection, this same drill instructor stopped before me and stated or asked something that I can't recall now. Without warning he hit me hard in the

Figure 6. (Photograph from Platoon 6 Graduation Booklet given to us upon graduating from boot camp, Parris Island, 1956.)

stomach with his ample fist, bending me to catch my breath, tears dropping directly onto the deck (floor of the squad bay). "Private Logue," he demanded, "are you going to cry! Why aren't you standing at attention!"

When a recruit marched out of step, the drill instructor compelled him to run around the entire platoon, his 9.5 pound M-1 rifle held high above the head, as his buddies marched smartly in unison. There were also the usual pushups for punishment. Those several who failed to qualify with the M-1 rifle at the range were required to wear their clothes backwards and straggle along behind the qualifiers, who at this stage of our training marched with marked precision, some 70 boot heels hitting solidly as one. Our Platoon 6 is pictured in Figure 6 marching in step at port arms at Parris Island.

Fortunately Daddy taught us to shoot the BB-gun and .410 and 12 gauge shotguns. Also nearly two years of Army ROTC at Auburn University were a benefit, although I took that training far less seriously than I did the Marine Corps. Because I had difficulty seeing the small target several hundred yards away, initially on the firing range I was sent to the base optometrist for glasses.

Figure 7.

If you blundered by calling your rifle a "gun," you were compelled to stand nude on a table in the squad bay before some 70 fidgety-footed recruits, holding the weapon high above your head with one hand, and your crotch with the other, repeating loudly with required accompanying gestures:

> This is my rifle,
> This is my gun.
> This is for killing,
> This is for fun.

Over two years after joining the Marines, when I had been promoted to sergeant, I was packed in a troop ship with hundreds of others all dressed down to t-shirts because of the heat. Tensions were high. While exiting a movie in an overly crowded passageway on the ship, I brushed the shoulder of a Black Marine. He grabbed me by the collar, shoved me against the bulkhead, and threatened, "White boy, who do you think you are shoving?" Frightened and anxious to improve my situation, I responded in my native Pine Apple speech: "I realli' wadn' tryin' to push inybody." When my assailant, who apparently was from the North, heard my Alabama accent, things got worse. He said to a few of his Black colleagues gathering around, "Hey man, look what we got here, a FARM BOY!" From such encounters, later, when designing and teaching my course on African American discourse, we could ask why under crowded conditions conflict between the races could flare so quickly. In what ways can such lack of trust be negotiated or resolved. Can it be? Why? Why not? Over the years how have African Americans addressed such incidents in their oral and written discourse?

I'm not sure what would have happened to me had this racial tension aboard ship accelerated. To my good fortune, Sergeant John Williams, a close friend in our small survey artillery unit and a Black resident of the Virgin Islands came along, placed his arm about my shoulder, and with a big smile and clipped speech deplored, "what have you gotten yourself into now, Logue," and then somehow walked me past the angry faces while, at the same time, identifying with their feelings. Figure 7 is a picture of Sergeant Williams of the Virgin

Figure 8. (Photograph from Platoon 6 Graduation Booklet, given to us upon graduating from Boot Camp, Parris Island, 1956.)

Islands, taken when we were practicing artillery fire for six months on Luzon Island, Philippines.

Near the end of my three-year tour of duty in the Marines, in 1958, after returning to Camp Lejeune from stints at Fort Bragg, North Carolina, California, Okinawa, Japan, and the Philippines, I was walking on the base one day and met Corporal Isaac Ward. We returned to my squad bay for a long chat about where we had been and what we had seen and experienced during our tour in the Corps. Figure 8 is a picture of Isaac Ward practicing the prone position with the M-1 rifle at the rifle range, Parris Island, South Carolina. He was a model soldier and person.

* * *

On April 8, 1956, soon after my boot camp training ended, a drill instructor marched 74 men of Platoon 71 from their barracks into Ribbon Creek, one of the tidal streams on Parris Island, and six of the recruits drowned. This unusual incident led to an investigation by the Marine Corps. Following this review, but after my departure from Parris Island, changes in the handling of recruits at boot camp were said to have been implemented. These planned improvements were designed to retain the drill instructor's authority while, at the same time, disallowing his abuse of it. Ironically, when I returned to Camp Lejeune after a 30-day leave at home, a delay in the cutting of my new orders necessitated that I go through combat training with some of the Marines who had survived the forced march through Ribbon Creek.

* * *

In the early 1960s, while teaching at Birmingham-Southern College, I attended a Billy Graham rally, said to have been maybe the first mass racially integrated public meeting in Birmingham, if not all of Alabama. The Reverend Billy Graham asked that we repent of our sins and accept Jesus Christ as our Lord and Savior, refrains I probably heard often in the Protestant churches our family attended regularly in Pine Apple, Greensboro, and Evergreen.

When exiting that Billy Graham revival along with thousands of others, I was shaken to see my former Parris Island drill instructor, dressed immaculately in civilian suit and tie, his some 6-foot 4-inch frame straight as a board, same bold face, towering head and shoulders above most others, marching briskly as if on parade past Blacks and whites leaving the huge football stadium. I hid in the crowd, seven years after Parris Island boot camp.

Several years later, while I was teaching at the University of Georgia, this ex-drill instructor, now disheveled, came unannounced into my office to inquire about a doctoral program in public administration. When he walked into my office, I quickly stood as erectly as I could manage at the time.

Despite its hardships, I am a better person for my voluntary service of two years, eleven months, and thirteen days in the Marine Corps. (I was allowed to leave the military a few days short of my three-year enlistment period to meet the deadline for enrolling in Auburn's forthcoming term).

My formal schooling in artillery survey motivated and taught me to study, also a novel experience for me. I served with a small artillery unit that measured and calculated distances and directions from 105 and 155 Howitzers—and once in the Philippines, an Honest John missile from the back of a truck—to targets using a 20-second transit. I applied trigonometric functions I failed to master in a mathematics course at Auburn three years earlier. I also benefitted significantly from interacting with African Americans on a daily basis on an equal status.

I will never forget my buddies—Ferguson, Walindoski, Moyer, Long, Schoen, Hagan, Blankenship, Murphy, Sneed, Wilson, Cantrel, Shoffit, Ackerman (the first Jewish person I had ever met), Boyce, Williams, Armstrong, and Ward.

While the formal instruction, challenging training, associations, and friendships were invaluable, at the same time, in a graduate seminar in sociology during my doctoral program at Louisiana State University, I could draw on firsthand knowledge to write a research paper on "Brainwashing at Parris Island." Dr. Vernon Parrington, instructor for that project, had been blinded by an artillery shell during World War II. That distinguished professor had graduate assistants read research literature in sociology to him in French and maybe German. He would serve on the committee to hear my defense of dissertation on Ralph McGill.

* * *

Back on Seventeenth Street North in downtown Birmingham, September 15, 1963, as we returned home from church, because of the threat from bricks being hurled against our car, we became increasingly desperate. There seemed to be little hope that Mary Jo, Michael, and I would get out of this dangerous situation safely. Suddenly there was a firm tap on Mary Jo's side window. We both grimaced and attempted once more to shift away from the thud, assuming a brick had bounced off the pane. The tap grew louder. We glanced over and saw the frantic face of a quite elderly African American man just one inch from the window. Not knowing what to do or what we could do, we looked at him fearfully, the motor of our Ford still running. He tapped again, and signaled urgently with his rotating hand for us to lower the window. Did we dare lower the window?

Most reluctantly, but with no good choice available to us, Mary Jo let the window down about one-half inch. The African American gentleman said firmly through the crack over the noise of the street, "Move over and I'll sit with you." Mary Jo crawled from the floor of our Ford, squeezed the door open, moved over next to me, and held Michael in her lap.

There sat Mary Jo, young Michael, and I amidst a storm that we could not comprehend, with bricks continuing to strike cars in front and back of us, the angry shouting unceasing. We were sweating, shivering, and crying in total fear, with a Black stranger sitting cheek-to-cheek with us in the front seat of our car for all to see, a rare sight in the Deep South under any conditions.

While Mary Jo, Michael, and I were concerned about ourselves, it is difficult to imagine what the elderly gentleman who rescued us was going thru. While our own child was frightened, four of the Sunday school children from the elderly man's church had just been murdered by a bomb, his sacred place of worship badly damaged. By the gentleman's age, one can probably assume the harsh discrimination he had experienced throughout his life. One would think that, after seeing the destruction and killing at his church, surely he must have considered picking up a brick and hurling it as hard as he could. When this incident ended, probably Mary Jo, Michael, and I would return to the safety of our home. This elderly gentleman, however, like other members of his church and community, were left with a life-time of grief and potential rage. "How long, oh Lord, how long," he must have wondered. Even so, somehow he willed himself to walk amidst a bombed site among the debris, smoke, and flying stones to rescue the enemy.

Figure 9. (Photograph property of Birmingham Public Library. Courtesy of Birmingham Public Library Department of Archives and Catalog number 85.l.l6.)

When the elderly African American gentleman entered our two-door car, sat down beside Mary Jo, and closed the door, the bricks stopped. Our volunteer passenger looked straight ahead. Finally the cars in front of us began to move forward, and we inched on past nearby 16th Street Baptist Church where, unbeknown to us, four African American girls, Denise McNair, 11, and Addie Mae Collins, Carole Robertson, and Cynthia Wesley, all 14, had been murdered at 10:22 a.m., the moment the dynamited church clock stopped. Sunday school was ending and the four girls were preparing to sing and usher at a worship service.

Many others were seriously injured by the bomb placed at the basement of the church by Thomas Blanton, Jr., Bobby Frank Cherry, and Robert Chambliss, all reportedly former members of the Ku Klux Klan. Among the injured was Sarah Collins Cox, 12, who had numerous pieces of glass removed from her eyes and eventually lost an eye.

One of the Church's stained glass windows that remained in place had the face of Jesus blown away, as pictured in Figure 9.

Wondering if it were safe, I stopped the damaged car down the road a block or two and, without a word, the African American gentleman opened the damaged door and got out. Bent over some from age, he began walking back slowly toward what we read later was the bloody site of the murders. I pray that we thought to thank him. Due to his moral courage and initiative, **we** were safe, but **not the children who had attended his church**. How could I not attempt to help students at the university examine the continuing efforts of African Americans to achieve equal rights, opportunities, and protection for themselves?

Note

1. I would like to thank my brothers (Mickey Logue, John Logue, and Lamar Logue) and sister-in-law (Helen Logue) for providing assistance with this chapter, and Eugene F. Miller for helping to edit the manuscript. I also draw from my "Teaching Black Rhetoric," Speech Teacher, XXIII (March 1974): 115–120.

References

Bobbs-Merrill. (1970). *Reprint series in black studies.* Indianapolis, IN: Bobbs-Merrill Co., Inc.

Kennicott, P. (1967). *Negro antislavery speakers in America* (Doctoral dissertation). Florida State University, Tallahassee, FL. [See also Kennicott, P. (1970). Black persuaders in the anti-slavery movement, *Journal of Black Studies, 1* (1), 5–20.]

Smith, A. L. [Molefi Kete Asante]. (1969). *Rhetoric of Black Revolution.* Boston: Allyn and Bacon, Inc.

Time-Life Films. (Grinker, C. & M. Koplin). (1970). *Black views on race.* United States.

Selected Publications by Calvin M. Logue

Logue, C. M. (1968). Ralph McGill: Convictions of a southern editor. *Journalism Quarterly, 45*, 647–652.

Logue, C. M. (1968). Political rhetoric [Theory] of Ralph McGill. *Communication Monographs, 35*, 122–128.

Logue, C. M. (1969). *Ralph McGill at work* (Vol. I of *Ralph McGill: Editor and publisher*). Durham, NC: Moore Publishing Co. [Biographical sketch plus eight texts of speeches by Ralph McGill.]

Logue, C. M. (Ed.). (1969). *Ralph McGill speaks* (Vol. II of *Ralph McGill: Editor and publisher*). Durham, NC: Moore Publishing Co. [Texts of speeches by Ralph McGill. Includes typescript of Logue's taped interview with McGill.]

Logue, C. M. (1974). Teaching black rhetoric. *Communication Education, 13*, 115–120.

Logue, C. M. (1974). Gubernatorial campaign in Georgia in 1880. *Southern Communication Journal, 40*, 12–32.

Logue, C. M. (1976). Rhetorical ridicule of Reconstruction blacks. *Quarterly Journal of Speech, 62*, 400–409.

Logue, C. M. (1977). Rhetorical appeals of whites to blacks during Reconstruction. *Communication Monographs, 44*, 241–251. [Abstracted in *Wilson Quarterly, 2*, 28–29.]

Logue, C. M. (1979). Racist reporting during Reconstruction. *Journal of Black Studies, 9*, 335–350.

Logue, C. M. (1979). Restoration strategies in Georgia, 1865–1880. In W. W. Braden (Ed.), *Oratory of the new South, 1865–1900* (pp. 38–73). Baton Rouge, LA: Louisiana State University Press.

Logue, C. M. (1981). Transcending coercion: The communicative strategies of black slaves on antebellum plantations. *Quarterly Journal of Speech, 67*, 31–46.

Logue, C. M. (1981). *Eugene Talmadge*. In C. M. Logue & H. Dorgan (Eds.), *Oratory of southern demagogues*. Baton Rouge, LA: Louisiana State University Press.

Logue, C. M. (Ed.). (1983). *Southern encounters: Southerners of note in Ralph McGill's South*. Macon, GA: Mercer University Press. [Essays by McGill on southerners. Includes typescript of Logue's taped interview with Ms. 'Reb' Gershon who knew McGill well from their school days.]

Logue, C. M. (Ed.). (1984). *No place to hide: The South and human rights* (Vol. I). Macon, GA: Mercer University Press. [Essays by Ralph McGill.]

Logue, C. M. (Ed.). (1984). *No place to hide: The South and human rights* (Vol. II). Macon, GA: Mercer University Press. [Essays by Ralph McGill.]

Logue, C. M. (1987). Alexander H. Stephens. In B. Duffy & H. Ryan (Eds.), *American orators before 1900: Critical studies and sources.* Westport, CT: Greenwood Press.

Logue, C. M. (1987). Eugene Talmadge. In B. Duffy & H. Ryan (Eds.), *American orators of the twentieth century: Critical studies and sources*. Westport, CT: Greenwood Press.

Logue, C. M. (1989). Ralph McGill. In W. Ferris & C. Wilson (Eds.), *Encyclopedia of southern culture* (pp. 964–965). Durham, NC: University of North Carolina Press.

Logue, C. M. (1989). Southern Oratory. In W. Ferris & C. Wilson (Eds.), *Encyclopedia of southern culture* (pp. 781–782). Durham, NC: University of North Carolina Press.

Logue, C. M. (1989). *Eugene Talmadge: Rhetoric and response.* New York: Greenwood Press.

Logue, C. M. (1992). Coping with defeat rhetorically: Sherman's march through Georgia. *Southern Communication Journal, 58*, 55–66.

Logue, C. M. (1992). The rhetorical complicity indigenous to winning the North Georgia Campaign [1864]. *Communication Studies, 43*, 124–131.

Logue, C. M. (2014). *January in slavery: An oral narrative of the South* (*as told by African Americans who lived under slavery*). North Charleston, SC: CreateSpace Independent Publishing Platform.

Logue, C. M. & Garner, T. (1988). Shift in rhetorical status of blacks after freedom. *Southern Communication Journal, 54*, 1–39.

Logue, C. M. & Miller, E. F. (1995). Rhetorical status: A study of its origins, functions, and consequences. *Quarterly Journal of Speech, 81*, 20–46.

Logue, C. M. & Miller, E. F. (1998). Communicative interaction and rhetorical status in Harriet Ann Jacob's slave narrative. *Southern Communication Journal, 63*, 182–198.

Logue, C. M., Miller, E. F. & Schroll, C. J. (1998). The press under pressure: How Georgia's newspapers responded to Civil War constraints. *American Journalism, 15*, 13–34. [A version of this essay, The press under pressure: Georgia newspapers and the Civil War, appeared in D. B. Sachsman, S. K. Rushing & R. Morris Jr. (Eds.) (2008), *Words at War: The Civil War and American Journalism* (pp. 165–178). West Lafayette, IN: Purdue University Press.]

Miller, D. H., Logue, C. M. & Jenefsky, C. (1996). Civil liberties: The expansion of white women's communication activities from the antebellum South through the Civil War. *Southern Communication Journal, 61*, 289–301. [Logue was awarded the "Creative Research Medal" by the University of Georgia Foundation for analysis of southern discourse.]

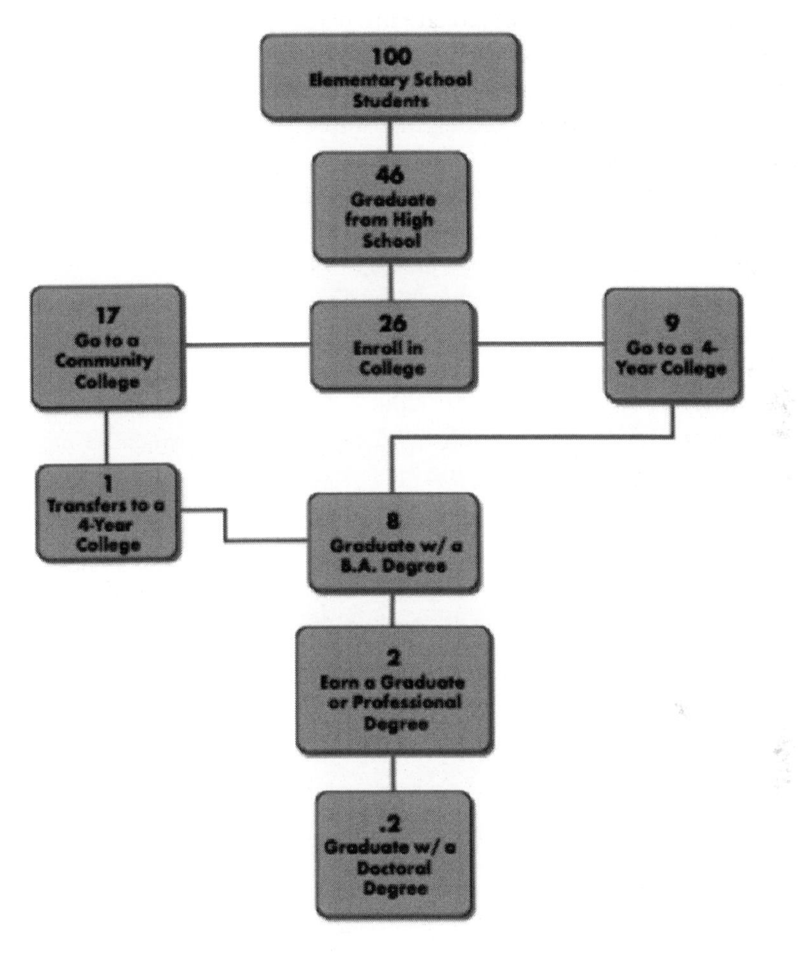

Figure 1. The Chicana/o Educational Pipeline illustrating low academic outcomes at each point along the educational pipeline in 2000. (Yosso & Solórzano, 2006a).

Chican@s ever enroll in four-year colleges, 8% graduate with a bachelor's, and less than 1% of the latter graduate with a doctoral degree. In 2010 the U.S. Department of Education's National Center for Education Statistics released a report on enrollment and completion trends based on the 2010 U.S. Census. Eight percent of Latin@s completed bachelor's degrees in 2010, compared to the 6% of Latin@s who completed bachelors in 2000, translating to an increase of 2% in ten years. Three percent of Latin@s completed doctorates in 2000 compared to the 4% who completed their doctorate in 2010. If this data were disaggregated to account for Chican@s as an isolated category, the 2010 data would likely not reflect a significant increase in completion reflective of enrollment trends.

In "On the Rhetoric and Precedents of Racism," Victor Villanueva cites field-specific numbers concerning Latin@s/Chican@s in rhetoric and composition. Villanueva reports that in 1995, 26 of the 1,373 individuals who earned doctorates in English language and literature were Latin@ which rounds out to 2% (1999, p. 651). In 2010 there were a total of 1,334 doctorates in this discipline with 40 earned by Latin@s, thus representing only 3% of the degrees conferred, so in all, an increase of 1% in fifteen years (U.S. Department of Education). As a more representative sample of the demographics specific to rhetoric and composition, Villanueva details the break-down of CCCC's membership, reporting that in 1999 Latin@s accounted for 1% of all members. As of 2012, Latin@ membership has risen to 2%, reflecting an increase of 1% in approximately 10 years (Suchor, K., email December 14, 2011, "FW: CCCC demographics," 2010). If I were to break down any of these statistics further, I am sure that someone like me—a first-generation Chicana, single mother of a teenage pregnancy—is an anomaly. Because of the numbers reflecting a disproportionate Latin@ enrollment to success and completion rates, institutions and their programs have a serious need to examine the disconnect preventing entire fields from best serving this burgeoning student demographic. These statistics, literature on Latin@ student success and retention, and my own personal experience reflect the fact that higher education, and particular to this study, rhetoric and composition, are in need of theory, practice, and methods that better serve individuals from underrepresented backgrounds.

A Call for Critical Race Theory

In "Working with Difference: Critical Race Studies and the Teaching of Composition," Gary A. Olson calls for greater attention in the field of rhetoric and composition to critical race theory (CRT) so as to assist writing programs and their instructors becoming better prepared, pedagogically and administratively, for underrepresented student populations (2003, p. 209). Olson contends that CRT provides our field with the tools by which to interrogate the effects of racial bias that actively impede success and retention in rhetoric and composition for marginalized students. Despite important contributions from scholars such as Keith Gilyard, Shirley Wilson Logan, and Jacqueline Jones Royster, Latin@s in this field have but two influences significantly referencing a theory on race scholarship concerning Latin@s—Gloria Anzaldúa and Victor Villanueva. Even so, as Olson suggests, "[Rhetoric and Composition] has witnessed no sustained examination of race, racism, and the effects of both on composition instruction and effective writing program administration" (2003, p. 209). Like Olson, I suggest we turn to CRT, but I extend this argument to focus on the field's methodology, counterstory, in our field's pursuit of actively challenging the status quo with all of its deeply institutionalized prejudices against racial minorities as it exists and continues to prosper in U.S. institutions of higher education.

Particular to critical race theory's counterstory, the methodology used in this essay, this method of research has potential for producing scholarship and informing pedagogy and mentorship in the field of rhetoric and composition studies. As an interdisciplinary method, CRT counterstory recognizes that the experiential and embodied knowledge of people of color is legitimate and critical to understanding racism that is often well disguised in the rhetoric of normalized structural values and practices. In this essay, I employ CRT counterstory as a hybrid form of scholarly inquiry and specifically rely on composite counterstorytelling as a writing genre. This form of counterstory differs from fictional storytelling. It instead critically examines theoretical concepts and humanizes empirical data while also deriving material for counterstory's discourse, setting, and characters from sources. These include, but are not limited to, statistical data, existing literatures, social commentary, and authors' professional/personal experiences concerning the topics addressed. As a writing form and a rhetorical methodology, I argue that counterstory has applications for both scholarly publication and craft in the composition classroom. However, the biggest hurdle to overcome in the present racialized era resides in programmatic and institutional recognition and acceptance of the ideology responsible for structural forms of inequality which are alive and well in the academy. In an effort to humanize this data, this essay illustrates, through two tellings, a "stock story" and a counterstory, that serve as tellings of Chican@ experience along the educational pipeline, with a focus on the .2% completion rate of Chican@ Ph.D.'s. In an effort to provide talking points for our field to engage in pedagogical but also in programmatic planning (including admissions/hiring practices and mentoring), my counterstory contributes a perspective that expands dialogue and understanding as to why this completion rate of doctoral degrees for Chican@s is nearly non-existent.

Richard Delgado and Counterstory vs. Stock Story

In his foreword to Richard Delgado's *The Rodrigo Chronicles,* Robert A. Williams, Jr., comments on Delgado's stories as being outsider stories. Williams says these stories "help us imagine the outside in America, a place where some of us have never been and some of us have always been, and where a few of us . . . shift-shape, like the trickster, asking the hard questions . . . without answers, questions about what it means to be outside, what it means to be inside, and what it means to be in-between in America" (1995, pp. xii-xiii). Delgado characterizes counterstory as "a kind of counter-reality" created/experienced by "outgroups" subordinate to those atop the racial and gendered hierarchy. While those in power, or as Delgado offers, the "ingroup," craft stock stories to establish a shared sense of identity, reality, and naturalization of their superior position, the "outgroup aims to subvert that ingroup reality" (1989, pp. 2412–2413). Delgado describes stock stories as those which people in positions of dominance collectively form and tell about themselves. These stories choose and pick among available facts and present a picture of the world that best fits and supports their positions of relative power (Delgado, 1989, p. 2421). Stock stories feign neutrality and at all costs avoid any blame or responsibility for societal inequality. Powerful because they are often repeated until canonized or normalized, those who tell stock stories insist that their version of events is indeed reality, and any stories that counter these standardized tellings are deemed biased, self-interested, and ultimately not credible. Counterstory, then, is a method of telling stories by people whose experiences are not often told. Counterstory as methodology thus serves to expose, analyze, and challenge stock stories of racial privilege and can help to strengthen traditions of social, political, and cultural survival and resistance.

Delgado outlines several generic styles counterstories can take: chronicles, narratives, allegories, parables, and dialogues (1989, p. 2438). In this essay I extend his discussion of counterstory by including dialogues, with a nod to sophistic argument, by presenting two tellings of the same event. The dialogue, as a theoretical device, is more than familiar in the field of rhetoric and composition and has been most notably employed by Plato to aid philosophical inquiry. Victor Villanueva reminds us that Plato's "writing is significant by virtue of its genre, an attempt at representation of dialogue, of storytelling . . . not as logocentric discourse but as [dialogue] as representation of discourse *in action*" (emphasis mine; 2004, p. 16). Also, Bizzell and Herzberg note the value Plato places on depicting oral exchanges because of their ability to respond "flexibly to *kairos,* the immediate social situation in which solutions to philosophical problems must be proposed" (2001, p. 81). Likewise, Delgado's specific method of placing two dialogues side-by-side provides him as author the opportunity to develop his ideas through exchanges between characters that represent and voice contending viewpoints about contemporary social issues. The audience is invited to first experience a version of the events from a status quo point of view, which in the case of this article's stock story represents that of the institution. Following the stock story, a counterstory is then presented to develop the author's marginalized viewpoint and to critique the viewpoint put forth by the stock story while offering alternative possibilities for the audience to consider. I call this method of placing two dialogues concerning the same events side-by-side "stock story vs. counterstory."

Beyond the styles of counterstory outlined by Delgado, Tara J. Yosso also explains these styles as generally composed in the autobiographical, biographical, or composite genre (2006, p. 10). For this essay, I compose my counterstories as composites dialogue, and an important feature of composite counterstory is the composite character. Composite characters are written into "social, historical, and political situations that allow the dialogue to speak to the research findings and creatively challenge racism and other forms of subordination" (Yosso, 2006, p. 11). Because these characters are written as composites of many individuals, they do not have a one-to-one correspondence to any one individual the author knows (Delgado, 1995, p. xix). In many cases, and as is the case for this particular stock story vs. counterstory, the composite characters are abstractions representing cultural or political ideologies, and could mistakenly be read as overly-stereotyped depictions of certain ideologies and politics. However, in the case of Delgado's work, and mine as well, composite characters in stock stories and the counterstories represent more than just a single individual and are intentionally crafted as composite characters that embody an ideology, such as institutional racism or a Chican@ academic identity. Accordingly, the stock story and counterstory crafted in this essay involve dialogues conducted among composite characters that represent university professor stocktypes, Chican@ students, and parents of underrepresented students.

A Stock Story Discussing a Chicana Graduate Student's Status as Qualified to Proceed in Her Ph.D. Program

In the particular graduate academic program providing the setting for this story, a qualifying exam is conducted to assess students' potential for joining the professional conversation in the field of rhetoric and composition. This exam consists of a meeting between students and the program director where the director engages in a qualifying assessment of each student's records in the program and the writing in her/his portfolio. The materials in the portfolio are meant to provide the director with a detailed sense of the student's analytical and writing skills. Aspects of the student's scholarship in the portfolio are evaluated based on a reflective essay and other academic writing (seminar papers) by the student. These writings indicate whether the student can step back from her/his writing and recognize her/his strengths and weaknesses as a scholarly writer and whether the student has developed a research trajectory indicative of her/his ability to perform graduate level work. In this story's program, the qualifying examination is intended as a mentoring opportunity for the participants to have useful conversations about the student's possibilities for writing and research. This particular step in the graduate school process was chosen because it serves a programmatic gate-keeping function for graduate students and can be especially problematic for underrepresented students, like the student discussed next.

The Stock Story

Setting. The program director and two professors are in a department conference room to discuss Alejandra Prieto, a Chicana graduate student who has failed her qualifying exam. In this program, as in others, if a student does not pass the qualifying exam, then a committee of professors will discuss the student, her portfolio, and her ability to continue in the program. The committee in this stock story consists of the program director and two professors, all of whom are white. The program director, D. Mosley, is male, from a middle-class background, and tenured. One of the professors, F. Hayden, is male, from a working-class background, and untenured, and the second professor J. Tanner, is female, from an upper middle-class background, and tenured. Alejandra has completed her first full year of the Ph.D. program after entering the program with a B.A. in sociology. The reasons for the committee's meeting are the student's failed attempt to pass her qualifying exam and also faculty concerns about the student's research interests, writing ability, and an assigned final grade of C in a core program course (C's in this graduate program constitute a failing grade; two C's can result in expulsion.)

Mosley: Thank you for finding the time to meet today. I know the beginning of the semester is a busy time for us all, so I'm glad we could all decide on a time at last. Now I know you are unfamiliar with this sort of meeting, but it's official procedure after a student has failed his/her qualifying exam.

Tanner [*teasing*]: Yes, Mosley, I went ahead and double-checked the program handbook to see that this meeting was a legitimate way to proceed, considering we've *never* experienced a student failing her qualifying exam, at least not in the sixteen years I've been program faculty, not to mention the four additional years I served as chair.

Hayden: Well, that's not exactly true; I recall other faculty saying some students have been of questionable qualifying status before, but I hear they usually leave the program before we have to come to this stage of committee discussion.

Mosley: Either way, Alejandra's progress and status in the program have become a concern for those of us in the room today. After reviewing her course schedules for the past two semesters, it seems she's taken all but one of her courses from each of us, all courses in rhetorical theory and one in composition pedagogy with Dr. Burton. Of the four courses she's taken so far, Alejandra's grades are three A's, and one C, which you Tanner assigned her. Now I met with Alejandra earlier this week regarding her qualifying exam and let her know concerns had been raised about her performance in class and about her writing. I also had specific questions for her about the C she earned in your class, Tanner, to which she did not have an adequate answer. So I guess I'd like to start there with what happened in your class; what's your assessment of this student?

Tanner: Well, to be honest, she's a sweet girl, she really is. You know she even brought some sort of Mexican cake to class one day to share with everyone. Sweet girl. However, as I recall, I raised a major concern about this student when we were in committee meetings about new admits, and it's the same concern I'm raising now: Is this student a good *fit* for this program? You both served on the program admissions committee with me back when we were forming Alejandra's cohort and you both . . .

Hayden: Yes, Tanner, we remember how you objected to her admission because she would be starting the doctoral program with only a B.A. in what you deemed an unrelated field. But I also remember that she was one of a very few minority applicants that year, and even, as an undergraduate, had impressive experience documented on her CV as a research assistant on nationally-funded projects. Plus, with the direction our field needs to go concerning the changing demographics of student and faculty populations, it couldn't hurt to admit a student whose focus is on social issues related to race and education, rather than the mostly literature and creative writing folks we usually get. We need to be more interdisciplinary, you know that.

Tanner: That aside Hayden, we're a top five ranked program, and we demand a lot from our students. Our curriculum is rigorous, and our students need to be the best and the brightest *in our field*, and it does nobody any favors to admit students who can't even tell you who and what the major theorists and journals of our time are!

Mosley: Okay, there's no reason to raise our voices. What we need is to return to the reason for this meeting, Alejandra's status as a student in this program. Talking about whether or not she should have been admitted is pointless because she's here, she's in the program, and we need to move forward and decide whether she should remain or go. Now, when I met with Alejandra for her qualifying exam, she was pretty emotional and not able to coherently discuss her progress in the program to this point. She even asked me outright if we admitted her as some sort of "affirmative action" recruit!

Tanner: [*mumbles something incoherent under her breath*]

Hayden: She didn't really ask that, did she? What did you say?

Mosley: She most certainly did, and I denied it, of course. This program, because of its ranking and rigor, is strictly merit-based, and I told her as much. Curiously, she somehow knew she wasn't a first priority admit and was on our second list of admits.

Hayden: Well, I always thought it a bad idea to have grad student reps on admissions committees. They gossip too much, and sometimes damaging information falls into the ears of those never meant to hear it.

Mosley: Yes, well, back to the original question, Tanner what happened in your class that resulted in this C on Alejandra's record?

Tanner: Right, well, did you ask her?

Mosley: I did, but I'd like to hear your perspective on the issue as well.

Tanner: Well, as I've said, again and again, Alejandra is just not a good fit for this program. She rarely spoke in my class, and the few times she did, her comments always drew the material back to her comfort zone of social oppression, particular to race. I mean sure, race is an issue, but it's all she wants to talk about! And then her writing! Her seminar paper was just not par with the rest of the students, not in content or quality. She tried, in my opinion unsuccessfully, to tie everything she read and studied in my course back to what I feel are likely recycled papers from sociology courses or projects. That aside, this attempt she makes to fuse her old discipline and ours comes across as awkward, at best, in her prose. It's just not clear writing; there's no focus and no connection or contribution to the field. Plus, she doesn't even use MLA and seemingly makes no attempt to do so. I stand my ground and still contend she is not a good fit for this program. She *earned* that C in my course.

Hayden: Ouch, Tanner, a C may as well be an F in this program, but I hear what you're saying regarding her participation in class. I experienced the same thing in the course she took with me. She rarely ever spoke, which made me begin to question whether or not she read and, more so, if she even comprehended the material? I mean she was practically silent the whole semester.

Mosley: Did she ever miss class?

Tanner and Hayden: No.

Mosley: Yeah, she never missed a day of my course either, but I recall her silence as well. So Tanner, did you ever speak to her regarding your concerns about her classroom performance or her handling of course materials?

Tanner: She knew as well as any other student that I hold an open door policy. I am *always* happy to assist students in any way possible, and I set office hours and appointments with students whenever needed.

Mosley: Yes, I asked her during our meeting whether she ever visited you concerning her progress in your course or if she ever discussed her grade with you. She said she hadn't.

Tanner: No, she didn't, and as I've said, my door is *always* open to students.

Mosley: Well as the handbook states, the official purpose for this meeting is for us to discuss whether the student has made satisfactory progress, maintained a 3.5 grade point average, or had other problems in the program. We need to assess Alejandra's potential for joining the professional conversation in our field, and this is based on her record in the program, her writing in coursework, and her meeting with me as program director. After hearing both of your concerns, I'm pretty sure she shouldn't continue on toward the Ph.D. I'll be meeting with her again next week for a follow-up to her exam, and she and I will discuss a plan of what she should do next. I'm thinking it'll be in *her* best interest to just take the master's and go. Are there any last topics either of you would like to discuss?

[*Tanner shakes her head no.*]

Hayden [*tentatively*]: You know, Mosely, I feel as if I'm pointing out the obvious, but I'm surprised this hasn't come up and that you're already considering she not continue in the program; despite Alejandra's C in Tanner's course, she did earn three A's in yours, mine, and Burton's courses. Does this not count as satisfactory progress? And come to think of it, for all the lack of contributions she made to course discussions, she did write really thoughtful, provocative reflection essays each week to the assigned reading in my course, so it was wrong of me to say and assume she didn't read or comprehend course material. And from what I remember, her seminar paper, while rough, was not any worse than those written by other first-years who came in with their B.A.'s and, in fact, wasn't too far off the mark from what some M.A.'s turn in. But Tanner, I think what makes her work . . . what's the word . . . difficult? Yes, I think her work is difficult for us to wrap our minds around because it's unconventional, probably by and large due to the fact that she approaches it from a perspective we're not trained in or accustomed to . . .

Mosley: Yes, Hayden, I hear exactly what you're saying. In fact, she did speak at least once in my course, and it was to ask what the "Eastern canon of rhetoric" is? [*laughing*] Different perspective indeed!

Hayden: So then, maybe it's not that she doesn't show potential for joining the professional conversation in our field, but perhaps it's that she has potential to say things we're uncomfortable with because her research interests are beyond our areas of expertise and her approach is something we've just not experienced before. Potential . . . I think she has it but just requires a better investment in mentoring—on our part.

Mosley: Tanner?

Tanner [*shrugs*]: I'm just not interested in her work. I don't understand it. And to be perfectly honest, I feel we've all done the most we can to help this student be successful. Her difficulties and failures in this program are hers, not ours. And Hayden, for all the positives you point out, do they in all honesty outweigh this student's shortcomings? Are you seriously suggesting we all, as faculty, shoulder the responsibility of teaching her *how* to be a student, a scholar, and a professional in *our* field. It's a little late in the game for her to play catch up in that regard, and I'm not paid enough to take on this task. You're either ready or not. You're a good fit, or you're not, and from what I've seen, she's not prepared to jump in and be the graduate student our program has such a successful record of bringing to degree and placement. So what does taking on Alejandra's lack of preparedness mean for us? More work. You, Hayden, of all people should be wary of this situation, what with your teaching load and the fact you still have quite a publishing quota to meet before you go up for tenure in a couple years. Do you honestly have the time it's going to take to mentor an underprepared student like Alejandra? Can you truly commit to mentoring this individual and showing her the ropes of this profession while also juggling the responsibilities you have to your own career and to the students who *are* prepared and *truly* need you? A student like Alejandra is unfair to us as professors who are pressed for time as it is. As I've already said, I'm not paid enough to teach someone how to be a student, and even if I were, I just don't have the time, none of us do.

Hayden: I never really looked at it that way . . . but how about if we . . .

Mosley [*interrupting*]: Good points Tanner, I believe Hayden and I hear you loud and clear [*winks at Hayden*] [*Hayden shrugs, shakes his head and looks down*], and we share your concerns. There's never quite enough time or money, now is there? [*chuckles*] Okay, I'd like to thank you both for taking the time to meet with me, and I'll take what you both have to say into serious consideration before meeting with Alejandra next week.

A Counterstory in which a Chicana Graduate Student and Her Mother Discuss Her Status as Qualified to Proceed in Her Ph.D. Program

Setting. Alejandra has just left the office of D. Mosley, program director, after their follow-up meeting. The meeting consisted of Mosley recounting various talking points from the committee meeting (described in the stock story) and asking for Alejandra's response to the concerns raised by each professor in that meeting. The meeting lasts nearly an hour and results in Mosley suggesting Alejandra consider finishing the program with the M.A. and perhaps seeking the Ph.D. in another program or field. Tearfully, Alejandra calls her mother to discuss the meeting.

Alejandra: *¿Hola Mami, como estáas?*

Mami [*concerned*]: *Bien. ¿Estás llorando mija? ¿Qué pasó?* Was it your meeting?

Alejandra [*defeated*]: Yes . . .

Mami: Why, what happened?

Alejandra: He told me I should just take the master's and go—

Mami: What?! And go? Go where? *¿Qué te dijo?*

Alejandra: I don't even know if it's worth getting into because he's right. I don't think I'm cut out for this program, maybe not even for grad school, I don't know . . .

Mami: Bullshit. *No es cierto mija*. You've worked too damn hard to start telling yourself "no" now . . .

Alejandra: I'm not telling myself "no" Mom; they are.

Mami: You have every right to be in that program, and no *pendejo* has the right to tell you that you can't . . .

Alejandra: But they're kicking me out.

Mami: Kicking you out? What exactly did he say?

Alejandra: Well, Dr. Mosley met with two of my professors to discuss my "progress and potential" in the program.

Mami: Which professors?

Alejandra: I've only taken four courses so far, and Dr. Burton is in Brazil for the semester, so beside Dr. Mosley, it had to be Dr. Hayden and Dr. Tanner.

Mami: Tanner? That *babosa* who gave you a C?

Alejandra: Yes, her . . .

Mami: Oh great.

Alejandra: So anyway, he said they all talked about my work in the program, and he told me they all "really like me as a person," and mentioned that Dr. Tanner had said how sweet I was because I brought Mexican cake to class one day to share with everyone . . .

Mami: That's nice *mija*, you did that?

Alejandra: No, I didn't; it was left-over cornbread from a barbeque place I went to the night before. And you raised me not to waste food, so I brought it in to share rather than throw it away.

Mami: What?! And because you're Mexican she assumes it's "Mexican cake"? Didn't you tell me once she's from the South? How can she not recognize cornbread when she sees it?

Alejandra: I don't know *Mami*; I think Dr. Mosley was just trying to give me a compliment before dropping the bomb.

Mami: Okay, so besides the cake, what else did he have to say?

Alejandra: He said each professor had specific concerns about my writing, my research interests, my classroom participation, and my overall "fit" for the program.

Mami: "Fit," what do they mean by that?

Alejandra: I don't know. Dr. Mosley's concerns about my research interests were really confusing. First, he asked how I think the fields of sociology and rhetoric and composition are related, but before he let me answer, he asked "Do you really think the discussion of 'race' *still* has a place in this field?" Which I guess was his way of saying this field has already discussed race?

Mami: And so by "fit," is he saying your research interests in "race" aren't a fit for this field?

Alejandra: I don't know, but if you remember, one of the most racist things that ever happened to me was in Dr. Mosley's class.

Mami: *¿Qué?* Refresh my memory . . .

Alejandra: He gave us a list of fifteen theorists from this book called *The Rhetorical Tradition,* for the fifteen of us in the class to choose from and present to the rest of the class on their major contributions to our field. I don't know if people of color gravitate toward likeness, but the two of us in Dr. Mosley's class (me and this guy from St. Lucia) sat in the back corner, and by the time the list got to us, we looked at who was left and then both looked at each other with ironic grins. Guess who was left for us "colored" folks to choose from?

Mami: Who?

Alejandra: Frederick Douglass and Gloria Anzaldúa. You know who Douglass is right?

Mami: *Sí*, the Black abolitionist, but I've never heard of Anzaldúa. *¿Es Mexicana?*

Alejandra: *Tejana,* and she identifies as Chicana, but isn't that crazy?

Mami: I know you're brown and got the *Tejana*, so does that mean the person who got Douglass is Black?

Alejandra: Yep, Chev looks like what we'd classify as "Black," but he's not African American. He's from the Caribbean, and me, well, I'm definitely not *Tejana,* and I've never called myself Chicana . . .

Mami: Right, you're Mexican. Your dad's Mexican, I'm Mexican, so you're Mexican.

Alejandra: Well, so I thought, but funny enough it was Dr. Mosley who called me "Chicana" today during our meeting. He said, "with your working class Chicana identity, you should have a wealth of cultural experiences to share and write about."

Mami: Why did he assume you're working class? If brown, then poor?

Alejandra: I know Mom; that's my point; it's all about assumptions in this program. No one bothers to ask me anything; they all just assume to know things about me, and it's like they all speak above me or around me, like I'm not here, as if it's easier for them to ignore me, unless I'm "sharing my wealth of cultural experiences" . . .

Mami: Like the Mexican cake?

Alejandra [*chuckles*]: Yeah. Exactly.

Mami: So let me get this straight: Mosley doesn't want you to talk about race as it relates to his classroom or the field, but instead prefers that you talk about your culture? What's wrong with this picture? Only talk about race if it has to do with happy topics like *tamales*, *mariachi*, and *folklórico*? *No cambian las cosas.*

Alejandra: I feel like my presence makes the professors and students uncomfortable.

Mami: Okay, so I can see *they* don't understand the "fit" of your research interests, but what was all this *cagada* about your participation being a concern?

Alejandra: Oh that. Dr. Mosley said the faculty is worried because I never speak up in class.

Mami: You don't speak in class?

Alejandra: No, not really, but here's why; in Dr. Tanner's course, for example, I genuinely tried to engage the material because I really identified with the gender and socioeconomic class issues brought up by the theorists she had us read, but when I would ask in class why race wasn't part of the discussion, since I know race, class, and gender are so interconnected in this country, Tanner would shut me down, every time. She'd say things like "Well that's not really rhet/comp material you're referring to," when I'd cite sociologists who discussed the same issues but with race as a focus. I felt unwelcome in her class, like the knowledge I brought with me, from sociology and from my personal perspective concerning race, was always automatically dismissed, because, according to her, I wasn't really using a rhet/comp perspective.

Mami: So you didn't feel like you could make a contribution to the conversation? But I thought they brought you into the program because of your sociology background, because it was—what was the word?

Alejandra: Interdisciplinary. Right, that's what I was told too, but now Dr. Mosley's saying they're unsure if I'm a good "fit." And maybe I'm not a good fit. In Tanner's class I just felt defeated. So silence became my refuge; it seemed like my only immediate option for survival.

Mami: Mija, I'm sorry, that sounds terrible, I had no idea . . .

Alejandra: It's alright, *Mami.* But what I guess I don't understand about the students I'm in class with is this constant chatter they engage in—and that, according to Dr. Mosley, they're expected to engage in. But it happens in every class I take, so I guess I understand the professors' concern that I don't speak, but Dr. Mosley actually asked if my silence was due to the fact that maybe I had trouble comprehending the material?

Mami: What?! What a terrible assumption to make!

Alejandra: *Mami,* to them silence equals lack of comprehension. And it wasn't that I didn't "get it"; I just wasn't prepared to contribute to half of the discussions taking place because I'm new to the field. I'm still learning. And the few times I did speak, I was either shut down or given strange looks as if I said something disturbing. So I decided silence would be my best strategy for the time being. It's as if there's some cultural standard in grad school that I don't understand and am completely out of place in.

Mami: It sounds more like a foreign country than just school, but what I don't fully understand yet is how you got to the point in the conversation where Mosley said you should take the master's degree and go.

Alejandra: Oh right, well, he brought up the C in Dr. Tanner's course and said Dr. Tanner claimed I never spoke to her about it and never sought her out during the semester for help in the course. But I basically told Dr. Mosley I'm terrified of Dr. Tanner, that she was so hostile, unwelcoming, and discrediting toward me in her class that the last thing I wanted to do was put myself in a vulnerable position like office hours with her, especially after the heinous grade she assigned me. *Mami,* a C in this program is pretty much an F, and an F-U, for that matter. I hope never to work with her again and will avoid her at all costs.

Mami: So what did Mosley have to say about that?

Alejandra: Well, Mosley didn't like that I haven't attempted to resolve this grade issue with Dr. Tanner and pretty much concluded the meeting with his recommendation that I finish the master's and perhaps look into other programs for doctoral work.

Mami: And how do you feel about his recommendation? I've noticed you're not crying anymore . . .

Alejandra: Well, to be honest *Mami*, now that I've had the opportunity to talk about it, I don't feel sad anymore. I'm kinda pissed. It makes me mad that these professors would rather be rid of me than face working with a student who is unconventional and is then what? Scary? Threatening? A waste of time? What is it they dislike about me?

Mami: It's not that they dislike you; they don't *get* you.

Alejandra: And I guess that would make sense; it's not like there are any other Latina/os or Chicana/os in the program, not as students or faculty, so their discomfort has to be about more than just the fact that I come from another field. I think it's because I'm the first Latina/Chicana/Mexicana they've ever had in their program, and they don't know what to do with me.

Mami: Yes, as if accepting you into their program was all the work they needed to do to diversify. But what about making sure you succeed? No, apparently your success is not their problem and is definitely not what they're prepared to do.

Alejandra: I'm not gonna let them tell me "no." I'm going back to Dr. Mosley's office tomorrow for another meeting. We need to discuss what it's going to take for me to succeed in this program. I'm going to talk about race, I'm going to be interdisciplinary, and I'm going to make these people *see* me.

Mami: Good *mija*, that's what you need to do—get mad and get to work. Call me tomorrow to let me know how it goes; I've got to hang up and get dinner going . . .

Alejandra: Mmmm, what are you making?

Mami: I was thinking of whipping up some "Mexican cake."

A Plea for Narrative: A Place for Counterstory in Rhet/Comp

When commenting on the conventions of academic discourse, Victor Villanueva notes the strength of logos but the pronounced weakness of pathos in academic exchanges. This leaning toward logic and reason to best communicate "serious" thought, and the pitting of logic against the assumed unreliability and volatility of emotion reaches far back into Aristotle's original suspicions that a too-heavy reliance on pathos leads the audience away from truth—the kind verifiable by facts and "proof." But as Villanueva argues, the personal, too often tied to emotions beyond logic and reason, "does not negate the need for the academic; it complements, provides an essential element on the rhetorical triangle, an essential element in the intellect—cognition and affect" (emphasis in original; 2004, pp. 13–14). For people of color, the personal as related through narrative provides space and opportunity to assert our stories within, and in many instances counter to, the hegemonic narratives of the institution.

Solórzano and Yosso characterize these hegemonic narratives as "majoritarian" stories that generate from a legacy of racial privilege and are stories in which racial privilege seems "natural" (2006, p. 27). These stories privilege whites, men, the middle and/or upper class, and heterosexuals by naming these social locations as natural or normative points of reference. A majoritarian story distorts and silences the experiences of people of color and others distanced from the norms such stories reproduce. A standardized majoritarian methodology relies on stock stereotypes that covertly and overtly link people of color, women of color, and poverty with "bad," while emphasizing that white, middle and/or upper class people embody all that is "good" (Solórzano & Yosso, 2006, p. 29).

Narratives counter to these majoritarian or stock stories, then, provide people of color the opportunity to validate, resonate, and awaken to the realization that we "haven't become clinically paranoid" in our observations and experiences of racism and discrimination within the institution (Villanueva, 2004, p. 15). In fact, as Villanueva points out, it is almost shocking to realize in the academic institution in which the sheer numbers of people of color are as exceptional as they are, how "our experiences are in no sense unique but are always analogous to other experiences from among those exceptions" (2004, p. 15). What's more, as these experiences are narrated through spoken and increasingly written and published work, people of color come to realize not much by way of diversity and inclusiveness in the institution has changed. Thus, my work in narrative counterstory within this essay is inspired by narratives specific to rhetoric and composition, such as Anzaldúa's *Borderland/La Frontera*, Villanueva's *Bootstraps*, Gilyard's *Voices of the Self*, Vershawn Ashanti Young's *Your Average Nigga*, and Frankie Condon's *I Hope I Join the Band*. Each of these scholars uses a narrative voice to relate racialized experiences, and as a necessary function of counterstory, these narratives serve the purpose of exposing stereotypes, expressing arguments against injustice, and offering additional truths through narrating authors' lived experiences. My work extends this narrative trend already in use in rhetoric and composition by crafting counterstory, but deviates from more familiar forms of autobiographical or biographical narrative through using a composite approach to the formation of these narratives, an approach most notably employed by critical race theorists Derrick Bell, Richard Delgado, and Tara J. Yosso, and constitutes the methodological basis for my greater body of work (Martinez, 2013).

As noted in my reference above to Condon's work, whites can and do tell counterstories, and people of color in contrast, can and do tell majoritarian stories

(Bonilla-Silva, 2003, p. 151; Martinez, 2009, p. 586). The keepers and tellers of either majoritarian (stock) stories or counterstories reveal the social location of the storyteller as dominant or non-dominant, and these locations are always racialized, classed, gendered. For example, Ward Connerly is African American, from a working-class background, male, and a prominent politician and academic. From his racialized position, Connerly is a minority, but speaks and represents himself from dominant gendered and present-day classed locations. From the position of an upper-class male, Connerly crafts stock stories to argue against affirmative action and to deny racial inequities. On the other hand, Condon's work narrativizes embodied whiteness and individual responsibility as a white ally. Although Condon is white, she is also a woman who speaks from a non-dominant social location, while as a white ally, she uses her dominant racialized location to craft critical race narratives that disrupt "discourses of transcendence" often responsible for leading audiences of white antiracists to believe they are somehow "absolved from the responsibility of doing whiteness" (2012, p. 13).

Condon makes an especially powerful case for the necessity of narrative by stating, "We need to learn to read, to engage with one another's stories, not as voyeurs but as players, in a dramatic sense, within them, and as actors who may be changed not only by the telling of our own stories, but also by the practices of listening, attending, acknowledging, and honoring the stories of our students and colleagues of color as well" (2012, p. 32). In my crafted dialogues above, I take up Condon's call to write and invite audiences into a dramatic engagement with these dialogues in hopes that through the detailing of the stock story vs. counterstory, my audience will locate their own subjective identities within the characters and thematic focuses of the text. Although I write the above narratives to commune with an audience of people of color who I assume will identify with and have academic experiences similar to those of Alejandra, this audience in not my primary target. My primary audience is the audience Condon herself identifies as the more difficult to persuade: "academics . . . who hope to join in the work of antiracism [who] need to stop minimizing the complexity and significance of narrative, stop depoliticizing the personal, and start studying the rich epistemological and rhetorical traditions that inform the narratives of people of color" (2012, p. 33).

Thus, I position my work in counterstory within social scientific interests with an active Humanities perspective, maintaining three main objectives, the first being that my work act as vehicle by which to raise awareness through counterstory of issues affecting the access, retention, and success of Latin@s in higher education, particularly in rhetoric and composition. Second, I hope this work will begin discussion concerning strategies that more effectively serve students from non-traditional backgrounds in various spaces and practices, such as the composition classroom, mentoring, and graduate programmatic requirements so as to *achieve* access, retention, and success. And third, I offer this demonstration of stock story vs. counterstory as a guide for counterstory not previously theorized by CRT, but which I believe will resonate with scholars in rhetoric and composition who are familiar with narrative forms spanning from Plato to contemporary scholars, and who seek options and variety in narrative forms to employ in the composition classroom and to publish work about these important issues.

As a narrative form, counterstory functions as a method for marginalized people to intervene in research methods that would form "master narratives" based on ignorance and on assumptions about minoritized peoples like Chican@s. Through the formation of counterstories or those stories that document the persistence of racism and other forms of subordination told "from the perspectives of those injured and victimized by its legacy" (Yosso, 2006, p. 10), voices from the margins become the voices of authority in the researching and relating of our own experiences. Counterstory serves as a natural extension of inquiry for theorists whose research recognizes and incorporates, as data, lived and embodied experiences of people of color (Solórzano & Delgado Bernal, 2001, p. 314). It is thus crucial to use a narrative methodology that counters other methods that seek to dismiss or decenter racism and those whose lives are daily affected by it. I have used personal stories as counterstory throughout this work to raise awareness about ongoing and historic social and racial injustices in the academy through reflection of lived experiences combined with literature and statistics on the topic (Yosso, 2006, p. 10). This essay in counterstory suggests a method by which to incorporate CRT in rhetoric and composition, as a contribution of other(ed) perspectives toward an ongoing conversation in the field about narrative, dominant ideology, and their intersecting influence on programmatic and curricular standards and practices. I offer this essay as a contribution and argument for using narrative in our field, and as an invitation to those who would continue the story.

Acknowledgments

I want to thank Jaime Armin Mejía, Cruz Medina, Adela C. Licona, and the Smitherman/Villanueva Writing Collective for providing feedback and encouragement with this essay through its very many and various stages and drafts. I want especially to thank my mother, Ana Patricia Martinez who took the time to sit with me and co-craft the Mami-Alejandra dialogue. The voices of the mother-daughter exchange would not/could not be genuine without my mother's touch.

Notes

1. This essay is reprinted with the permission of its original publisher, the journal, *Composition Studies*, Fall 2014, 42(2).

2. Sandra K. Soto (2010) states that her use of the "@" ending in Chican@ "signals a conscientious departure from the certainty, mastery, and wholeness, while still announcing a politicized collectivity" (p. 2). This "@" keystroke serves as an expression of the author's "certain fatigue with the clunky post-1980s gender inclusive formulations" of the word and announces a "politicized identity embraced by man or woman of Mexican descent who lives in the United States and who wants to forge connection to a collective identity politics" (original emphasis, p. 2). It also serves to unsettle not only the gender binary but also the categories that constitute it.

3. Chican@ and Chicana/o are used in my work synonymously with Mexican American. These terms are used in my work to refer to women and men of Mexican descent or heritage who live in the US. According to Yosso "Chican@ is a political term, referring to a people whose indigenous roots to North America and Mexico date back centuries" (p. 16). Also see Acuña (2010) for more on the history and origins of this term.

References

Acuña, R. F. (2010). *Occupied America: A history of chicanos* (7th ed.). New York: PearsonLongman.

Bell, D. (1987). *And we are not saved: The elusive quest for racial justice.* New York: Basic Books.

Bell, D. (1992). *Faces at the bottom of the well.* New York: Basic Book.

Bizzell, P. & Herzberg, B. (2001). *The rhetorical tradition: Readings from classical times to the present* (2nd ed.). New York: Bedford/St. Martin's.

Bonilla-Silva, E. (2003). *Racism without racists: Color-blind racism and the persistence of racial inequality in the United States* (2nd ed.). Boulder, CO: Rowman & Littlefield.

Condon, F. (2012). *I hope I join the band: Narrative, affiliation, and antiracist rhetoric.* Logan, UT: Utah State University Press.

Connerly, W. (2000). *Creating equal.* San Francisco: Encounter Books.

Delgado, R. (1995). *The Rodrigo chronicles: Conversations about America and race.* New York: New York University Press.

Delgado, R. (1989). Storytelling for Oppositionists and Others: A Plea for Narrative. *Michigan Law Review, 87*(8), 2411–2441.

Delgado Bernal, D. (2002). Critical race theory, Latino critical theory, and critical raced-gendered epistemologies: Recognizing students of color as holders and creators of knowledge. *Qualitative Inquiry, 8*(1), 105–126.

Delgado Bernal, D. & Villalpando, O. (2002). An apartheid of knowledge in academia: The struggle over the "legitimate" knowledge of faculty of color. *Equity and Excellence in Education, 35*(2), 165–180.

Ennis, S. R., Ríos-Vargas, M. & Albert, N. G. (2011). *The Hispanic population: 2010.* Washington, DC: U.S. Department of Commerce: Economics and Statistics Administration, U.S. Census Bureau. Retrieved from http://www.census.gov/prod/cen2010/briefs/c2010br-04.pdf.

Martinez, A. Y. (2009). "The American way": Resisting the empire of force and color-blind racism. *College English, 71*(6), 584–595.

Martinez, A. Y. (2013). Critical race theory counterstory as allegory: A rhetorical trope to raise awareness about Arizona's ban on ethnic studies. *Across the Disciplines.* Retrieved from http://wac.colostate.edu/atd/race/martinez.cfm.

Olson, G. A. (2003). Working with difference: Critical race studies and the teaching of composition. In L. Z. Bloom, D. A. Daiker, E. M. White (Eds.), *Composition Studies in the New Millennium: Rereading the Past, Rewriting the Future* (pp. 208–221). Carbondale, IL: Southern Illinois University Press.

Solórzano, D. & Delgado Bernal, D. (2001). Examining transformational resistance through critical race and LatCrit theory framework: Chicana and chicano students in an urban context. *Urban Education, 36*(3), 308–342.

Solórzano, D. & Yosso, T. J. (2002). Critical race methodology: counter-storytelling as an analytical framework for education research. *Qualitative Inquiry, 8*(1), 23–44.

Soto, S. K. (2010). *Reading chican@ like a queer: The de-mastery of desire.* Austin, TX: University of Texas Press.

U.S. Department of Education, National Center for Educational Statistics. Integrated Postsecondary Education Data System. (2010). *Completions Survey.* Washington: U.S. Department of Education.

Villanueva, V. (2004). *Memoria* is a friend of ours: On the discourse of color. *College English, 67*(1), 9–19.

Villanueva, V. (1999). On the rhetoric and precedents of racism. *College Composition and Communication, 50*(4), 645–661.

Yosso, T. J. (2006). *Critical race counterstories along the chicana/chicano educational pipeline.* New York: Routledge.

Yosso, T. J. & Solórzano, D. G. (2006a). *The Chicano and Chicano educational pipeline* (CSRC Policy and Issues Brief No. 13). Los Angeles: UCLA Chicano Studies Research Center Press.

Yosso, T. J. & Solórzano, D. G. (2006b). Leaks in the chicana and chicano educational pipeline. *Latino Policy and Issues Brief, 13*, 1–4.

Reframing Race in Teaching Writing Across the Curriculum

Mya Poe

> A graduate Health Policy class is discussing *The Immortal Life of Henrietta Lacks* by Rebecca Skloot. The book traces the life of Henrietta Lacks, a cancer patient, a poor African American woman, a mother, a wife, and likely the world's most important cell donor. Lacks' cells were taken without her consent and were used to create an "immortal" cell line, which has led to major advances in biomedical research and huge profits. Lacks died shortly after her cells were taken in 1951, although her cells are still used today in labs around the world.
>
> In discussing the ethics of using a patient's cells, a white student argues that taking the cells of an African American cancer patient and using the cells without her consent was acceptable "because it was legal at that time." An African American student bristles and questions, "Just like slavery?" Two Indian students in the class are puzzled at this exchange. The remainder of the class is silent.

Last spring, John, a faculty member in Health Policy and Administration, shared this story with me during one of our discussions about teaching writing. John was disturbed by the interaction among the students in his class; not only had the white student missed an important point about bioethics but she had also missed seeing how bioethical issues could be related to race and socioeconomic status. The retort from the African American student did not further the conversation, and John could not get any of the students to meaningfully discuss issues related to patient consent, ownership of genetic material, and the implications of these issues for different groups after this class exchange. Although John was frustrated by this event, he also saw it as an important window into student learning and thought this incident would make an ideal writing opportunity. So, he contacted me to help him design a meaningful writing assignment around this class exchange in hopes that it might help students understand the ways that a professional in the discipline might think through these issues. The bioethical issues presented in *The Immortal Life of*

Henrietta Lacks are complex, and John wanted his students to think more critically about those issues, especially as they relate to poverty and race, before writing their final papers for the semester. The goal for John was not for students to write about their personal feelings on the topic but to use writing to think through the ethical issues in the Lacks case from a professional point of view.

In my time as a writing across the curriculum (WAC) director, I have worked with many faculty like John who have an interest in using writing to help students think through technical issues of identity, ethics, and policy. In John's case, the topic of race could have served as a roadblock to writing instruction; he could have dropped the class discussion and moved on. Instead, he saw the exchange as an opportunity for writing and reflection.

Stories like John's have led me to believe that we need to anticipate these moments where race and writing come together across the curriculum and share ways of working through these moments as we work with faculty and teaching assistants in helping them design, deliver, and assess writing. The WAC literature, however, offers little help in understanding these intersections. While the WAC literature provides a stunning number of resources on developing faculty workshops, tracking changes in student writing over time, and managing successful programs (McLeod, Miraglia, Soven & Thaiss, 2001; Soliday 2011; Young & Fulwiler, 1986), it is decidedly less helpful in attending to issues of students' racial identities. In "Black holes: Writing across the curriculum, assessment, and the gravitational invisibility of race," Chris Anson explains that the dearth of information on racial identity is "puzzling," given WAC's openness to diverse forms of discourse and the populations who produce those forms (2012, p. 16). Anson provides an extensive search of the WAC literature, including the WAC Clearinghouse, CompPile, collections, and annotated WAC bibliographies, to find information related to WAC and race. His search yields only a handful of references. For example, the WAC Clearinghouse does include a bibliography related to "diversity," but most of the entries are related to gender, not racial identity. Anson notes that WAC leaders are not disinterested in issues related to race but that "the subject of race is perceived to generate layers of additional complexity over principles, theories, and pedagogies already challenging to faculty in various disciplines to interpret and apply to their teaching" (2012, p. 19). Likewise, WAC scholars may worry about being perceived as foregrounding the values of composition studies over those of other disciplines. Besides, when WAC principles are distilled to brief faculty workshops with a focus on best practices in generic assignment design and assessment, issues of diversity seem "beside the point" (Anson, 2012, p. 19).

More recently, a number of WAC articles have been devoted to multilingual writers (Cox & Zawacki, 2011; Johns, 2005), but often these articles ignore students' racial identities in favor of their linguistic identities. Our field's interest in literacy practices makes a focus on linguistic identity understandable, but as scholars in English Language Learning have noted, "Through teaching and learning a second language, racialized images of the teacher, students, and people that appear in teaching materials get produced and reproduced" (Kubota & Lin, 2009, p. 1). Indeed, ESL/EFL researchers have begun to acknowledge that a critical perspective on multilingual writers also means paying attention to issues of power and racial identity. (For example, see the special issue of *TESOL Quarterly*, Kubota & Lin, 2006, dedicated to the topic.) Ryuko Kubota and Angel Lin (identify four areas for study, including learner/teacher identities and race; manifestations of race in pedagogy, curriculum, materials, and technology; language policy, language ideology, and race; and critical (classroom) discourse analysis and race (2009, p. 15–16). Each of these reminds us that language teaching is merely not about the dissemination of technical skills but about the interactions that inform those instructional contexts both in the classroom and in the ideologies that pervade those contexts.

To take a racialized perspective on WAC suggests a critical stance toward the field. Scholars such as Donna LeCourt (1996), Victor Villanueva (2001), and Michelle Hall Kells (2007) have called for critical perspectives on WAC practices, especially as related to ethno-linguistic identity. LeCourt, for example, has called for changes that allow students to bring in their alternative literacies. The Writing Across Communities initiative at the University of New Mexico is attempting to do just that by integrating WAC and service-learning through an eco-composition agenda that is meaningful to students from the local community. Kells writes of the program:

> The challenge for the Writing Across Communities initiative at UNM is enhancing opportunities to build identification with the cultures of the academy as well as to cultivate appreciation across the university for the cultures and epistemologies our students bring with them. (2007, p. 96)

WAC's limited engagement with race stands in contrast to the rich body of literature in composition studies on ethnic rhetorics and literacies. One gesture to bring race to WAC scholarship is to draw on this body of research. However, because WAC operates throughout the university community, it is also important to consider that simply importing theory into our practices will likely fail. We have to engage the other frames about race that circulate in the university community—frames that are often deployed by administrators and other powerful stakeholders in the university community.

My goal in this chapter is to offer specific ways that we can integrate discussions about race in our interactions with faculty, graduate students, and administrators across the curriculum. First, I explain several other frames about race that operate in the university. I then go on to explain three ways that we can reframe race within

WAC to make race a meaningful part of our discussions about teaching writing across the curriculum. In my discussion, I use examples from faculty workshops and writing intensive courses to illustrate these points. By understanding the new diversity, recognizing how stereotypes matter, and drawing on linguistic diversity, I contend that we will better help faculty teach writing and improve their ways of responding to student writing.

Existing Frames

As Chris Anson (2012) notes, one of the reasons that WAC scholars may be reluctant to engage with the topic of race is that it complicates existing relationships with faculty in other disciplines. This is true but not because composition scholars are the only ones who bring racialized frames to the table. Quite to the contrary, we can find quite powerful other frames for race in university communities.

In *The Activist WPA: Changing Stories About Writing and Writers* (2008), Linda Adler-Kassner explains how framing—"the idea that stories are always set within and reinforce particular boundaries" (p. 4)—allows for the creation of larger narratives and help individuals make sense of everyday experiences (p. 11). Quoting Deacon, Adler-Kassner goes on to write that "frames define stories that both reflect and perpetuate dominant cultural values and interest rather than 'stimulating the development of alternative conceptions and values' that are 'critical' to those values and interests" (2008, p. 12).

Drawing on the notion of frames allows us to interrogate the stories we already have available to discuss race and writing as well as related notions about achievement and language use. Ironically, often the most powerful, visible frame for race on university campuses are not those deployed by faculty researchers but frames deployed by university administration. For instance, a common frame for discussing race comes as the *multicultural* frame. A multicultural frame about race might go as follows:

> The challenges in working with an ever-growing pluralistic school population encompass many areas. The provision of relevant multicultural curriculums, the use of culturally sensitive assessment and intervention strategies, the training of school staff in the provision of these services, the recruitment and retention of multicultural and diverse professionals, and the integration of diverse communities and parents in an authentic and empowering manner are only a few of the critical issues facing those working with today's students. (Sanchez et al., 1995, para. 3)

In the multicultural frame, the term race is often synonymous with diversity or a number of other ways that we might characterize individuals in a pluralistic society (gender, ethnicity, religion, etc.), thus race is just one of many variables through which we may recognize difference. The stories in this frame emphasize "cultural sensitivity" or awareness, suggesting that increased understanding of our differences will lead to a more tolerant society. As a result, multicultural approaches tend to focus on training and community building. Even very good initiatives, such as antiracism initiatives, however, don't engage with student literacies (St. Cloud State University, 2015; University of Puget Sound, 2015).

Although the multicultural frame has been a powerful way to open up discussions of difference, it not free from problems. The approach conjures notions of attending "diversity workshops" that include "warm and fuzzy conversations about diversity that raise consciousness but rarely upset or threaten" (Denny, 2010, p. 33). As Jennifer Trainor notes, attempts in multicultural education to interrogate white privilege have fallen short with white audiences (2008, p. 7) and can actually have the effect of fortifying existing identities and refocusing only on the struggles of working class whites (p. 19).

Another common frame in discussion about race is the *achievement gap* frame. An achievement gap frame might sound like the following:

> Black ghetto students will get statistically significant higher scores on measures of abstract thinking when they have mastered the grammar of standard English . . . the mean IQ scores of black ghetto students will go up when they learn to speak and write standard English. (Farrell, 1983, pp. 479, 481)

In the achievement gap frame, race is an identifying marker for grouping individuals who share a set of physical characteristics. For example, in the quote above, Black individuals who live in poor, urban areas share a common set of attributes. By changing the linguistic practices of this group, the story goes, there will be a change in their cognitive abilities. Achievement gap frames, such as the example above, employ a comparative approach to race; for example, race is tied to a trait, such as IQ, that can be contrasted to the IQ of another raced group.

The achievement gap frame can be found in high-profile books such as the *Bell Curve: Intelligence and Class Structure in American Life* (Herrnstein & Murray, 1996) and, more recently, *Academically Adrift: Limited Learning on College Campuses* (Arum & Roska, 2011). To be fair, arguments such as the one in the *Bell Curve* suggest a biological rationale for differences in performance while *Academically Adrift* makes no direct argument. However, *Academically Adrift* like many such publications works within the achievement gap frame, deploying a language of static racial identity correlated with assessment results without considering whether the decisions being made from those assessment results are valid. In the end, the achievement gap frame can be difficult to challenge because administrative audiences gravitate to stories that rely on statistical evidence that seems irrefutable.

In addition to the multicultural frame and the achievement gap frame, other frames that circulate in academic contexts include the post-racial frame and a post-structural frame. In the post-racial frame—a frame that students often work within—racial identity should no longer be a factor in selection processes because U.S. culture no longer operates through the lens of racial prejudice (Trainor, 2008; For a critique of color blindness, see Bonilla-Silva, 2006). In the humanities and social sciences, it is not uncommon to find researchers working within a post-structural frame in which identity is a fluid, discursive construction that has meaning in cultural contexts only because individuals in those contexts assign value to racial constructions (Hall, 1996). Other faculty may bring an antiracist frame or a culturally-responsive one (Ladson-Billings, 1997). For social scientists like John in Health Policy, race may be a social construction, but it has very real material consequences as related to access to healthcare, quality of care, health outcomes, and legal and civil rights implications. For faculty like John, I do not need to bring him a theory of race from composition studies; he already has an understanding of race that is meaningful in his disciplinary context. He needs help teaching writing.

In the end, all of the above frames have meaning to the audiences who deploy them, and we are unwise not to acknowledge that these frames shape individuals' views of teaching culturally-linguistically diverse populations. Each frame provides the language and logics that make certain conclusions seem commonsensical. What interests me is not locating one "right" frame for race but identifying a frame that allows for meaningful discussions of teaching writing to culturally-linguistically diverse students. For example, none of the above frames tells us how to turn the heated Health Policy discussion in John's class into a meaningful writing assignment. In what follows, I suggest ways that we can reframe race in our work with faculty, administrators, and students across the curriculum so the place of racial identity (and its intersections with gender, language, socioeconomic status, geography, and so on) "make sense" in understanding how to better teach writing. My suggested reframing of race draws on three inter-related principles: (1) making race local, (2) identifying expectations, and (3) acknowledging the racial aspects of linguistic diversity and its meanings in the disciplines.

A Frame for Race and Writing Across the Curriculum

Brian Huot (2002) argues that assessment of writing should be site-based, locally-controlled, context-sensitive, rhetorically-based, and accessible. Huot's taxonomy is a good model for thinking about how we might reframe race in WAC scholarship;

reframing race means reframing the way we think about teaching and responding to student writing across the disciplines. My proposed frame is about what race means in teaching writing, not a theory of race that sits outside of writing. Such a frame makes research locally meaningful, whether we focus on classroom or program-level concerns. Thus, the stories that we should tell about race and writing are ones based on the specific needs of students and teachers at our specific institutions. The research we propose should be based on sound principles of writing research, namely that writing is a rhetorical act, shaped by our linguistic-cultural backgrounds. The writing instruction we propose—be it assignment design, peer review practices, or assessment—should not be based solely on generic best practices, but on practices attuned to the contexts in which writing is taught at our institutions and the students who are the recipients of that instruction. Finally, the conclusions that we draw about students writing abilities across the curriculum should be validated at our institutions with our own values and not solely through external measures.

Situating Race Locally

Instead of starting with generalizations about teaching writing to racially diverse student populations, it is better to start with discussions about local students and local needs. By describing specific students—students in our classrooms and programs—we can root our conversations locally, where all teaching and assessment stories should begin. The specificity of these discussions is key because terms like "international" or "minority" do not really give us much useful information in these local situations. Moreover, it's too easy to over-generalize our students' motivations and performances when we use generic labels. Instead, a conversation that begins as follows is more helpful:

> The students in my Health Policy class include two African American women, four Euro-American men and four Euro-American women, two Asian American women, and two men from India. In talking to my students, I've found that at least half them know another language and use it on a regular basis. One of the African American women comes from a privileged background and already has a job with a pharmaceutical company. The other African American woman is a returning student; she's interested in becoming a hospital administrator. Of my Euro-American women, one is a former nurse and a widow whose husband died in Iraq. The other three women are traditional college-age students who are interested in pursuing a

> master's degree in Health Administration. One of those students speaks Russian at home and is interested in health policy because her mother was diagnosed with breast cancer.

By talking with greater specificity about the actual students in our classrooms, we can move past generalizations about "international students," "basic writers," or "transfer students." Of course, we often need help in figuring how out to elicit such information from students, especially in large classes. Informal writing prompts can be used to gather some of this information. Rather than using close-ended surveys, I prefer to use open-ended writing prompts so that students can articulate their identities in ways that make sense to them (although research such as by Araiza, Cárdenas & Garza, 2007, show that surveys can yield very good context-specific information). In asking students to articulate their identities in ways that make sense to them provides us emic descriptions of identity.

By describing students with greater specificity in our classrooms, we will likely find that initial notions about race become more complicated. Those more complicated notions of race allow us to respond more meaningfully to student writing. For example, a first year writing teacher explained in a WAC workshop how a peer review discussion went awry when a Dutch Indian student who grew up in Tanzania used the term "mulatto" in her essay. What was the student's reasoning in selecting the term "mulatto" and how could the instructor guide a class conversation in such a way that would acknowledge the various ways that different students understood that term and its historical legacy in different national contexts?

Working locally, we will also likely find that within the disciplines, the monolithic constructions of students starts to pull apart. For example, my colleagues in the sciences do not simply work with "Asian" students in their labs. They work with Indian-American, Indian, Chinese, Taiwanese, Asian American, and American-Sri Lankan students who come with various linguistic backgrounds (and possibly cultural expectations about the nature of scientific research). Each of those students brings specific writing needs that cannot be addressed with broad characterizations as English as Second Language (ESL) learners or as "Asian" students.

Finally, by describing the students in our programs with greater specificity, we can design multiple levels of support that are meaningful to those populations. For example, if our students are Hmong, Generation 1.5 learners from the local area, then how does that make us rethink the guidance we are giving new teachers about responding to student writing, training our teachers about peer review, and what kinds of program support we need for these new teachers to help them support the local Hmong students who are in our classrooms? In attempting to describe students in our programs with greater specificity, we often find that existing institutional identifiers are insufficient. Comparing our emic definitions with those etic labels can be enlightening in revealing institutional frames for racial identity.

In the end, asking about context-specific demographics allows us to think about racial identity as more dynamic, especially when we bring together "domestic diversity" and "international diversity." It also allows us to make connections to the multiple, shifting identities that students bring to writing classrooms (Canagarajah, 2004). Most importantly, by reframing race as one situated within the specific contexts in which we teach writing, we can move to specific strategies for teaching writing across the curriculum that is attuned to the identities of the students at our institutions.

Understanding What Expectations We Bring to Writing Instruction

Once we have greater specificity as to our understanding of students in our classrooms, then we can design writing instruction that is better suited to those students. The next question, then, is how good are those assignments and our assessments. What do we do when we find that some students do not perform as well as other students? What do we do when performance seems to be linked to race? Rather than using an achievement gap frame and explaining differences through static identity groupings, it's more useful to consider what expectations teachers and students bring to rhetorical situations across the curriculum. Turning questions of difference into moments of dialog aligns with WAC's emphasis on "pedagogical reform rather than curricular change" (Townsend, 1994, p. 1301); our goal is to help improve the teaching of writing, not tell departments what their students should be writing.

On one hand, it's simple enough to argue that students come with different motivations to learn and different ability levels. Some students take more easily to the expectations of a writing intensive class, for example, than others. Differences in writing development are normal; learning to write is a complex activity and students' personal and cultural identities sharply affect their relationship to writing (Herrington & Curtis, 2000; Ivanič, 1998). Problems arise, however, when systemic barriers or our own biases lead to erroneous conclusions about race and writing ability. It goes without saying that race does not cause individuals to perform in certain ways because of some innate ability associated to that person's race. But racial stereotypes can lead to performance differences.

What is needed is a better understanding of what expectations faculty and students bring to writing classrooms. For example, at one institution where I gave a workshop, instructors of the first year seminar courses brought up the subject of race; African American, Native American, and Latino/a students in their first year writing classes needed more help but would not approach them, they explained. After some discussion, I found that instructors were making an implicit connection between students' race and a university-sponsored bridge program. They assumed that all Latino/a, Native American, and African American students in first year courses were from the bridge program and came with a common set of writing issues. I questioned if they were making assumptions about students too quickly and ignoring the writing needs of other students—namely, white and Asian students who were also in the bridge program. We also talked about how their expectations for those students—expectations that those students came to recognize very quickly—effectively shut down dialog about teaching writing with those students.

While the notion of stereotypes may seem simplistic when discussed in general terms, stereotype research has actually been quite compelling when done in context. Stereotype research on teaching practices has shown that stereotypes do impact teaching and learning (Ferguson, 1998; McKown & Weinstein, 2007; Pollock, 2001; Rose, 1989). Sandra Kamasukiri (1996), for example, showed that teachers' attitudes toward language use had a direct impact on the way that they taught students. Meredith Bulinski et al. (2009) found that white teachers provided more comments to white students than to students of color but that Latino/a students received more comments on grammar than other students. What was surprising in the Bulinski et al. study was that white teachers typically shied away from commenting extensively on the writing from students of color. Arnetha Ball (1997), on the other hand, found that African American teachers were more likely to score the writing of African American students lower than white teachers because of their sense of expectations for writers.

The research on teachers' assessments of second language writing is mixed. Donald Rubin and Melanie Williams-James (1997), for example, found that raters favored Asian writers over other native writers. On the other hand, they also found that teachers' ratings of non-native writers "were best predicted by the number of surface errors they detected" (1997, p. 139). And Deborah Crusan (2011) in a study involving more than 100 faculty across the disciplines found that altering racial/national identifications on student papers influenced the scores that readers gave to writers; scorers gave writers who they believed were born in the US lower holistic scores on their essays.

In addition to research on teachers' assessment practices, Claude Steele's research on stereotype threat (1997) has been influential in understanding how students bring stereotypes to learning contexts. According to Steele, stereotype threat is "the threat of being viewed through the lens of a negative stereotype, or the fear of doing something that would inadvertently confirm that stereotype" (1999, p. 798). Contrary to the belief that low-achieving students are likely to have difficulty on academically difficult tasks, Steele has shown that students who are aware of stereotypes about their group and who highly identify with a domain—e.g., school ("high achievers")—are the students who are most likely to be affected by "threat." It is not that such students believe the negative stereotype; quite to the contrary, such students understand that the negative stereotype is a social construction of their identity, not an actual representation of their ability. As Claude Steele and Josh Aronson write, "It is important to understand that the person may experience a threat even if he or she does not believe the stereotype" (1995, p. 798). For these students, the desire to overcome the perception of a negative stereotype leads to depressed performance.

Writing researchers have also sought to understand what expectations students bring to writing classrooms. Jennifer Mott-Smith (2009), for example, looked at the experiences of five Generation 1.5 students on a writing proficiency exam and found that her students were keenly that they were labeled as "high risk." Zandra Jordan's research (2012) on African American language (AAL) at a historically Black college showed that negative stereotypes were common in such contexts. When Jordan interviewed students about their use of African American language, she found that students characterized AAL as "not professional" and described it as "ignorance that plagues the African American community and allows other races to believe 'we' are less intelligent" (2012, p. 98). Yet, Jordan also found that students did not passively accept negative stereotypes. They sought to change stereotypes, as one student explained, "I do believe that professors should realize that students come from different walks of life . . . speaking 'African American English' is a cultural thing, not meant to harm anyone" (Jordan, 2012, p. 98).

In my own work on racial stereotypes and writing assessment, I found that students were aware of stereotypes about race and academic performance. For example, one African American student explained:

> Schools give minority students a benefit over the white students because they feel the minority student can't compete with the white student, for this reason white professors will look at the test of a minority student and if they sound the least bit intelligent, the professors are surprised and hype up their grade a few notches. So I feel that the grading professor will grade me on the fact that I'm a black male. (2006, p. 93)

What is telling about research on ethno-linguistic stereotypes from students' perspectives is the persistence with which students feel stereotypes are perpetuated and their resistance to those stereotypes. The research also suggests that students carry their understanding of stereotyping into subsequent classroom interactions. For example, in a study conducted by Geoffrey Cohen, Claude Steele, and Lee Ross (1999), they found that African American students did not respond to the typical "buffered" feedback offered by white teachers. Students did not believe in feedback that they perceived to be insincere platitudes. Instead, Cohen, Steele, and Ross found:

> When feedback was accompanied both by an invocation of high standards and by an assurance of the student's capacity to reach those standards, Black students responded as positively as White students and both groups reported enhanced identification with relevant skills and careers (1999, p. 13)

In sum, both teachers and students bring raced expectations to educational contexts, and those expectations shape the ways that teachers respond to student writing and the ways that students respond to teacher feedback. Often simple practices in understanding stereotypes can lead to meaningful changes in practice. For example, simply counting the kinds of comments we provide different students provides a self-assessment tool for understanding how we respond to writing. Likewise, marking student papers with the names removed is a useful exercise to see if our judgments are affected by subtle biases. Getting students to articulate their own assumptions about learning and disciplinary content can reveal their raced expectations.

Situating race locally is critical, but only a starting point. Understanding what expectations we bring to writing classrooms—be they first-year writing courses, writing intensive courses, or disciplinary courses in which writing plays a role—is important if we are to think about what kinds of changes we make in teaching practices. Rather than thinking of race as an added complexity to WAC workshops or individual consultations, a focus on the raced expectations that we bring to classrooms can improve teaching and even lead to department-led initiatives to better support student writing in the major.

Understanding the Connection Between Multilingualism and Race

The third element in reframing race across the curriculum is paying attention to the connection between multilingualism and race. In making the connection between language and racial identity, however, I do not want WAC practitioners to explain linguistic and rhetorical practices through essentialized cultural explanations. Instead, I want us to think about how to make connections between home and professional literacies. In doing so, I want us to pay greater attention to how our characterizations of linguistic diversity are often raced in subtle ways. As Lan Hue Quach, Ji-Yoen O. Jo, and Luis Urietta, Jr. argue, "U.S. linguicism creates inferior identities for nonnative English speakers and ethnolinguistic minority groups . . . Policing Standard English as the only valid linguistic form subordinates and devalues the identities and experiences of ethnolinguistic-minority students" (2009, p. 121).

In disciplinary writing contexts, there are many instances when paying attention to the racialized assumptions of linguistic diversity is critical. In professions such as Health Policy understanding linguistic diversity is enormously important. As John explained to me, hospital administrators as well as nurses, doctors, and other hospital workers interact with individuals from diverse backgrounds. Too commonly, misconceptions arise based on patients' linguistic practices—misconceptions that are located at the intersection of a patient's linguistic and racial identities. Those misconceptions can lead to disastrous consequences, or at the very least, distrust of the healthcare system. Thus, teaching Health Policy students about that connection between race and language use and its implications for professional practice are an essential part of disciplinary education.

Two bodies of literature are useful in integrating linguistic diversity and its racial implications in WAC practice. First, we can draw on the large body of research in linguistic, education, and writing studies on the rhetorical and language patterns of various groups. Such research, for example, has shown us that language patterns are codified and taught, often implicitly through everyday practice. For example, Shirley Brice Heath's ethnography of families in Roadville and Trackton, Ways With Words (1983), illustrates the ways that children learn to use language through the patterns and practices found in their own families. Some of these practices map onto language and literacy practices found in school while many do not. Thus, for scholars like Heath, writing is a cultural practice and the diversity of language use is a cultural resource, not error-ridden linguistic patterns that need to be swept away (see also Genishi & Dyson, 2009; Purcell-Gates, 2007; Taylor, 1983). Narratives by Keith Gilyard (1991) and Victor Villanueva (1993) critique the ways that attempts to eliminate linguistic variation reap social and personal tolls and remind us that purely cultural explanations for writing practices do not sufficiently account for the personal and social ways that individuals use language.

Second, contemporary theories of multilingualism are valuable. Such theories posit the "multiple and fluctuating character of English as not a single, unchanging world language, or lingua franca, but a constellation of ever changing Englishes" (Horner, Lu & Matsuda, 2010, p. 2). Multilingual researchers have turned their attention to global Englishes, investigating the varieties of English spoken and written internationally (Lu & Horner, 2004). Even when the end-goal is still Standard English, multilingual theory asks us to consider, "Whose version of Standard English?" Through such questioning, we can move beyond absolutist positions on grammar and move to practices that recognize language use in context: When and where is linguistic variation a standard part of disciplinary practice? When is it more limited and why? Whose interests are represented in those differences?

Understanding the racialized implications linguistic diversity, thus, can be a valuable resource for teaching writing in many disciplines. If the goal is to help prepare students for real-world rhetorical situations, then teaching writing across the curriculum means preparing students for the multilingual spaces in which they will be writing and working. In classroom interactions, we can ask students to identify their own grammatical and spelling patterns, noting when and where they find certain patterns more effective and where deviations from a particular dialect can be strategically useful (Young, 2007).

In writing classrooms, a place where difficulties over linguistic variation often surfaces is in peer review (Leki, 2001). For example, in a biological engineering course I co-taught, students wrote a grant for their final class project. At the end of the semester, students participated in a "study section" that was modeled on the National Institutes of Health process for peer review of grants. In their reviews, students were asked not to make specific comments about the researcher and only focus on the criteria of significance, innovation, and approach. However, when commenting on the writing of Ye-jun, a Korean student, another graduate student (herself a second language writer) commented:

> Overall, this proposal is well organized and clearly planned. However, there are many missing words and grammatical errors in the background section PROOFREAD! (e.g., "every year, it cause over five hundred million people," etc). SCORE: 2.5 (without the language errors, I would give this grant a higher score).

While it is certainly plausible to argue that this writer could have gotten additional editorial help with his writing, the student reviewer's belief that the errors were a matter of the writer's lack of effort (PROOFREAD!) shows a misunderstanding of language use. To our and our students' detriment, we did not take this chance to initiate a class discussion about linguistic diversity in professional contexts. For example, it is worth debating why this reviewer felt compelled to comment and score the grant on a feature that was not indicated on the scoring rubric—a choice that meant this grant would not be funded in our class scenario. Finally, it's useful to ask if such reactions are stronger toward students of certain racial identities than others.

Ultimately, simply asserting that linguistic diversity is a good thing does not help us teach writing better. In fact, many faculty may agree with the spirit of linguistic diversity but reject multilingualism in disciplinary contexts because of the belief that Standard English is the only dialect used in professional work. Thus, in reframing race in relation to linguistic diversity in teaching writing across the curriculum, several points are important. First, the linguistic diversity that our students bring to writing classrooms across the curriculum is a reflection of the shifting demographics of higher education. It does us little good to think of linguistic diversity in terms merely of error. To help students learn writing, we need to recognize that language use is tied to identity and that students may conflate our responding to their writing as a statement about their racial identity. It is not unreasonable to ask students to learn the linguistic conventions used in disciplinary writing, but it's also useful to recognize that those patterns may be broken or "meshed" with other linguistic forms in specific contexts. Moreover, we have to consider what we want to teach students about the connection between linguistic diversity and professional practice. The myth of linguistic homogeneity is strong in the disciplines as English language publishing is now common in many disciplines. But just because Standard English is required for publishing doesn't mean that it's used all the time in professional practice, and, in fact, encountering linguistic diversity is a normal part of daily practice for many professionals.

Conclusion

Integrating race in WAC practice has the potential to address very real teaching problems that are experienced by teachers across the curriculum. For this reason, I believe it is essential that we ground discussions of race in local contexts and in ways that have specific meaning for teaching writing. By talking about students in specific contexts, we can help teachers like John develop meaningful writing assignments and assessments of student writing. In John's case, we devised a writing assignment for his Health Policy students in which they were asked to review an informed consent document from a local hospital. Although informed consent is now required for medical procedures, its usefulness remains debated, primarily because many patients do not understand the documentation, and doctors will not treat patients under normal circumstances unless given consent. Students were not asked to speculate how Henrietta Lacks or other patients might read the document. Instead, they were asked to provide their personal interpretation of the document, articulating their analysis through their own identities. Those analyses illustrated the varied expectations that readers bring to rhetorical situations and the subtle ways that race and other identities inform those interpretations. In the end, whether it be researching the expectations that teachers and students bring to writing situations or drawing on linguistic diversity as a resource in contemporary disciplinary practice, re-framing race in writing across the curriculum means being attuned to the contexts in which writing is taught at our institutions and how race is meaningful for us and our students at the institutions at which we teach.

References

Adler-Kassner, L. (2008). *The activist WPA: Changing stories about writing and writers.* Logan, UT: Utah State University Press.

Anson, C. (2012). Black holes: Writing across the curriculum, assessment, and the gravitational invisibility of race. In A. Inoue & M. Poe (Eds.), *Race and writing assessment* (pp. 15–29). New York: Peter Lang.

Araiza, I., Cárdenas, H. & Garza, S. (2007). Literate practices/language practices: What do we really know about our students? In C. Kirklighter, D. Cárdenas & S. W. Murphy (Eds.), *Teaching writing with Latino/a students: Lessons learned at Hispanic-serving institutions* (pp. 87–97). Albany, NY: SUNY Press.

Arum, R. & Rosa, J. (2011). *Academically adrift: Limited learning on college campuses.* Chicago, IL: University of Chicago Press.

Ball, A. F. (1997). Expanding the dialogue on culture as a critical component when assessing writing. *Assessing Writing, 4*(2), 169–202.

Bonilla-Silva, E. (2006). *Racism without racists: Color-Blind racism and the persistence of racial inequality in the United States* (2nd ed). Lanham, MD: Rowman & Littlefield Press.

Bulinski, M., Dominguez, A., Inoue, A. B., Jamali, M., McKnight, M., Seidel, S. & Stott, J. (March 2009). *"Shit-plus," "AWK," "frag," and "huh?": An empirical look at a writing program's commenting practices.* Paper presented at the Conference on College Composition and Communication, San Francisco, CA.

Canagarajah, S. (2010). An updated SRTOL? [CCCC diversity blog]. Retrieved from http://cccc blog.blogspot.com/2010/11/updated-srtol.html.

Cohen, G., Steele, C. M. & Ross, L. D. (1999). The mentor's dilemma: Providing critical feedback across the racial divide. *Personality and Social Psychology Bulletin, 25*(10), 1302–1318.

Cox, M. & Zawacki, T. (2011). WAC and second language writing: Cross-field research, theory, and program development [Special issue]. *Across the Disciplines, 8*(4). Retrieved from http://wac.colostate.edu/atd/ell/index.cfm.

Crusan, D. (October 2011). *The problem of bias: Achieving fair and equitable L2 writing assessment.* Paper presented at the Conference on Writing Education Across Borders, State College, PA.

Denny, H. (2010). *Facing the center: Toward an identity politics of one-to-one mentoring.* Logan, UT: Utah State University Press.

Farrell, T. (1983). IQ and Standard English. *College Composition and Communication, 19*(4), 470–484.

Ferguson, R. P. (1998). Teachers' perceptions and expectations and the black-white test score gap. In C. Jencks & M. Phillips (Eds.), *The black-white test score gap* (pp. 273–317). Washington, DC: Brookings Institution.

Genishi, C. & Dyson, A. (2009). *Children, language, and literacy.* New York: Teachers College Press.

Gilyard, K. (1991). *Voices of the self: A study of language competence.* Detroit, MI: Wayne State University Press.

Habib, A. & Mallett, K. (2011). *Diversity at Mason: The pursuit of transformative education.* Fairfax, VA: George Mason University.

Hall, S. (1996). Introduction: Who needs identity. In S. Hall & P. Du Gay (Eds.), *Questions of cultural identity* (pp. 1–17). London: Sage Publications.

Heath, S. (1983). *Ways with words: language, life, and work in communities and classrooms.* Cambridge, UK: Cambridge University Press.

Herrington, A. & Curtis, M. (2000). *Persons in process: Four stories of writing and personal development in college.* Urbana, IL: National Council of Teachers of English.

Herrnstein, R. & Murray, C. (1996). *The bell curve: Intelligence and class structure in American life.* New York: The Free Press.

Horner, B., Lu, M. & Matsuda, P. (2010). *Cross-language relations in composition.* Carbondale, IL: Southern Illinois University Press.

Huot, B. (2002). *(Re)Articulating writing assessment for teaching and learning.* Logan, UT: Utah State University Press.

Ivanič, R. (1998). *Writing and identity: The discoursal construction of identity in academic writing.* Amsterdam: John Benjamin Publishing Company.

Johns, A. (2005). The linguistically diverse student: Challenges and possibilities across the curriculum [Special issue]. *Across the Disciplines, 2.* Retrieved from http://wac.colostate.edu/atd/lds/index.cfm.

Jordan, Z. (2012). Students' right, African American English, and classroom writing assessment: Considering the HBCU. In A. Inoue & M. Poe (Eds.), *Race and writing assessment* (pp. 98–110). New York: Peter Lang.

Kamusikiri, S. (1996). African American English and writing assessment: An Afrocentric approach. In E. M. White, W. D. Lutz & S. Kamusikiri (Eds.), *Assessment of writing: Politics, policies, practices.* New York: Modern Language Association of America.

Kells, M. (2007). Writing across communities: Deliberation and the discursive possibilities of WAC. Reflections: A Journal of Writing, Service-Learning, and Community Literacy, *6*(1), 87–109.

Kubota, R. & Lin, A. (2006). Race and TESOL [Special issue]. *TESOL Quarterly, 40*(3), 471–493.

Kubota, R. & Lin, A. (2010). *Race, culture, and identities in second language education: Exploring critically engaged practice.* New York: Routledge.

Ladson-Billings, G. J. (1997). *The dreamkeepers: Successful teachers of African-American children.* San Francisco, CA: Jossey-Bass.

LeCourt, D. (1996). WAC as Critical Pedagogy. *JAC, 16*(3), 389–405.

Leki, I. (2001). A narrow thinking system: Nonnative-English-speaking students in group projects across the curriculum. *TESOL Quarterly, 35*, 39–67.

McKown, C. & Weinstein, R. (2008). Teacher expectations, classroom context, and the achievement gap. *Journal of School Psychology, 46*(3), 235–261.

McLeod, S., Miraglia, E., Soven, M. & Thaiss, C. (2001). *WAC for the new millennium: Strategies for continuing writing across the curriculum programs.* Urbana, IL: National Council of Teachers of English.

Mott-Smith, J. (2009). Responding to high-stakes writing assessment: A case study of five generation 1.5 students. In M. Roberge, M. Siegal & L. Harklau (Eds.), *Generation 1.5 in college composition* (pp. 120–134). New York: Routledge.

Nieto, S. (2010). *The light in their eyes: Creating multicultural learning communities.* New York: Teachers College Press.

Omi, M. & Winant, H. (1994). *Racial formations in the United States: From the 1960s to the 1990s* (2nd ed.). New York: Routledge.

Poe, M. (2006). Race, representation, and writing assessment: Racial stereotypes and the construction of identity in writing assessment (Doctoral dissertation, University of Massachusetts, Amherst). Retrieved from http://scholarworks.umass.edu/dissertations/AAI3206201.

Pollock, M. (2001). How the question we ask most about race in education is the very question we most suppress. *Educational Researcher, 30*(9), 9–12.

Purcell-Gates, V. (2007). *Cultural practices of literacy: Case studies of language, literacy, social practice and power.* Mahwah, NJ: Lawrence Erlbaum.

Quach, L. H., Jo, J. & Urrieta, L. (2009). Understanding the racialized identities of Asian students in predominately white schools. In Kubota, R. & Lin, A. (Eds.), *Race, culture, and identities in second language education: Exploring critically engaged practice* (pp. 118–137). New York: Routledge.

Rose, M. (1989). *Lives on the boundary: A moving account of the struggles and achievements of America's educationally underprepared.* New York: Penguin.

Rubin, D. & Williams-James, M. (1997). The impact of writer nationality on mainstream teachers' judgments of composition quality. *Journal of Second Language Writing, 6*(2), 139–153.

Sanchez, W., et al. (1995). Working with diverse learners and school staff in a multicultural society. Washington, DC: United States Department of Education. Retrieved from http://www.eric.ed.gov:80/PDFS/ED390018.pdf.

Smitherman, G. & Villanueva, V. (2003). *Language diversity in the classroom: From intention to practice.* Carbondale, IL: Southern Illinois University Press.

Soliday, M. (2011). *Everyday genres: Writing assignments across the disciplines.* Carbondale: Southern Illinois Press.

St. Cloud State University. (2015). Anti-Racist Pedagogy Across the Curriculum (ARPAC). Retrieved from http://www.stcloudstate.edu/arpac/.

Steele, C. M. (1997). A threat in the air: How stereotypes shape intellectual identity and performance. *American Psychologist, 52*(6), 613–629.

Steele, C. M. & Aronson, J. (1995). Stereotype threat and the intellectual test-performance of African-Americans. *Journal of personality and Social Psychology, 69*(5), 797–811.

Steele, C. M. (1999). *Thin ice: "Stereotype threat" and black college students. The Atlantic Monthly (August).* Retrieved from http://www.theatlantic.com/issues/99aug/9908stereotype.htm.

Taylor, D. (1983). *Family literacies.* Portsmouth, NH: Heinemann.

Townsend, M. (1994). Writing across the curriculum. In A. Purves, L. Pap & S. Jordan (Eds.), *English studies and language arts* (Vol. 2, pp. 1299–1302). New York: National Council of Teachers of English.

Trainor, J. (2008). *Rethinking racism: Emotion, persuasion, and literacy education in an all white high school.* Carbondale, IL: Southern Illinois University Press.

University of Puget Sound. (2015). *Race and pedagogy initiative.* Retrieved from http://www.pugetsound.edu/academics/academic-resources/race-pedagogy-initiative/.

Villanueva, V. (1993). Bootstraps: From an American academic of color. Urbana, IL: National Council of Teachers of English.

Villanueva, V. (2001). The politics of literacy across the curriculum. In S. McLeod, E. Moraglia, M. Soven & C. Thaiss (Eds.), *WAC for the new millennium* (pp. 165–178). Urbana, IL: National Council of Teachers of English.

Young, V. (2007). *Your average nigga: Performing race, literacy, and masculinity.* Detroit, MI: Wayne State University Press.

Young, A. & Fulwiler, T. (1986). *Writing across the disciplines: research into practice.* Portsmouth, NH: Boynton/Cook Publishers.

Zawacki, T., Hajabbasi, E., Habib, A., Antram, A. & Das, A. (2007). *Valuing written accents: Non-native students talk about identity, academic writing, and meeting teachers' expectations.* Fairfax, VA: George Mason University.

Section Two
Identity Matters

p. 47), neglects to examine how race indeed shapes different life experiences and opportunities for people. Nieto and Bode critique the diversity approach by stating, "To be effective, multicultural education needs to move beyond diversity as a passing fad. It needs to take into account our history of immigration as well as the social, political, and economic inequality and exclusion that have characterized our past and present, particularly our educational history" (2008, p. 5). Without attending to issues of inequity and particularly the role race pays in constructing social inequities, we remain unaware of and thereby unwittingly reproduce racist discourses and practices in our classrooms.

The diversity approach, without the deconstruction of race and white privilege, can do more harm than good in classrooms. When composition instructors include and discuss "multicultural texts" in their writing classrooms without analyzing race as a social construct, they risk reifying race as a biological term (Gilyard, 1999, p. 47). A classroom discussion on race under the false idea of race as an objective, biological fact leads students to "pedestrian interpretations and constructions inside a bankrupt race-relations model, thus leading to a sort of King to King solution, students dreaming and all getting along—rhetorically" (Gilyard, 1999, p. 49). This false notion of white people and people of color needing to "just get along" stops any analysis concerning the deep-rooted systematic racism in the university system and society. It prohibits any critical analysis of race and eliminates any opportunity by the educator or the student to acknowledge white privilege, while at the same time strengthening white privilege. What needs to happen is a deconstruction of race, but perhaps most importantly the white race. Goodburn urges educators "to move beyond defining texts as multicultural because they are written by those other to ourselves and begin thinking about how all discourses are inherently raced, through social constructions of whiteness as well as social constructions of color" (1999, p. 84).

If a compositionist brings in essays by bell hooks, Percival Everett, Malcolm X, Sherman Alexie, Sam Edgar Wideman, and Richard Wright as a way to illustrate the power of the social construction of race to oppress and marginalize, then a foundation about race must be set. What could be the result if the compositionist had brought these writers into the classroom without first illustrating to students how race is socially constructed? Including these works without deconstructing race reifies these writers' place on the cultural fringe. The compositionist's attempt to incorporate multicultural texts into the classroom without first deconstructing race and his/her own racial position make him/her culpable in marginalizing and othering these writers. In bringing in multicultural texts and not examining their own racial place, the white compositionist is telling students of color, "although I profit every day from white privilege, I am still sensitive to their place within the racial discourse." This is disingenuous and hypocritical. It is tantamount to the old clichéd defense by whites—"I'm not a racist. Some of my best friends are Black."

The result of using multicultural texts within a classroom accepts the antiquated and false notion of race as biological because the teacher's failure to prove otherwise.

Antiracist Approach to Teaching Writing

Antiracist pedagogy centers on racism and "insists on criticism of racist domination and its impact on education, including composition curricula" (Gilyard, 1999, p. 47). An antiracist pedagogical approach allows students and professors to evaluate their own places of privilege or non-privilege within society while trying to displace instances of racism both in the composition classroom and in the larger society.

When writing instructors and their students either individually or collectively deconstruct how racism works, they must avoid the common assumption that racism is a set of beliefs and practices that only "racist" individuals participate in. This conceptualization of racism, as residing in someone, allows us to dismiss the relevancy of race in our own lives, as most individuals firmly claim, "I'm not racist." Whether one is racist or not, one produces racist discourses. The "new racism" locates race in the ideologies of language or more specifically in rhetoric (Villanueva, 2006, p. 5). Rhetoric, intentionally or not, is always ideological (Berlin 2003, p. 717), and we cannot avoid reproducing the ideology within the rhetoric. Within this understanding of rhetoric, the individual can never act with complete freedom, but rather, all action is a product of the cultural forces at work (Berlin, 2003, p. 731).

Given the pervasive nature of rhetoric, it is naive to think that when writing instructors shut the door to the classroom and class begins that teachers and students alike are suddenly free of the cultural and societal ideologies constantly working on them. Students and teachers do not leave their race, ethnicity, sexuality, gender, or class in a heap outside the classroom door, so nor can they dismiss themselves from their inclusion in dominant discourses. Racial discourse influences rhetoric and composition pedagogies, so not to examine its influence in the classroom not only reifies its dominance, but ignores the context in which writing is produced. It also completely ignores the marginalization of people of color. To ignore the effect racial discourse has on the "othering" of students of color erodes the trust between educator and student, potentially destroying the environment of the classroom as a place that should "build students' confidence and competence as writers" (Hairston, 2003, p. 698).

Just as multicultural texts should not be inclusive of only those who are marginalized in our society, whiteness theory reminds us that racial analyses should not only focus on those who are marginalized by racism (Thompson, 1999, p. 145–146). Rather, racial analyses should also focus on the benefactors of racism: whites. As such, writing instructors must examine how their pedagogical practices reproduce or challenge whiteness. Imagine a large group of WEAs discussing the issue of race and then focusing the discussion on themselves and how they have been constructed racially.

To begin the process of examining whiteness, white instructors must first deconstruct their own privilege before leading students in a discussion on race as a social construct. Just because white educators are in authoritative positions does not mean they can escape the scrutiny of their own racial position and privilege. White educators must embrace this scrutiny as it will lead them to evaluate their own biases and prejudices and make them better teachers because just as we (teachers) are "read," upon entering the classroom, we (as teachers) also read our students and recognize these students' placement in relation to the dominant culture. Although it is imperative to recognize difference and its importance, it is also important to analyze "how we, as teachers and researchers, read and write our students as 'raced' texts" (Goodburn, 1999, p. 72).

Once WEAs recognize instances of whiteness and how they benefit from it, whiteness begins to lose its invisibility and its power to influence. "To redesign social systems we need first to acknowledge their colossal unseen dimensions. The silences and denials surrounding privilege are the key political tools here" (McIntosh, 1990, p. 6). Once white instructors begin to identify how whiteness operates in their own lives, they can begin to deconstruct how white privilege operates within their writing classrooms.

As an illustration of an antiracist approach that deconstructs whiteness, and thereby displacing a colorblind pedagogy two writing instructors use critical autoethnography to record and analyze their daily teaching practices in their First Year Writing classes. The following two sections provide narrative analyses of Victoria and Michael's classrooms as they examine whiteness in their own teaching pedagogy.

Victoria's Class

I am teaching a typical first year composition class at a state university in the Southwest. I have 21 students, mostly freshmen (18–19 years old), with almost an equal mix of males and females, and only a few ethnic minority students (two Mexican Americans and one African American). My class is at 8 AM, so I am ambitious to create an interactive classroom experience early in the class hour. To begin class, I ask a daily attendance question.

This activity does not directly solicit race talk, however because I ask students questions about themselves, their cultural, linguistic, and racial experiences often surface nonetheless. Some of the questions I ask include: "What is something that people do that really gets on your nerves? What is the best excuse you have given to

get out of something? What is the most embarrassing thing you have done during a class session?" One morning I asked, "What was your favorite television show while you were growing up? As I read the role sheet alphabetically and called out the names of several WEA students, they responded with shows like Saved by the Bell, The Brady Bunch, or Full House. When it came time for Francisco[1] (Mexican American) to respond, he said in a soft voice, "It's a Spanish show." Seeking an answer to the question, I asked, "What show was it?" Francisco, again in a soft voice said, "It was a Spanish comedy show." Persistently I asked, "What was the name of the show?" He responded, El Chavo del Ocho.[2]

In my attempt to break away from a colorblind perspective and conduct a racial analysis in my writing classroom, I later reflected on the sequence of events that occurred during that class session. As a result of my analysis, it became clear that Francisco did not perceive our classroom as race-neutral or colorblind. Being one of only two Mexican Americans in the classroom, he was likely keenly aware of the white dominance that permeated the classroom.

As I reflected about the question and answer activity, it became clear to me that whiteness was embodied in our white bodies [white students and teacher], as well as in our race talk. As I read the role sheet and called out students' names to answer the question, I called on several white students before I called on Francisco. In the process of naming several shows that were entirely in English and made up of white cast members, the class participated in a process of cultural bonding (McIntyre, 1997). After each student named a show, a few other students chimed in with their personal reflection about the said show. For example, students spontaneously responded about the shows in general, "Oh, I loved that show," or "I remember watching that show every day after school." Alternatively, they commented on specific cast members, "I was so in love with Zack [Saved by the Bell]," or "Weren't the Olson twins so adorable [Full House]." Sometimes they would solicit a response from other students' knowledge on the show, "Didn't Greg end up sleeping with Marcia [Brady Bunch]?" And then another student responds, "No. He slept with the mother. What is her name? . . . Florence Henderson." Having watched all these shows myself, I would sometimes contribute to the conversations. For example, when a student posed the question, "Didn't the dad [from The Brady Bunch] end up dying," I responded, "Yes. He died from complications arising from AIDS."

By the time I called on Francisco, the class, including myself, had set the parameters for the type of response that was expected: the naming of an English language show with white cast members followed by student/teacher personal reflections about the show. Since Francisco's favorite childhood show did not fit neatly into the parameters of white talk that we had set up prior to his answer, he withheld the name of his favorite show, and instead simply told us that it was a "Spanish show." As a result of the previous class discussions, Francisco likely believed that we [white students and teacher] would not be familiar with the show and thus could not respond to it in a personal manner in the way we related to the other shows. When I asked him again to tell us what the show was, he still avoided naming the show and instead gave a response that would be meaningful to the mostly white, English-speaking group, "It was a Spanish comedy show." For Francisco, simply naming the show, El Chavo Del Ocho, to a WEA group would not be meaningful because most would probably not know anything about the show. In an attempt to give meaningful answers to an English-speaking, white classroom, he tailored his responses to give us (WEAs) information we might want to know about his favorite childhood show—namely that it was a Spanish comedy.

After reflecting on this classroom experience, it became painfully obvious that I was contributing to the production of whiteness in my classroom, thereby creating a context in which Spanish and Mexican cultural practices had little meaning. While I am fully aware that I cannot forego the benefits of whiteness or cease my own contribution to the meaning of whiteness, I nonetheless disappointed myself. After all, yes I am white, but I grew up in and currently live in a Mexican community wherein I am known as Chavela, not Victoria. I am fluent in Spanish, have three children who speak Spanish only. I am very familiar with El Chavo del Ocho (La Chilindrina is one of my favorite all-time television characters) and I consider myself hyper-attentive to issues of racism and multiculturalism.

Hoping to displace a colorblind perspective, I took the information I learned from the attendance question activity and paid attention to the ways in which race and language were operating in my classroom and to whose benefit. In my future discussions with Francisco, I spoke to him in Spanish. During our conversations we often discussed the politics of language and agreed that society unfairly marginalizes minority languages. In one conversation, he said:

> The schools and government say they want immigrants to learn English but when they [immigrants] do, they don't necessarily get a better job or graduate from high school. I don't think they really want us to learn English. I think they just use the English language issue as an excuse to keep us in poor paying jobs.

I was excited about Francisco's critical perspective on race and language, so I continued to discuss these issues with him throughout the semester.

For the final assignment in the class, I assigned a group research paper. This research paper required all the common elements of a research paper; including a claim, evidence, library research, proper citation, etc., but in the end it would be one paper, written by a group of people. With several students deciding the topic and claim for the paper, I was hopeful white students would not silence Francisco's critical perspectives. I monitored his group's discussions closely, often adding my own critical perspective to their conversations. I was delighted when "minority languages" came up and eventually became this group's research topic.

After much discussion, the group decided to focus on the role "minority languages" play in the work place, which turned out to be rather complicated. For example, shortly after this meeting a white male student named George sent the group (and me) an email telling them that he wanted to change groups. He elaborated by saying that although he did feel this topic was important, he was a strong advocate of "English Only." The group was now down to three people: Francisco and two white women (Amanda and Alyssa). Once the group met again, they reassigned responsibilities to each individual. Amanda and Alyssa, who were assigned the task of conducting outside research, reported back to the group, stating they spent ample time researching the "important roles of minority languages," but could not find anything. According to them, they could only find articles that supported the removal of foreign languages and assimilation into English as quickly as possible. It was not until they contacted the librarian directly that they, according to them, were able to find research that supported the importance of minority languages in the US.

The final research paper resulted in a critical research paper that confronted common language stereotypes, such as "Immigrants do not want to learn English" and unfair hiring practices, such as hiring undocumented workers who do not speak English and then paying them a fraction of what "documented" workers earn for the same work. The white students in Francisco's group learned a lot about language practices and politics in the United States. While their research paper confronted many myths about language, their presentation of the research to the larger class revealed further complexity to their views of language. In one of the group meetings about the presentation, Francisco suggested that they start off the presentation speaking Spanish. The women responded enthusiastically to this idea, stating that speaking Spanish was a good idea since the research addressed the importance of minority languages. In subsequent group meetings, Francisco started to teach and rehearse the lines in Spanish that they would use in the presentation. Within these group meetings, the three group members had a good time laughing at Amanda's and Alyssa's English accents in Spanish, but Francisco seemed content that they were trying nonetheless. As an instructor, I felt good about their decision to speak Spanish in their research presentation. I was convinced that my own modeling of speaking Spanish in the classroom to Francisco, helped set the precedent that speaking Spanish in class was acceptable.

To my surprise, when it came time for Francisco's group to present their research to the class, Spanish was never spoken. I asked the group about this after class and learned that the women had convinced Francisco that speaking Spanish in the presentation was not a good idea because nearly no one in class would understand what was being said. In the end, even though their research presentation emphasized the preservation of minority languages, the group simultaneously conformed to WEA ideology that has us believe that only English can be spoken in an academic setting. Thus, at the same time they were speaking to the importance of minority languages, they were indeed marginalizing a minority language—stipulating through performance in their presentation that Spanish can be spoken at home or when needed in work environments, but not in formal academic settings.

Throughout the semester I took notes on many different examples of how race operated in my writing classroom and by no means was I aware of all the ways in which race and whiteness manifested in my classroom. By attempting to be color-attentive, instead of colorblind, my hope is to disrupt the normalcy of whiteness. In my work with Francisco, I disrupted whiteness by speaking to him in Spanish and by discussing language issues that displaced the assumption that English is the only legitimate language that can be used in the contexts of academia. However, based on their research presentation, it is unclear to what extent my anti-racist teaching practices interrupted the logic of WEA ideologies.

Michael's Class

I presented my freshmen composition students with University of Texas journalism professor Robert Jensen's white privilege article. Jensen, an American citizen of northern European descent argues he has been the benefactor of unearned white privilege within academia. After discussing the article, I asked my students if they believed white privilege exists. The students who spoke out during this discussion were white students who claimed there is no white privilege.

During this discussion, the students of color were largely silent. To prove white skin does not come with unearned privilege, the white students listed examples such as affirmative action and designated periods of multiculturalism such as Black History Month and Hispanic Heritage Month. I pointed out to the students that these were programs created to combat systematic racism and the marginalization of minority voices and did not disprove the concept of white privilege. Then I admitted to the classroom that I, a white male like Robert Jensen, was a benefactor of white privilege. This put an end to the discussion. All the students, white students and students of color, did not know how to react to such an admission. I had broken white privilege's first rule—I acknowledged it.

As Russell Ferguson writes in the introduction to Out There: Marginalization and Contemporary Cultures, "In our society dominant discourse tries never to speak its own name. Its authority is based on absence" (1995, p. 11). Acknowledging my own white privilege was the first step in confronting white privilege within the classroom and inviting students to embark on a critical discourse about race. It would be impossible for me to teach multicultural texts, to deconstruct race as a social construction, and attempt to empower white students and students of color to critically analyze racial issues without first admitting my own privileged position and subsequent power within what Ferguson calls the "invisible center" (1995, p. 9). To not do so and then engage students in a conversation on race would come across as hypocritical and disingenuous and more nefariously would reify the dominant discourse. Not to deconstruct race "in the contexts in which we work, is to confirm the prevailing discourse and to be implicated in the maintenance of an exploitative social order to the exact extent that said discourse promotes exploitation" (Gilyard, 1999, p. 49).

I have had some success in deconstructing my own white privilege and race in my freshmen composition classroom. During the initial discussion about white privilege, I heard the response that there is no such thing as white privilege, but I heard nothing from the students of color. However, I did witness a few students of color react non-verbally. One such reaction was from Sofia, a self-described Mexican-American woman. She fidgeted in her chair when the white students said white privilege did not exist and then offered the program of affirmative action as evidence. She hesitated to talk, so I did not push the issue. I gathered from private discussions with Sofia that she felt her views would be judged as biased because they come from a woman of color. She knew whatever she said would be measured by her positionality as a Mexican woman. Her voice would be marginalized because it was in her interest to argue the idea white privilege certainly existed.

Through private conferences and written feedback in papers, I made it clear to Sofia that I believed race was a social construct and white privilege certainly existed. I have to admit this was not an easy process. I shared with her some of the privileges that even as a working class male I had received. Initially, it was apparent that she did not fully trust me. Although she never disrespected me in any fashion, I noticed that she often just listened attentively not knowing if she should believe me or not. It was not until I spent many hours with her that I slowly got her to have faith in me.

I require my students to write a reader response for each assigned reading. In these reader responses, I intentionally do not mark grammatical or mechanical mistakes, and I never tell students that they are wrong, but instead I provide encouraging comments, pose questions as prompts for them to look at an issue in a different light, or show empathy for what they have experienced. Although this was my choice, my students often did not like this practice because some of them felt that being a "good writer" meant being a proficient grammatician. From these response papers, many students and I started one-on-one dialogues. Students like Sofia used these dialogues to engage some of the race issues I had brought up in previous class sessions. For example, in response to an essay about remedial education, Sofia confessed, she was placed in remedial classes at a young age. I posed the question, as to whether she thought this was racially motivated. In her response, she mentioned that although she did not want to sound racist, it seemed suspicious that most of the students in her developmental writing class were students of color. As our communication continued through these reading responses, I saw that her writing became stronger.

As the semester continued, she often spoke her mind in her reading responses as well as in class discussions. Toward the end of the semester, while discussing the portrayal of women and minorities in mass media, Sofia initiated a class discussion on the portrayal of Latinas as either sex objects or maids. She did not hesitate during the discussion, but rather was forthright in her opinions about how the dominant culture defines Mexican women as objectified sexual objects or domestic workers. She placed the blame for this at the feet of a dominant culture controlled by white men. One comment she made was very critical and seemed to be directed right at me, both in terms of content and her nonverbal delivery of the message which was physically directed at my body. She stated, "I know there are a lot of good white men out there who recognize these problems, but they do nothing about it." Sofia's comment was so meaningful to me in terms of my own self-reflection as an antiracist instructor. While Sofia was discussing media and the dominant Latina image, there were direct implications from her statement for my own teaching. I realized that while I may recognize that I have white male privileges, and even can name a few of those privileges, I was left with the sober reality that I do little to disrupt a system that provides me those privileges. As the semester ended, I felt encouraged to explore new antiracist pedagogical practices—ones in which I not only recognize my privilege, but also find ways to give up those privileges, to whatever extent that is possible. I am hopeful that my pedagogical practices somehow empowered Sofia to speak and write about issues she felt strongly about. While Sofia's experience in my class seemed to be a positive one, I am not so optimistic about the several other Latinos in my class who continued to remain very quiet over the course of the semester.

Color-Attentive Approaches to Teaching Writing

As evidenced in Victoria and Michael's case studies, their classrooms were not race neutral contexts. Even when not intentionally discussing race, Victoria's class nonetheless participated in "white talk" and white cultural bonding. This "white talk," especially because it was never identified as such during the class discussion, served as the unspoken cultural norm in the classroom. White talk serves to inconspicuously keep white students' experiences, both cultural and linguistic, at the center of classroom practices, while simultaneously limiting the ways ethnic and linguistic "others" can logically participate. Left unanalyzed, the white talk in Victoria's classroom likely flies under the radar of white participants and is rendered as business as usual. After all, Victoria was merely taking class attendance.

Unlike Victoria, Michael purposely discussed race in his writing classroom. It is important to point out, however, that the decision to openly discuss race does not necessarily lead to the disabling of racism. To the contrary, classroom discussions on race may act to invite the reproduction of racist discourses. As Michael explained in his case study, his invitation to talk about white privilege and his own admission that he is a benefactor of white privilege did not produce racial harmony in his classroom. Rather, white students dominated talk time and reiterated racial rhetoric that served to silence the students of color in the class. Ultimately, Michael's discussion on race and white privilege was with the white students in his class, who authoritatively claimed racism does not exist, and if anything, people of color have advantages given to them through programs like affirmative action. If nothing else had been done, this discussion on race would have done nothing more than reestablish a racial hierarchy in class, with white students not only speaking on behalf of their own racial experiences but also on that of people of color. Similar to the effects of the colorblind logic, this "race talk" discredits students' of color experiences of racism and likely resulted in their silence during this discussion. Michael, however, did not drop the race issue there. Rather, he used the open class discussion to plant the seed in the minds of students of color that he was critical about racial issues and could potentially serve as their ally. Michael's one-on-one interactions with students of color provided a potential "safe space" for students of color, as seemed to be the case for Sofia, to critically discuss race. The white students, however, never did engage critically with the issue of race.

In both case studies, Victoria and Michael engage in pedagogical practices that attempt to debunk the colorblind approach to teaching writing, and experience varying degrees of success. What is clear from these case studies is that antiracist pedagogies are never simple or complete. Rather, writing instructors must be intentionally reflective on their pedagogical practices and constantly adjust their practices to address newly realized forms of whiteness and/or racism. Important here is that writing instructors must first seek to understand how, rather than if, race operates in their writing classrooms. With this knowledge, writing instructors can develop strategies to displace practices that allocate privilege to some students while marginalizing others. As stated at the beginning of this chapter, inattention to issues of race, also known as colorblindness, ignores the unique set of experiences students of color and linguistic minorities bring to the writing classroom, including cultural knowledge (e.g., biculturalism), language competencies, and experiences with racism. An instructor's inattention to race also allows him/her to remain unaware of how racial discourses are produced in his/her classroom and to what effect. In our efforts to construct writing classrooms that are receptive to all students' experiences, we need to enact pedagogies of inclusion. That is, our pedagogical practices and curricula need to be inclusive of students of color and/or linguistic minority students' cultural and linguistic resources as well as include racial analyses that take into account how racial constructs shape students lives inside and outside the writing classroom.

Conclusion

The blindness in the colorblind approach to teaching writing does not shut down racism, but rather metaphorically closes our eyes and our consciousness to the ways race actually works in our classrooms. Ironically, despite its meritocratic intentions, the colorblind logic inconspicuously reinscribes the status quo. In this article we urge writing instructors to become more color attentive in their classroom practices. The move to become more color attentive involves including texts that validate the cultural and linguistic knowledge all students bring into our classrooms and analyze how race is embodied in the discourses and practices students and instructors produce in the classroom. While the antiracist approach best meets these expectations, we caution educators from uncritically assuming that any approach will help them achieve a status of non-racism in their classrooms. Perhaps the most important lesson we can take from Victoria and Michael's narratives is that writing instructors can make progress in their antiracist endeavors, but they cannot completely debunk racism in their classrooms. Clearly, Victoria and Michael identify themselves as antiracists and adopt antiracist pedagogical practices in their writing classrooms; however, as they acknowledge, they can never work outside the logic of racism and white privilege.

Notes

1. Pseudonym.

2. A Mexican sitcom that focused on the mischievous actions of the apartment complex tenants, but it especially focused on "Chavo" a child who lived in apartment number eight.

References

Berlin, J. (2003). Rhetoric and ideology in the writing class. In V. Villanueva (Ed.), *Cross talk in comp theory* (pp. 717–737). Urbana, IL: National Council of Teachers of English.

Ferguson, R. (1995). Invisible center introduction. In R. Ferguson, M. Gever, T. T. Minh-ha & C. West (Eds.), *Out there: Marginalization and contemporary cultures* (pp. 9–14). New York: The New Museum of Contemporary Art.

Gilyard, K. (1999). Higher learning: Composition's racialized reflection. In K. Gilyard (Ed.), *Race, rhetoric and composition* (pp. 44–52). Portsmouth, NH: Boynton/Cook Publisher.

Goodburn, A. (1999). Racing (erasing) white privilege in teacher/research writing about race. In K. Gilyard (Ed.), *Race, rhetoric and composition* (pp. 67–86). Portsmouth, NH: Boynton/Cook Publisher.

Gordon, J. (2005). White on white: Researcher reflexivity and the logics of privilege in white schools undertaking reform. *The Urban Review,* 37, 279–302.

Hairston, M. (2003). Diversity, ideology, and teaching writing. In V. Villanueva (Ed.), *Cross talk in comp theory* (pp. 697–713). Urbana, IL: National Council of Teachers of English.

McIntosh, P. (1990). White privilege: Unpacking the invisible knapsack. *Independent School, 49*(2), 31–36.

McIntyre, A. (1997). *Making meaning of whiteness: Exploring racial identity with white teachers.* Albany, NY: State University of New York Press.

Murray, R. D., Jr. (1999). Power, conflict, and contact: Re-constructing authority in the classroom. In K. Gilyard, *Race, Rhetoric, and Composition* (pp. 87–103). Portsmouth, NH: Boynton/Cook Publisher.

Nieto, S. & Bode, P. (2008). *Affirming diversity: The sociopolitical context of multicultural education.* New York: Pearson.

Thompson, A. (1999). Colortalk: Whiteness and off white. *Educational Studies,* 30, 141–160.

Villanueva, V. (2006). Blind: Talking about the new racism. *The Writing Center Journal, 26,* 3–19.

Deconstructing Whiteliness in the Globalized Classroom

Dae-Joong Kim and Bobbi Olson

In this chapter, we share our own experiences of enacting whiteliness and its effects for teaching in the globalized classroom. We engage in a dialogue to deconstruct our own whitely identities and consider the unearned authority imbued in this position, which, left unchecked, reinscribes oppressive race relations in the globalized classroom.

University classrooms in the contemporary United States are an increasingly globalized space: no longer are the seats within these classrooms reserved solely for the white sons (and, more recently, daughters) of America; rather, classrooms today represent a diverse student population: white students, yes, but also people of color from the US and several countries across the globe. The teacher, too, has increasingly come to embody globalization. The white man wearing elbow patches is still often found facilitating student learning, but so too are those whose home countries are thousands of miles from the classroom they are in. The globalized classroom represents a rich opportunity for student learning, but it is also a complex space, one that requires consideration of the multifaceted ways identities are intersecting at any given moment for both students and teachers. In this chapter, we share our experiences of teaching in the globalized classroom to consider its complexity, particularly in terms of race and racism.

We share our experiences in what follows of being raced as white and non-white, and of racing our students as white and non-white. Though one of us is not white and one of us is, we find that both of us have enacted whiteliness in our teacher role. Whiteliness is not just about the physical characteristics of one's perceived skin color: "Whiteliness is not necessarily a product of being white. Whiteliness is, rather, an articulation of epistemologies that have been racialized; whiteliness is a rhetoric" (Condon, 2011, p. 3). As Frye has described it:

> Being whiteskinned (like being male) is a matter of physical traits presumed to be physically determined; being whitely (like

> being masculine) I conceive as a deeply ingrained way of being in the world. Following the analogy with masculinity, I assume that the connection between whiteliness and light-colored skin is a contingent connection: this character could be manifested by persons who are not "white;" it can be absent in persons who are. (2001, p. 87)

This "way of being in the world" of course manifests itself in our classrooms. While it's expected that different ways of being are represented in a globalized classroom, it is important to consider the particular effects of whiteliness, especially when enacted by instructors since "Whiteliness is connected to institutional racism . . . by the fact that individuals with this sort of character are well-suited to the social roles of agents of institutional racism" (Frye, 2001, p. 87). Both of our experiences represent the prevalence of whiteliness in the U.S. academy. This may be in part because the "teacher role" is closely related to middle-class values, which share many characteristics with whiteliness (such as a belief in and the enforcement of rules, and a belief in one's own authority)—though whiteliness and "middle-class-ness" are not one and the same (Frye, 2001, p. 93).

We have chosen to use the term "whiteliness" purposely while acknowledging the fact that there are several terms, often with overlapping (and sometimes contradicting) connotations. In particular, whiteliness is different from white privilege in that whiteliness is an epistemological worldview, a lens of judgment, whereas white privilege is a systemic structure that Peggy McIntosh (1989) has claimed is often invisible. Yet, as Sara Ahmed has discussed, this invisibility is limited to those who benefit from it; white people may not notice the ways in which their skin color manifests itself in certain privileges, but for people of color who do not "inhabit" it, "it is hard not to see whiteness; it even seems everywhere" (2004, n.p.). In contrast, whiteliness, as discussed above, is not limited to one's skin color (or the reading of it). Whiteliness "is the epistemological frame that enables and reproduces this invisibility [of whiteness]" (Condon, personal communication, August 18, 2014, n.p). In other words, "part of the work whiteliness does is to sustain the invisibility of whiteness as a normative racial identity as well as the invisibility of white privilege to whites" (Condon, personal communication, August 18, 2014). The introduction to this collection also offers a discussion of these differences.

"One can be whitely," Frye has explained, "even if one's beliefs and feelings are relatively well-informed, humane, and good willed" (2001, p. 88). Whitely people—and often teachers, we argue—"generally consider themselves to be benevolent and good-willed, fair, honest and ethical" (Frye, 2001, p. 89). Whitely teachers do not see themselves as perpetuators of institutionalized racism in the classroom, though they are discursively connected to institutional racism at a deeper level. We did not imagine ourselves as perpetuators of institutionalized racism. Rather, whitely people are taught to consider their roles as a "judge—a judge of responsibility and of punishment," a "preacher" who "point[s] out wrongs and tell[s] others what to do," a "martyr—to take all responsibility and all glory" and finally a "peacemaker," one who "could see all sides and see how it all ought to be" (Frye, 2001, pp. 88–89). These roles offer a façade for our behaviors, allowing us to see our behaviors as not racist, but in students' "best interests." The best interests, however, are whitely interests.

We share our experiences and those of others not to self-deprecate or exalt, but rather in an attempt to deconstruct the ways in which our own and others' whiteliness permeates the globalized classroom and to demonstrate that "Whiteliness is a narrative not only about language but also about white supremacy" (Condon, 2011, p. 4). In sharing our stories, we do not presume that the act of saying we have been racist through our whiteliness excuses us from the act. "[I]f we say we are ashamed," Ahmed warns, "if we say we were racist, then 'this shows' we are not racist now, we show that we mean well. The presumption that saying is doing—that being sorry means that we have overcome the very thing we are sorry about—hence works to support racism in the present" (2004, n.p.). Meaning well does not change the conditions of racism. However, through our conversations, we have found that whiteliness is shared and prevalent within the "teacher" position and within power structures in and out of the classroom whose boundaries expand into the global space. And in such powerful roles, teachers need to recognize and understand these positions, though recognition alone is not enough, for "understanding racism will [not] necessarily make us non-racist or even anti-racist . . . But race, like sex, is sticky; it sticks to us, or we become 'us' as an effect of how it sticks, even when we think we are beyond it. Beginning to live with that stickiness, to think it, feel it, do it, is about creating a space to deal with the effects of racism" (Ahmed, 2004, n.p.). To "deal with the effects of racism in a way that is better" (Ahmed, 2004, n.p.), then, we believe teachers must consider their own involvement within the racist structures in which they operate.

Bobbi's narratives demonstrate the authority granted white and whitely teachers and the attending costs of this unearned authority; DJ (Dae-Joong Kim)'s accounts are grounded in aspiring to be whitely and enacting whitely values since it seems "whitely" is what teachers are "supposed to" be in personal, as well as discursive and institutional power structures where whiteliness dominates largely due to asymmetries in the dominant power structure and its biased rhetoric. In what follows, we use our own narratives in attempt to do the work we are calling for: to deconstruct our identities and consider whitely teachers' unearned authority, which left unchecked, reinscribes oppressive race relations in the globalized classroom.

Furthermore, our narratives and their attending analyses represent the evolution of our thoughts as we've conversed with each other—moments of "unlearning" in order to learn our own roles in the classroom. These conversations and moments of unlearning have been possible for us because of the globalized classroom; otherwise, we would not have gotten this chance to explore our roles as teachers in this space. For us, the globalized classroom is not a utopia or dystopia but a space of hope because it is always in on-going construction, disagreement, and movement of transnational beings. The globalized classroom is not what the first world romantically embellishes as the space of consensus, fair exchanges of knowledge without tariff (all forms of discriminations), or beautiful plains without obstacles. On one hand, as a miniature of the global space, here students and teachers are exposed to doubts, instability, unfair exchanges, and dominance and resistance, on which border-crossing unidentifiable Others raze down racial, national, linguistic, cultural, gender, economic, and political stone walls in every U.S. classroom. On the other hand, this does not mean that local difference and its significance can be ignored in the classroom. Local difference is always already mediated by globalization. In the globalized classroom, global and differential race and racism is a local/global phenomenon hidden under and covered by euphemistic ideas of mutual understanding, global collaboration, hospitality to cultural differences, multicultural awareness, diversity for efficiency, and so on which morally, politically and ideologically strengthen the positions of subjects (those who hold global whiteliness). In this classroom, exchange students, international students, international teachers, and teachers with global backgrounds tend to be excluded from "us" to be regarded as "they" whose visas prove their only legitimate presences here (the US).

We shared ideas and thoughts about these problematic spaces we experienced in seemingly opposite contexts: Bobbi as a white teacher within a non-white multilingual space and DJ as a non-white international teacher in a monolingual (with some exceptions), and largely racially, nationally homogeneous space (except for some ethnic students). Sometimes, we had to go through disagreements and logical and practical cul-de-sacs, but that helped us engage with these issues with our central aim for social justice. Thus, this chapter is about a journey to open a space of hope in a future where whiteliness in the classroom gives way to internationally democratic encounters of differences by which global justice can occur. In what follows, we share our dialogue over time; though we have written from a "we" perspective in this introduction, we have done so because we are both drawing from the same theoretical idea of whiteliness to ground our experiences. When relaying and reflecting on our individual personal experiences, however, we must keep our voices separate. A unified "we" cannot accurately account for the range of differences we embody due to our different personal backgrounds and experiences and how those are read onto us. Furthermore, a "we" voice might conflate and expunge our differences, when in fact we believe the opposite is necessary in a globalized world: we need to know our differences in order to engage in a dialogue with others, not to erase difference but to understand and create a new space/conversation. Our choices for this format go beyond our own interests; we also wanted to invite readers into our conversation in order to reflect on their own experiences in the globalized classroom. In short, we use this format in order to welcome readers to participate in rather than merely be informed by what we're saying. We return to a unified voice in the conclusion to come together on the idea that this work is ongoing and that no matter our individual experiences, we must commit to it together.

DJ: What I am and where I am located share one similar discourse—I am an Other[1]-in-class. This is an ontological discourse[2] that defines the significance of my presence as a teacher and a learner in this space to the extent that this fundamental position can be discussed, which also makes possible our (Bobbi's and my) dialogic conversations in this writing. Discourse is the space where Otherness and disagreements emerge, deconstructing subjectivity and unity. Our dialogue in this sense is not purporting unity but antagonisms against our socially determined teaching identities and positions. I use the word "ontological" because here my presence itself becomes highly problematic, and on this foundational instability, discourses of race, nation, and globalization are embedded. Indeed, this is the starting point to explain my transnational or trans-spatial experience I have gone through teaching in the US; without this positioning, I remain a dis-identifiable being. Pivoting on the question of the connections between a teacher's linguistic, national, and cultural identity and pedagogy, this chapter also saunters around an untraditional experience—how a non-native-English-speaking teacher teaches English (more specifically composition) to native-English-speaking college freshmen. More specifically, I will talk about what it's like to be a non-white teacher of mostly white students. However, readers should not expect to glean a success story in which a subject with a linguistic disability achieves excellence as a teacher of English.[3]

Rather, in this chapter, I am testifying here what I experienced as a desubjectified (racial and national) Other meeting Others[4] (American/other international students and colleagues) in the swamp of unexpected conflicts mostly related to racism and globalization. The best analogous example that represents a similar experience to mine is Entre les Murs (The Class) directed by Laurent Cantet.[5] In this movie, a French teacher is struggling with his internalized prejudices and racism, only to be locked in his own racial, gendered, and national wall by insulting and punishing an African student and a rude but dauntless white female student. Each time the instructor tries to avoid racism, classism, and other discriminations, he falls into a trap of self-righteousness. However, this movie is not stuck in blaming one's self or others. The best scene in the movie is when the teacher tries to keep a heated and precarious discussion, aimed for disagreement, going with his students. Though his position is unstable and his arguments get slippery and sloppy, he refuses to end his endeavor to engage in discussion with his students.

In this respect, the movie presents a hard but positive truth that the classroom can be a space not of consensus but of dissensus (disagreement) and radical equality. The radical equality happens when a teacher courageously abandons the assumptions about his own authority and students' unrecognized unstable identities to get in a debate off guard with students. This can be possible only when the teacher discovers and realizes how his position is ultimately (over)determined by prefabricated layers of oppressive (racial, national, gender, etc.) formations on the state and global levels. Disorientation is a necessary pedagogical step in this sense, especially in the globalized classroom where culture shock, misunderstanding, misrecognition, alienation, and dislocation happen regardless of a teacher's assumed position.

In truth, I have experienced these kinds of quandaries several times while teaching in the US and have had unexpected learning moments in these classes. I at first felt disoriented because this radically shook the foundation of my being's "there" that I had thought I belonged to nationally, racially, linguistically, culturally, and ontologically. When I was in Korea, I was a racially and nationally unproblematic being; I was one of "we," namely, an ordinary Korean speaking Korean among other Koreans. Though I experienced class or regional discrimination sometimes, I was never exposed to racial issues and never thought of myself as a racial Other in Korea. But here in the US, walking, talking, sulking, and eating, I feel disoriented and sometimes discriminated against. It takes time to bear people's suspicious looks, pretentious kindness, hospitality hiding hostility, and the racial assumption that I am a shy, sly, and effeminate Asian male, the most prominent stereotypes of Asians. Yet, this disorientation and estrangement are not negative experiences. No, these were, are, and will be positive trans-spatial experiences. Going through these experiences, I have been able to attain authenticity because of my experience of being an Other without a solid identity. In fact, I have been able to find a real "I" under the "otherization" that put my identity into more complex (racial, national, gender) discourses. Also, heterogeneity and becoming an Other has uncovered my hidden ethos (dwelling place in Greek) where globalization is embodied. If I kept living in Korea as a being in a nationally, racially homogenous space, I could not have had this chance to speculate on potential alterity in my presence because I was inured to colorblindness and internal racism in Korea.[6]

For the most part, my experience is a result of globalization. I can be here because I am a body moving across borders—a trans-spatial being. But, as Negri posits, "Globalization must be met with a counter-globalization" (2000, p. 207). In fact, the U.S. town where I belong to now is an un-global space, though it is slowly globalizing. In this Midwest town, whiteness was and is dominating, albeit it's going through an influx of gaining more ethnically and nationally diverse people. For example, when I arrived, I inevitably noticed that my foreignness, like pollen from Asia, caused some to have allergic reactions such as "Why are you here? Studying English?" I tried to explain, but in many cases, those explanations did not satisfy questioners' curiosity because my position was recognized as an unconventional one.

Moreover, after I started teaching, all the contextual positioning of my presence in the classroom became more complex. Always, becoming an "Other" as a teacher in the classroom was not easy. For example, when I first entered the classroom to teach a first-year composition course, students looked at me, but they did not pay attention. One of them loudly said the instructor must be late. When I walked to the front seat and sat on the supposed instructor's chair, students stopped talking and looked at me with puzzlement. When I opened my mouth and spoke to introduce myself, one of the students loudly said, "Can you say that again?" I felt intimidated, though I knew (hoped) that she only wanted to catch clearly what I was saying. The hierarchical relations between students and me seemed to be reversed; I felt like I was an English Language Learning student in front of all native-English-speaking teachers. Then, one of the students vividly asked, "When did you first come to the US?" I answered without hesitation, "Five years ago." Facing a doubtful expression on her face, and sensing awkwardness in the class, I declared, "But you don't need to worry too much about communication with me. I can understand what you say mostly." I knew that "mostly" would not be convincing, but that was the limit of confidence I could offer. I perceived that this linguistic otherness determined my linguistic identity, which led to determinations of my other national and racial identities. I was marked as a yellow foreigner whose English was not his mother tongue.

From then on, while teaching a few classes, I sometimes could not resist the tempting desire to gain, amplify, and stabilize my authority in the classroom to escape from the unstable position I held. I tried to stand tall and speak with authority, which negatively disoriented me from my own pedagogical idea to create a democratic classroom—namely, ultimately equal relationships between teacher and students. Not only did I try to behave like a whitely teacher, but I also tried to erase my foreignness, clunky accent, and different facial expressions to show that I was qualified as a teacher in the context I was in. Though I did not have whiteness as a physical color, I held an ideological belief that I was situated in the context of whiteliness where whiteness meant authority. Ahmed put it well: though I studied whiteness and antiracism in an academic setting, this did not mean that whiteness was something to be academically deconstructed. Though critically engaged with racism and whiteness, I did not recognize that whiteliness was deeply rooted in my performance. The more I pretended, the less I felt confident and secure. My Otherness would not go away easily. Rather, what I found out, through painful self-reflections, were really devastating results. I endeavored to gain authority as if I were a white/whitely teacher. Clearing this mesmerizing effect of pretension was painful but revealed that I was an Other, which is truly problematic as well as fruitful.

By and large, I learned that I was an Asian Other in a classroom of American Others, but I failed to learn how to reflect on my own position in terms of others' positions. Among what I learned, related to my learning of the significance of the instability of my teaching identity as a (racial and national) Other in the U.S. academy, the most interesting things for me while teaching three classes for two semesters have been the moments when I have engaged with issues related to my quandaries—race and nationality and their problematic contextualization with pedagogical acts in the classroom.

As such, race and racism is a generic, but unstable, topic in every classroom in the US. Maybe it is because race itself is an unstable discourse as a product of constantly changing transnational power structures. The idea of race in the classroom has changed over time and has forced us to conceive ourselves in various discourses. For instance, Everyday Anti-Racism (2008), a comprehensive book written by various writers with foci on practical and theoretical understandings of racial issues in the classroom, purports to present a broad picture of these issues in primary and secondary educational institutions. But all the writings in the book cannot satiate my thirst for an explanation of my untraditional position. The reason of this limit is simple—most writers in the book do not challenge but firmly hold on to a seemingly self-evident thought that he or she is able to teach students and readers race and racial issues because they think that those issues are teachable. Are they? What does something that is teachable mean? It might well mean that students can be convinced or persuaded to think in ways a teacher purveys. To many teachers, acceptance, acknowledgement, and reflection are what teachers would like to evince from students. However, this idea of "teachable" presupposes that a teacher's knowledge about race and racial issues are deliverable and truthful. For example, Priya Parmar and Shirley Steinberg, in discussing their positioning in class as a white Jewish teacher and an Asian Indian teacher in public high schools, state, "As teachers, we have found that identifying ourselves to students in terms of our own positionality . . . has been a way to carve a safe space for students in which to discuss sensitive racial and ethnic matters" (2008, p. 283).

Although mostly accepting their statement, I personally cannot agree to the idea that teachers' positioning will produce students' safe space for learning. My experience tells that it did not. Sometimes leading discussions about racism or immigration during class, I was located in a volcano of debates where these interstices and fissures occurred and magma of unconscious prejudices flew and were ossified into obstacles for communication. One time, reading and discussing Malcolm X's essay, a white female student claimed that white people were really racially discriminated against.[7] I was shocked and dumbfounded by her explicit comment. Another white student said that because of scholarships for ethnic students, she could not get one; a student retorted that maybe President Obama's daughter did not need to pay tuition because of these scholarships. Debates went on, and I really felt frustrated by the unconscious racism in students' mindsets. Yet, I admit that the class really disclosed where I was living and in what situation I was located; I was living in a location where racism was and is prevalent. Then, what is the significance of my pedagogical practice of raising issues most of the students are not familiar with? My answer is that I have tried to render a differential discursive location and create a new location where students can engage with new thoughts and new ways to understand the world they live in. In short, I have tried to create differential spaces. Differential space is a space where difference functions to switch teachers' and students' mindsets from internalized racism to deconstruction of everyone's whiteliness to face up to the truth of one's own unearned privilege by virtue of whiteliness. This differential space can be created and cognitively mapped within differential racism in globalization. Yet, differential space occurs within global racism. This version of racism in global context can be called differential racism according to Balibar.[8] This differential racism is more complicated racism than the previous one because it is global racism mediated by colonial and local difference, as well as ideologies of multicultural difference.

Before I could create a differential space, I was located by the institution and read by my students because of differential racism. This positioning in my case brought about confusions, alienations, denials, awkwardness, and so on for both me and my students. Maybe it was because I was an Other; I did not speak English as fluently as they did, and I might not (to them) have had the authority to talk about American history and racism. Though these explanations cannot answer the previous question of whether race or racial issues are teachable or not, especially for a teacher who is an Other in the US, through my frustration with students I could tease out that there was something "wrong" with my "teaching." In fact, I was not "teaching" but creating "disagreements" in class, which produced a differential space, because to me those issues were not "teachable" regardless of my lack of knowledge, experience, linguistic accuracy, or authority.

As a result of my experience, I radically posit that race and racial issues are not "teachable" but in permanent disagreement because they are not subject to consensus or convergence of relevant knowledge. Teaching cannot accompany learning inasmuch as a teacher asserts that race and racism is a topic of the past to be learned for preparation of a history test, denying that whiteness (or whiteliness) is property[9] or forcing students to accept the idea that they are living in a colorblind society. The moment of teaching comes as soon as a teacher recognizes that consensus is not possible but that only disagreements can shake up the unverified hypothesis that race and racism is a subject to be taught. What's more, contemporary race and racism is expanding its interactive discourse, keeping up the pace of globalization and its products of (post) colonialism and asymmetrical power structures in the global space perpetrated by global capitalism. Race and racism becomes a more complicated issue on the global expanse where new immigrants, migrants, refugees, and all other border-crossing beings, such as Gloria Anzaldua's (1987) mestizos/mestizos, Negri's (2000) multitude (as a new global nomadic proletariat), post-colonial subalterns, etc., run into new and differential racism. Differential racism is covered up by cultural pretentions that minorities' differences are tolerable insofar as they do not implement their power to change the majority.

Upon these conditions, a need to deconstruct seemingly stabilized racial discourses in the classroom and expand this discourse into broader and more complex issues of globalized differential racism against immigrants, migrants, refugees, and all the other border-crossing people becomes more urgent. In this context, I have tried to deconstruct my own positioning and whiteliness in local and global contexts and rebuild an untraditional position to create an instable space of discussion in classes. But this turns out to be mixture of success and failure necessarily. Going through this pedagogical experiment, I realize that this deconstruction and unstable construction of a new space might not be possible without collaboration with a colleague who can provide a second glance on my position. That's the reason I started this conversation with a white female colleague, Bobbi Olson.

Bobbi: I am a white American citizen,[10] raised and educated in predominantly (and often overwhelmingly) white environments. English is my first and only language. I tell my identity because these markers influence how my students perceive me and how I act and have acted as a teacher. In telling my race—and in telling the narratives I include throughout this chapter—I acknowledge the fact that "declaring whiteness, or even 'admitting' to one's own racism when the declaration is assumed to be 'evidence' of an anti-racist commitment, does not do what it says" (Ahmed, 2004, n.p.). Rather, a white person stating her race is often a further demonstration of white privilege (Ahmed, 2004). But, I declare my race and other identity markers because ignoring the ways in which my race manifests itself is also an act of white privilege. To work against the racist structures I benefit from, I must "stay implicated in what [I] critique" (Ahmed, 2004, n.p.). In other words, as a white person, I "must recognize in an ongoing and enlarging sense the extent to which the humanity of those of us who are raced white depends on learning to be conscious as well as critical of and resistant to racial states of thinking, organizing, being, and doing" (Condon, 2012, p. 17)—including within myself and the structures within which I operate. A step in this process is to understand the ways in which my race is read and the resulting implications. For example, I need to not only consider how I enact whiteliness in my teacher role, but also how the institution of higher education operates from a whitely perspective—and what I can do to resist both my own individual perspective and behaviors and that of the institution's.

Throughout my teaching career, I have taught composition courses at four different institutions of higher education. Most of my students have been white, although there have been multilingual students—both international and American citizens, but none of whom were white[11]—in some of the classes I've taught in the past. I have also taught a class open only to international students, in which all of my students were multilingual, and I was the only white person in the room. My experiences teaching multilingual students in the classroom has made me think more critically and wonder what I can do to be a more effective teacher of all of my students present in the classroom and their worldviews, worldviews that do not always align with the whitely ones I've embodied and that have served me well throughout my own education.

Part of my feeling that I need to be a better teacher to all of my students comes from my experiences hearing and learning from many multilingual writers when working with them in the one-with-one context of the writing center. Through conversations in this context, I have been granted insight to the position of multilingual students in the U.S. university structure, though of course I cannot fully realize this position since it is not one I share. The experiences multilingual students have in the U.S. university that they have revealed to me, however, demonstrate the ways in which multilingual students in this context are often invisible, except for when teachers view multilingual students as "problems"—which seems to be the predominant perspective voiced about multilingual students by their (white) teachers. (They're "problems" because they do not behave "normally"—i.e., as white students do.)

DJ's perspective offers what it means to be an "Other" teaching in a mostly white classroom in the US; my perspective focuses on what it means to be a white teacher of multilingual students, all of whom, in my experience, were not white. While this makes me an Other in the classroom[12] in that I was the one who was different from my rather homogenous group of multilingual international students, it does not make me Other to the extent DJ was in his classroom due to the racial order that is prevalent both in and out of the classroom. For DJ's white students, his Otherness indicated foreignness and racial difference; for my students my Otherness was valued for it was white. To my students, my white face and native-speaking use of English represented a point of access to the power structure dominant in the U.S. university, as well as in the global power structure more broadly as the use of English consistently spreads internationally. To my students, my native-English-speaking use of the language "represent[ed] capital and power" but also "symbolize[d] a kind of dividing rod of class and racial disparity within the United States and around the world" (Grant & Lee, 2009, p. 45). DJ and I both consider our race because teaching in a globalized classroom necessitates a consideration of it, both our own and our students'.

Why must we think about race? The short answer seems to me that whether it is acknowledged or not, race is present in the classroom: our behaviors as teachers stem from the presence of race, and our students similarly operate within race structures. To reach the teaching goals DJ and I share—which means considering not only how our own presences in the classroom affect student learning but also calling out the structures that underlie institutions in the US—race has to be explicitly addressed. To remain silent on how race affects social and institutional structures in the US ignores the reality that race has infiltrated the ways students are treated in the classroom and university writ large. According to Omi and Winant, in order to advance toward racial progress, "we should think of race as an element of social structure rather than as an irregularity within it; we should see race as a dimension of representation rather than an illusion" (1994, p. 55). We need to help students see the ways in which their race affords them privilege or denies them access in often invisible ways. We need to, as teachers, think about how our own race and ways of being reinscribe oppressive racist structures, structures that many whitely teachers would say we're fighting against. To do this work, though, both DJ and I recognize that "Challenging the dominant racial ideology inherently involves not only reconceptualizing one's own racial identity, but a reformulation of the meaning of race in general" (Omi & Winant, 1994, p. 91). To "reformulate the meaning of race in general," we must first understand race as it currently exists. For my work, this means calling out that part of the "problem" of multilingual writers in the American classroom is their race.

Although no one seems to name the racializing of multilingual students, the fact is, they are raced in American classrooms, though it's not usually explicitly acknowledged because their national differences and linguistic identities cover their racial identities so that the racial structure seems to be hidden from their positions. But, this is not true—multilingual students' racial presences are scanned and mapped in race discourse where their presences are marked by non-whiteliness. Even white multilingual students from Europe will be exposed to global racism because their whiteness is not immediately regarded as whiteliness. Multilingual students feel "different" from their white classmates, and their white classmates often treat them as such. (White students will talk about the "Asian" student in the classroom or the "foreign" kid—even when these students are just as American as them—but seldom, if ever, the "white" boy who sits in the corner. I've never heard a white student describe a white classmate with white as a defining characteristic.) Yet conversation about multilingual students is often framed around their linguistic "deficiency,"[13] and race goes unnamed. A focus on linguistic "deficiency"—in which multilingual students are "problems" because of their "different" use of the English language—means that teachers, administrators, and other "normal" (i.e., white) American students don't have to name what else they perceive to be different about multilingual students, which is particularly telling in that in my experience, most of these teachers, administrators, and students who complain about the "difficult" multilingual students are white and/or act in whitely ways. (That, too, often goes unacknowledged.)

The focus on multilingual students' "deficiency" in English permits instructors, administrators, fellow students, etc., to hide behind that reasoning in order to deny the reality that multilingual students are viewed and treated as Other because of other uglier reasons—multilingual students are often not American, not native-English speakers, not-white, and not-the-same. This tactic, much like the paradigms of race Omi and Winant explain, "neglect[s] the specificity of race as an autonomous field of social conflict, political organization, and cultural/ideological meaning" (1994, p. 48). In short, race is never named and therefore never addressed. (And therefore the actors can believe there are no bad teachers and/or students being racist in the classroom.) This omission is problematic in its own right, for as Bonilla-Silva (2010) reveals in his discussion of "colorblind racism," little advancement toward racial progress can occur when privileged parties refuse to recognize or admit their involvement in racism. This omission goes beyond the fact that no progress can be made, though—omission provides space for the ongoing practice of implicit racism because we negate the relevance of race to people's lived experiences. For multilingual students in the American university, that race is never named means that there isn't an easy end or transformation to the discrimination multilingual students face in U.S. institutions of higher education, a discrimination that I believe is more deeply seeded than how multilingual students use the English language.[14]

I believe it is imperative to think about my own teaching and the possibility I have for replicating racial structures in the classroom because I have heard the individual stories of multilingual students feeling Othered, and conversely, I have heard instructors do the Othering in both written and oral form. For these individuals, I think it matters to try and help whitely teachers understand how race affects multilingual students' experiences. On a broader level, though, I think it matters because they're not just individual cases: racism happens on a systemic level. International student enrollment in U.S. universities has been consistently on the rise, and it is reasonable to expect it will continue to do so. As multilingual students become a larger percentage of our student population in the US, I think it is only right that we think about how to teach them well, especially given that international multilingual students are often recruited by universities for profit. If capitalizing on many multilingual students' increased international tuition rate and additional fees, it seems at the very least an ethical demand that we consider multilingual students' particular needs and experiences in the U.S. university. It seems at the very least we need to look for ways that we do not make them feel as if they do not belong in American classrooms, for it's very likely they feel that way in many other spaces in the US.

One thing that comes up for me as a white instructor, however, is that I could very well choose NOT to talk about race. Because white and whitely is perceived as "normal" in the US, it is rare that students would bring up (or ask questions based on) my race and behavior. For DJ, this hasn't been true. He is viewed as Other (not white) the moment he steps into the American classroom. But white and whitely teachers, because they don't often think about race in connection to their lived experiences very often, often don't consider the way their race is read and how that manifests itself in the classroom. There have been several instances where I didn't.

So yes, I can "choose" to talk about race in ways that DJ cannot because his (white) students recognize his non-whiteness (yet grant him more authority when he acts whitely), but not talking about race is an act of white privilege, and in particular, a form of unearned authority—authority granted to white instructors not by virtue of their actions, but by the perception of their skin tone.

What concerns me about my role as a teacher is how much of this role is based on characteristics I cannot control, on a sense of perceived authority I did not earn, but which is "central to whiteliness" (Frye, 2001, p. 91). When my classroom of all multilingual international students saw me walk in the door the first day of our class, they viewed me as Teacher before I ever introduced myself, for "Whites symbolize power and privilege and all forms of capital" (Grant & Lee, 2009, p. 57). This symbolized whiteness is whiteliness, and once I began to speak—and my status as a native-English speaker became clear without me ever stating that fact—the students had already granted me full authority in the classroom. But what happens when white (and whitely) instructors do not think about this unearned authority, when they operate as if the treatment given them is automatically expected? More specifically, what happens when white/ly teachers are not even aware of this unearned authority and behave as if it is natural and neutral? The repercussions of unexamined unearned authority is that this authority goes unchecked; in these cases, students don't learn, or perhaps more accurately, what they learn is who has the right to authority based on race structures. Here's an example:

> Ali,[15] an international multilingual student, came to the writing center with a paper he had labored over for several weeks. He sat there dejected as he handed me the graded product, fully marked up in red pen with many curt comments but no explanations behind them. In the top corner, the instructor had written "Don't you listen to what I say? Your grammar never improves." In this moment, Ali didn't learn grammar: he learned he didn't belong.

In this moment with Ali, I could not erase the teacher's comments, nor could I as a writing center tutor change his grade to reflect the thoughts I had about what he had written, which did not line up with the instructor's assessment. (It has helped me rethink my own presentation of self and authority in my written feedback to my students, though.) Yet in this moment, Ali and I could still disrupt the implication that Ali didn't belong. As I reflect on this session, I realize that in this space we could have interrupted the instructor's whiteliness and belief in his "rightness" by talking together about what perspective those comments might have come out of. In this moment, Ali and I could have still done the work of deconstructing the comments from the instructor and our own identities to critically reflect on the authority granted white and whitely teachers and why. In doing so, I believe we would have made an attempt toward disrupting the racial order by critiquing it, even if in our work together we could not ultimately change that instructor's previous comments.

The unearned authority accorded to white teachers comes in part from their race, but this authority is represented by teachers and students as coming from other things: the credentials a teacher has earned through graduate degrees, for example, or in multilingual students' teachers' cases, the teacher's native-English-speaking status. Riffing on Peggy McIntosh's metaphor of unpacking the knapsack of white privilege,[16] I have composed a list of the ways my teaching body—based on a perception of my race and whiteliness—is experienced differently in the classroom than I believe DJ's and other people of color's to be even if they are whitely, too.[17]

My Unearned Authority:

1. I can expect that my students assume I have the necessary credentials to be their teacher.
2. I can feel assured that my students will not question the legitimacy of my degree since it is from an American university.
3. I can expect that my students will not wonder where my degree is from in the first place.
4. I can assume that my students will not question my spoken language, and that I won't have to think that carefully about my pronunciation.
5. I can expect that my students will not question my course design or teaching approach based on their perception of my credentials.
6. I can expect that most of my students will not question my ability to grade their work, lead class discussions, answer their questions, and so on.
7. I can expect that students will respect the expectations I set forth without questioning or challenging me.
8. I can enter the classroom and not be mistaken for another student.
9. I can admit when I do not know something and not perpetuate the idea that my race is less intelligent.
10. I can choose to disclose where I was born if I want to, but it is not an immediate question that comes to my students' minds.
11. I can expect that when I speak, my students are not making judgments of my intelligence based on my pronunciation.[18]
12. I can expect that my students will assume the feedback I provide them is the "correct" answer.
13. I can expect that if I want to converse with my colleagues about a particular teaching situation, most of them will look like me and have a similar worldview (Rothenberg, 2000) as me.
14. I can feel assured that my students will not assume I earned my teaching position because of a commitment to "diversity" (Geller et. al., 2007, p. 98).

15. I can expect that my students will not ask me how many languages I know because it is clear I am a native-English speaker, which is the only language they care that I know.

DJ: In response to Bobbi's consideration of the shadowy, covert authority of whiteliness in the multilingual classroom and its ideological connection to racism: I fell into complex sequences of thoughts about Bobbi's idea of difference and white teachers' (un)intentional omission of racial issues in class as well as her self-deconstructing ways of addressing her unearned authority in terms of whiteliness as a property. Her arguments of instructors' Othering reveal a common ground I am standing in as much as it also shows how we could continue our conversation on this issue. I think we can have conversation because we have the courage to deconstruct our own positioning. And, this equal deconstruction results in more troubling but helpful thoughts on how our idea of difference is related to radical equality in our classes also. Then what is the fundamental aim of this conversation? My answer is "racial (including global) justice in the classroom." My ideas of racial justice are mostly influenced by Catherine Prendergast's titanic study on "how literacy has been accepted as White property in crucial contexts that helped shape the country" (2003, p. 7). As she testifies, literacy has been biased and manipulated by the state to exclude people who do not possess whiteliness as property. However, agreeing with most of her arguments, I could not personally agree with her last remark in the introduction that "A literacy that creates rather than threatens unity in this country, I maintain, will be one that takes this insight, and its mandate to confront and end a history of injustice, to heart" (2003, p. 15).

Though I agree that someday we might be able to accomplish this utopian task, I resist the idea of unity as the final goal. What's more, our project here goes beyond racial justice in the US, purporting to address differential racism in the global classroom and to create differential space. In this context, as a theoretical account of our conversation, I would like to delve into the meaning of difference per se. Our conversations about the global situation embed and embody our differences rather than reveal a way to converge those differences. All those differential conversations are possible because of radical "equality" based on "difference" between us.

Nowadays people hesitate to express the overtly discriminative idea that difference is difficult. But, in fact, difference is always difficult to understand because difference razes down reasonably beautiful concepts of unity, identity, consensus, collaboration, mutual understanding, and so on. In a sense, difference can be powerful when it has an affinity to equality. History and current local and global situations prove that equality originates from and sustains on totally different prepositions; disagreement, revolution, constant debates—namely all efforts to render difference be difference. As such, in history equality is a bloody word aiming for pure difference without unification; endless demonstrations and revolutions have had to have people in the past and in the present shed immense tears and blood to make this term survive in this world because equality denies our utopian belief in unity.[19] Equality is a process, not a result of changes. In global history, a region of activists has fought to actualize equality only to crawl into this unattainable goal because it is against given social systems on the state or global levels that purport to build a unity uprooting differences. More importantly, even difference itself as a concept without its context has become a catchword for differential racism to the extent that this term is imbued by ideals of peace, coexistence, multiculturalism, cosmopolitanism, salad bowl, melting pot, etc.

Difference is not a noun but a verb because it disagrees to any unified system, e.g., whiteliness, as an individual praxis. What's more, difference as praxis against racism presupposes its equal dissemination for everyone for radical democracy. Prevalently, difference loses its power whenever people who hold whiteliness deny that difference exists in class in forms of disagreement and equal difference between teacher, colleagues and students. People possessing whiteliness are afraid to admit that racial difference in power structures exist as much as their unearned authority as a teacher with whiteliness is disrupting an equal chance of true education for both teachers and students. To my surprise, many white students—and even some non-white students and colleagues I have met—have told me that race and racism is played-out in the US because racism was a phenomenon of a historical phase that has since died out. Colorblindness is a filmy illusion of whiteliness.

In addition, many are afraid to discuss race and racism even when they do acknowledge its remaining prevalence. For example, most of my colleagues in a class I took for first-year composition teachers said that they were avoiding racial issues in their classes because they did not know how to initiate or continue these conversations, and it was awkward for them, as mostly white teachers, to discuss in their classes. Thus, when I said that I had tried to bring up issues of racism and xenophobia in my classes, they looked shocked and worried. One colleague even said that when she raised a racial issue, students, who were mostly white, stayed in a dead silence, showing embarrassment. As a result of her experience, this teacher doubtfully asked me how students could actively participate in discussions about race and racism in my class. The professor who led this class guessed that students might have actively spoken out their opinions about racism freely in front of me because I was a foreigner and an Asian.

Frankly speaking, I felt confused by these reactions. I thought the intentional omission of race and racism in our first year writing classes denies the possibility that each student has different perspective about race and racism. Those colleagues easily presupposed that students were ignorant because "they" looked hesitant to speak about race or racism. My experience tells that it is not true. The problems lie on how to approach these issues. Right after a teacher holds on to a common sense that race is indifferent to him or her so that he or she can teach impartially, he or she falls into a deception and an unintentional complicity to systemic racial formation. Bobbi's attempts to deconstruct her own whiteliness also prove this. She is trying to abandon her pretentious impartiality and unquestioned authorities in order to start discussion with racial (national) Others because she realizes that she could turn into an Other in global race system. Her listing of unearned authorities—whether shared with students or not—is a way to think about and open discussions about race and racism in the globalized classroom. Still, this requires, as Bobbi's case shows, painful differentiation and deconstruction of identity, consensus, and unity. Indeed, differentiation of an authoritative subject position as a teacher with unearned authority via her whiteliness (though it is undeniable that some authority is earned given a teacher's position) is a constantly on-going deconstruction of unity and consensus; even difference itself has to be differentiated in order not to be forcibly integrated into conceptual, ideological unity. Speaking in the voice of Jacques Rancière (2010), a French philosopher, I claim that equality and difference, for this reason, is dissensus. And, dissensus is a way to actualize democratic justice in the racially hierarchical global classroom.

Race and racial issues are subject to dissensus[20] which Rancière (2010) coined to explain how consensus is detrimental to political efforts to create more democratic space and how disagreement as dissensus is important to make real difference in politics.[21] Dissensus deconstructs the ideology of consensus and germinates radical equalities that deconstruct hierarchical, hegemonic structures; it destructs hierarchical ideology in the classroom of "you have to agree to my idea because you are students." This does not mean that teachers are unnecessary, nor can Rancière's arguments be universally adaptable. Rather, the lesson I learned by my teaching is that most students already "know" TOO MUCH about race and racism in terms of consensus, and their racial experiences are already too realistic and unified to be discussed in class only via fixed textbooks. What the students and teachers need is to first unlearn their knowledge manipulated by media that promulgates racial prejudices so that they are able to explore meaning of their experiences in terms of whiteliness and structural racism. Differentiation and dissensus presupposes unlearning in the classroom. This is a way to create radically democratic equality in the classroom so that everyone realizes they all are in the same rhetorical position to create differential space—"I don't know, but I need to learn why I have the potentialities to become racist easily and how to disagree with these potentialities." Yet, this is not just applicable to me but to all teachers regardless of their racial, national identities. In Bobbi's case, unless she unlearned those unearned authorities international multilingual students might have about her and learned simultaneously how those students could learn and unlearn their own problematic positions, a democratic struggle to create equality and differentiation might not occur in Bobbi's teaching and learning experience in the classroom, writing center, and everyday life. Bobbi has deconstructively reflected on her own unearned authorities and other white teachers' hidden racism to assume potential Otherness (i.e., I am white and/or whitely and I am different from you, but I feel also the same Otherness in this class), and brought about thinking of the ways she could create space for dissensus, for example, with Ali in their writing center session (i.e., though I am not different from other white teachers racially, I admit that I am situated in the global racial structure which forms me as a potential racist, but I am able to disagree with and deconstruct these positions and can participate in discussions about racism with you in moments of dissensus). This is an example of the simultaneous process of unlearning and learning as well as a creation of differential space for radical democracy to create radically equal articulations to disrupt teachers' whiteliness. Whiteliness is a rhetorical, personal and institutional system from which every individual with singular differences, regardless of their color or position, can detach themselves in order to articulate hegemonic antagonism, though this requires painful deconstruction of one's whiteliness. Bobbi's and my experiences could be on the same page not because we are in the same discourses (I am different from Bobbi in terms of gender, nationality, race, and language) but because we are in the same pedagogical situation where we are potentially Others in the globalized classroom. We are sailors of different colors in the same boat crossing borders as we are on the sea of equal potentiality of disagreements.

Along with this theoretical linking of difference and equality for desubjectified teachers' roles and their engagement with students' dissensus to bring up race and racism in classroom and my interpretation of Bobbi's case, henceforth I also reflect on my own cases. In these cases, I consider the whole complexity of issues and the endless search for ways to unlearn my prejudices and learn new perspectives about my position as an Other in class. Class discussion was not easy in these moments. Sometimes, going through these moments, I felt vertigo as if I was standing on a precipice looking down to abyss of ambiguity of my positions and identities as a teacher. For example, in my second semester writing class, there were two African American students in the class and a Chicana student; the rest of the students were white. In this class, I read a paper written by Jewel,[22] an African American female student. The assignment was a rhetorical analysis about a text students chose. Reading through Jewel's paper about rap culture in the US, I was dumbfounded by her African American English vernacular. The content of the paper was great; she intelligently analyzed the significance of rap culture as a resistance against the majority. However, based on my knowledge of prescriptive English grammar, her writing seemed to have too many grammatical "errors," and sentences were confusing and sloppy from my perspective. I, who had learned grammar in high school and struggled with mastery of my command of English, could not help but doubt my ability to grade her writing.

Though I learned about African American vernacular and its difference from so-called "standard" English and why this is historically relevant to racial justice in the classroom, I did not know how to handle Jewel's paper.[23] Eventually, I decided to talk about this with her, but she, mostly shy and quiet in class, said she had not thought before that her writing used African American vernacular. I gave her a better grade than I thought I should at first, but still I am confused whether I did right or not. Did I Otherize her because of my linguistic incapability to recognize vernacular differences? Did I racialize her? In another class, we discussed Fredrick Douglass's essay, "How I Learned to Read and Write." I asked an African American male student his opinion about racism and racist history several times, but he rejected talking about that issue and just said that the US does not have racism today. I was also embarrassed. I now realize that it was "I" in the subjective, dominant position as a teacher that embarrassed these students; in truth I could not abandon and unlearn my prejudiced belief that those students would like to talk about their ethnic identity and culture in a white-dominated, but globalized classroom where an international teacher was talking about race and racism based on his own prejudice. The realization happened when I was also Otherized.

A few weeks later, while discussing Asian American experience in an essay by Amy Tan, out of curiosity a student asked for me to speak Korean. This was another embarrassing moment to me, though I could not pinpoint exactly how and why I felt embarrassed. After a long hesitation, I finally translated part of the essay from English to Korean and spoke out loud (even though, in fact, Amy Tan is a Chinese American writer). Students listened carefully and said that the sounds and pronunciation were much different from those in English. Then, one student asked if I felt more comfortable speaking in Korean or in English; I said absolutely I felt more comfortable whenever I spoke in Korean because it was my mother tongue. Discussing the meaning of mother tongue, I wondered in my deep heart why I had to feel awkward when I spoke in my mother tongue in front of those native-English speakers.

After I left school that day, I thought about my experiences with my African American students and my own experience of speaking Korean in the classroom, and I finally realized why I felt embarrassed and why they did also. I felt embarrassed because I had to declare my national (and linguistic and racial) identity in front of mostly white and almost all American students, uncovering my foreignness and Otherness. I felt naked in public because it made me self-realize that I was different. The cases with my two African American students and my own reversed situation revealed that I did not recognize that asking those questions created a hierarchical structure of assuming teacher's authority, which prevented further discussion and learning. I unintentionally endeavored to create a consensus, forcing those two African American students to articulate their thoughts about race and racism in front of their white classmates; I acted as if I had been a whitely teacher in a white students' class. In truth, I held firmly to an authority of racial dominance over those African American students—so that my position was overdetermined by whiteliness, in the form of racial consensus in the classroom.

Denying my assumptions, those two African American students created dissensus against my hegemonic consensus. By their reactions, I could realize I did not go through unlearning my prejudices, and I was counting on my authority of whiteliness in classroom. I had to unlearn those assumptions and engage with these issues by deconstructing my internalized racism, recognizing how my own lacks turned them into Others so as to cover my Otherness in the classroom. At the moment when I thought that I could pose those questions to these two African American students, I held on to the seemingly neutral position I assumed I held—Asian, foreigner, and a middle-aged male teacher. In fact, I painfully had to acknowledge that I became a racist at those moments and could not deconstruct my seemingly safe, neutral position. But this is not self-blaming. Self-blaming is a way to ascribe structural polemics onto an individual situation, which is bound to result in losing a chance to scan and map the constantly changing and heterogeneous global, racial discourses of whiteliness, my Otherized, and sometimes Otherizing presence is situated in. My feeling was much closer to "shame," a shame that I could fundamentally feel.

All in all, in the broadest sense, all of us are singular, different beings in a globally racial system. I mean we are all trans-spatial beings (those beings crossing discursive or physical borders); in particular, we are equally vulnerable, and we are on the verge of becoming Others and the victim of various systems. In the racial system—which is the framework for every social space in the US formed throughout racial history—I am as vulnerable as my African American students who also possessed different positions. Those vulnerable positions also uncovered the ontological equality in race and national discourses. Then, how can I constantly unlearn these prejudices and learn and participate in dissensus with students? I listen to Bobbi's account to find a way to break through this quandary.

Bobbi: I include here an example of faculty speaking about multilingual students to highlight the attitudes often present—though perhaps unspoken—in U.S. universities regarding multilingual students. While this example is an individual one, I think it is representative of the thoughts on many college campuses across the U.S. DJ's experience certainly speaks to these same sentiments.

I was invited to speak to a group of faculty from a department other than my own to share my experience in working with multilingual writers. What I think these (all white) faculty wanted were some tips and strategies for responding to and assessing multilingual students' writing—writing and behaviors that they viewed as very different and unacceptable in relation to their American, native-English-speaking students. These faculty members claimed that their main concern was the ways in which multilingual students' use of English deviated from what the instructors viewed as "standard" English. (Their notion of "standard" English was really just a prescriptivist use of English grammar, and one that did not consider how the language acquisition process worked, or that there is no one absolute "standard" as language is living, not static.) As we conversed, frustrations in working with multilingual students rose to the surface:

> "*They* don't know how to do group work."
>
> "*They* don't participate in class."
>
> "*They* don't know English."

One participant's final remark "They don't belong here" finally speaks to the sentiment I think all of the other concerns were hinting at: these students don't look like the students I thought I would be teaching. In DJ's case, his students were thinking this teacher doesn't look like the teacher I thought I would have. How can this teacher teach me?

It is easy in this moment, I think, to judge. To say that the remarks I heard and that are implicit in DJ's telling of his classroom experience are indicative of a widespread viewpoint in which multilingual writers are Others is a simple move to make: the speakers' use of the pronoun "they" signals a clear differentiation in their minds as being not-the-same as the rest of their students. While there are differences, the problem is that these thoughts then manifest themselves in treating multilingual students as not-the-same, which almost always means less-than.

I don't tell this story in order to point out how "bad" these instructors were. Within our conversation about this situation, DJ asked me "What makes you any different?" And that's the million-dollar question. I cannot undo the fact that my white face is read as one of power. What I can undo, or begin to unsettle, is my whiteliness in an attempt to disrupt the attitudes that permeated beneath those instructors' comments. I can disrupt my own thoughts in order to not recreate what I heard those instructors saying in that moment. To disrupt the I-am-right-and-Others-are-wrong whitely perspective evidenced in a "we" versus "they" mentality, I can attempt, as Frye suggested:

> [To] refuse to enact, embody, animate this category—the white race—as I am supposed to, I can free up my energies and actions from a range of disabling confinements and burdens, and align my will with the forces which eventually will dissolve or dismantle that race as such. If it is objected that it is an exercise of white privilege to dissociate myself from the white race this way, I would say that in fact this project is strictly forbidden by the rules of white solidarity and white supremacy, and is not one of the privileges of white power. It may also be objected that my adoption or recommendation of this strategy implies that the right thing to do, in general, for everyone, is to dissolve, dismantle, bring an end to, races; and if this indeed is the implication, it can sound very threatening to some of the people whose races are thus to be erased. (2001, p. 98–99)

Neither DJ nor I (nor Frye) want a unified classroom in which difference is dissolved; if I disrupt in the ways Frye describes, however, I have a chance of unsettling my own whiteliness and disrupting them in the classroom. I have the chance at not continuing to Other raced students in the classroom and instead create a new space, one that values difference instead of trying to expunge it or focus solely on it.

One way of disrupting my pattern of whiteliness has been re-examining my classroom materials, such as the readings and essay prompts I assign. Thinking about our classroom materials and experiences, I believe, is necessary in order to notice the values and worldviews they reflect, particularly because we probably did not even notice that they reflect/promote certain values and worldviews in the first place. In her examination of the way her gender, class, and race led to her own (at the time unnoticed) privilege throughout her life, Paula Rothenberg (2000) reflects on how this privilege affected how she taught and what students learned—her worldview made the readings she selected seem "natural," for instance, though she realizes now they were decidedly Eurocentric. Rothenberg reminds us of the importance for teachers to consider what type of information they disseminate to their students, for students don't just learn "content" in the classrooms; rather she cites Edgar Friedenberg's argument "that the real lessons our students learned in school were not in the curriculum but in the school culture—the kinds of treatment they received, and thus came to expect, from those in authority" (2000, p. 134). What are multilingual students learning in the American classroom, when, like Ali, they are made to feel as if they don't belong? I imagine they are learning just that: that they don't belong. When students do not see their own experiences and perspectives included in the classroom materials they are a part of, it is a signal that these experiences and perspectives have no worth in that space. It's clear, then, that we are in the position to perpetuate institutional racism after all.

I've found that beginning by asking myself questions helps distance me from the ingrained attributes represented in my classroom materials. For instance, what are the readings I've chosen to assign? Will multilingual students (and/or other raced students) identify with any of them? Is a multilingual student's perspective included or even acknowledged? In my own past as a teacher, for example, I think of the ways in which a course centered on "argument" sponsored an exclusively Western notion of argument—one that is linear and direct. Some of my students in those previous classes who were schooled to construct arguments more subtly and indirectly surely did not see their previous experiences and knowledge included in my syllabus or course design. The signal to them in those moments was that their prior experiences were wrong. But I had never realized there were other styles of argument. I was too entrenched in my own thinking and schooling—based on white, Western standards, just as I was white and had a Western mindset—to think that there was anything beyond that I could present to my students. In so doing, I as a teacher did what I've heard done to many multilingual students: reinforced the feeling that they didn't belong, that their ways of knowing (and being) had no real place in the American classroom.

Here's another example of the ways in which what we do in the classroom may exclude students—in particular multilingual students—when we as teachers do not think beyond our own experiences (including race and culture). As a new teacher, I often borrowed assignment ideas from more experienced instructors. I mostly adopted them as they were, with perhaps just a few changes in order for me to get my own head wrapped around what I was asking students to do. One such assignment required students to analyze political cartoons of their choosing. After class on the day I explained the assignment, Sami,[24] the only multilingual student in the course, came and talked to me. He expressed that he could not do the assignment, as he had no familiarity with the genre of political cartoons or understanding of the knowledge of the politics in which the humor was dependent upon. In his home country, it was illegal to make comments about government actions and/or leaders. I simply hadn't thought of this. I had realized that this assignment might be difficult for students because political cartoons are often laden with implications rather than direct statements. Yet when I thought about the difficulties, I was viewing them through my own framework: as a white American. Perhaps the more experienced instructors who taught this assignment had thought of how it might be ethnocentric, but I don't recall that that idea had ever been raised in any discussions among teachers I had been a part of, and I naively had not thought of it on my own. If the assignment was presented in other classrooms similarly to how I presented it, it is likely that many international multilingual students struggled with this assignment. And unlike Sami, many of those students probably did not voice their concerns because of the authority they perceived their instructors to have. (I believe Sami did speak to me because being such a young female at the time meant that my authority was more tenuous.)

Although my assignment was naïve and lacked thinking on my part about all of my students' perspectives, I think there are cases too where assignments created with good intentions to help students think about and dismantle racism can still be problematic. Matak[25] came to the writing center[26] wanting help thinking about how to approach an assignment. His instructor had asked his students to think about the ways in which white privilege affects education, housing, or employment. (I don't think the assignment specifically said in America, but it was clear that was the assumption. The assignment was complicated, and both Matak and I were confused as to where to start: Matak because he was unsure of what he was being asked to do, and me because I was uncomfortable with having the conversations I knew we'd have to have.) Matak asked me what white privilege was, for he didn't understand the phrase. In trying to explain it to him, at one point Matak interjected with "but in America, anyone can be president." Matak was a refugee who had lived through more horror and atrocities than I could begin to imagine;

I didn't want to be the one who disclosed the fallacy of the ideal that had brought him to this country, that "equality for all" was a myth in action. As I think about Matak and our afternoon together, struggling to think about what race means in America and how it affects people's lives in unequal distributions of power, I think about how I imagine that that teacher was trying to do good work, trying to do just what DJ and I think is so important: to call attention to the ways in which race affects daily life in America.

But it seems that this whitely teacher's assignment did good work for a select group of students. What was Matak going to gain in this moment? In his book Faces at the Bottom of the Well (1992), Derrick Bell shows through his narratives that change in America is often in service of whites. (Furthermore, narratives OF change are often in service of whites.) Matak's assignment seems to skirt on this as well, at least in application. White students probably did gain an increased understanding in the ways in which they were privileged, and that what they believed they had "earned" in life came as a result not just of their achievements but also of their race. In her memoir Lit, Mary Karr (2009) writes of her father's metaphor for the privileged. Though in this case, she is referring specifically to class privilege, because of the ways in which race and class are intertwined in the US, I think the metaphor is apt to discuss white privilege more generally: "Born on third base, my daddy always said of the well off, and think they hit a homerun" (Karr, 2009, p. 41). This assignment helped the white students realize they didn't hit the homerun, but what did it make Matak realize? That he was on first, with no hope of catching up? The questions here are not easy, but I think the beginning step of questioning is a start: asking ourselves questions like how all of our students might approach an assignment and anticipating the range of possibilities and incorporating them into our assignment and course designs helps create a more inclusive space, one not bound to the hierarchical constitution of whiteliness. And it's important, I think, to share with our students our own unease and uncertainty regarding race matters.

In addition to how we design our courses and assignments, I think it's also important to think critically about the language used when referencing multilingual students. Since "the use of language and how we signify is central to circulating, enforcing, and performing difference" (Denny, 2010, p. 122), how teachers talk about multilingual students reflects teachers' ideas about the position of multilingual students in the university (and America). The faculty who signaled their belief that multilingual students are Other by using the pronoun "they" then perpetuate the belief that multilingual students are Other when using that language in conversation. The infamous example of the UCLA student who posted her self-proclaimed "rant" on YouTube about "Asians in the library"[27] demonstrates the ways in which language use positioning multilingual students as Other influences how (white) people behave toward multilingual students. This young (seemingly white) woman states that "The PROBLEM" as she sees it, "is these HORDES of Asian people that UCLA accepts into our school every single year—which is fine—but if you're gonna come to UCLA, then use AMERICAN manners." The rest of the "rant" is filled with her feelings on "them" and reveals just how much she does not see herself as a part of "their" world and vice versa—"they" are not truly a part of "our" (white, American) school. They, they, they versus we/our/my. The division evident in these statements and underlying mindsets only perpetuates racism and racist structures. If we follow Frye's advice for feminists' fight against racism, then instead of maintaining the rigid divisions patent in this young woman's spiel, it may be possible to:

> [C]ontribute to the demise of racism if we upset the logical symmetry of race—if Black women, for instance, cultivate a racial identity and a distinctive (sexually egalitarian) Black community (and other women of racialized groups, likewise), while white women are undermining white racial identity and cultivating communities and agency among women along lines of affinity not defined by race. Such an approach would work toward a genuine redistribution of power. (Frye, 2001, p. 99)

We can create a genuine redistribution of power by creating a differential space in our classrooms; clinging to "us" versus "them," however, only maintains the existing racial space.

What I have just said is my theoretical analysis of this situation; the personal reactions I had to this particular case are harder to articulate, but important to the work of thinking about dissensus and radical equality. My difficulty of articulation is not caused by my whiteness alone but also by the whiteliness present in the young woman's rhetoric that uncovered my own structural involvement in this global racism. When hearing this young woman talk for the first time, I immediately bristled. I bristled partly because of her obvious Othering, a phenomenon I'm trying to work against. But hearing her, I also realized that she was not different from me in as far as racism is not something differentiated from me—I am entrapped in it as well. While I heard her words and flinched, I also resented this viral speech for making the work that much harder. My multilingual international students may have feared that I secretly had the same thoughts as this young woman, despite my friendly demeanor in the classroom. Without investigating issues such as these—without probing into uncomfortable places—my students and I are merely replicating the structure that is already is. What we need to do instead is to create a new structure, one that asks all of us to remove ourselves from the assumptions of "normal" within our identities and consider the effects of those identities together. This is where Frye's "redistribution of power" can occur.

All of this is not to say deconstructing one's whiteliness in order to create a differential space in the globalized classroom—one not entrenched in racism, but aware of it—is easy, however. It has been very difficult for me both here on paper and in my conversations with DJ to explore my whitely positions and what effects those have had on my students. It's been uncomfortable, challenging, and troubling to turn inward in those ways. I have been hesitant to move into information too personal, instead relying on "objective" analysis. DJ has pushed me to go further, and it has been in those moments that I have begun to unlearn my whitely behaviors in order to disrupt them. But my resistance to digging deeper is an effect of my white privilege as well: by virtue of my structural involvement in whiteliness, I haven't had to consider my perspective and experiences as anything but "normal." I haven't had to talk about my race before, so when trying to do this work, I have been scared, defensive, and conflicted. Who am I to talk of these issues? I've thought. Who am I to say anything back to DJ, a person of color? Antiracist work is scary, and I realize I will continually "mess up." That does not seem a justified reason to not continue this work, however—it would indeed seem another act of white privilege.

DJ: Reading Bobbi's struggle and quandaries, I think about the different kind of stalemate I encountered as an international teacher. Bobbi's thoughtful articulation of complex polarity between "we" and "they" and her pedagogical strategies to deconstruct these institutional systems by designing more inclusive courses and assignments as well as critical reflections on language in the globalized classroom guide me to think of my own classes and think over how complexly globalized these classes have been. But one thing I have struggled with in her story and explanation is the more complex discourses in our classrooms influenced and overdetermined by the global politico-economically asymmetrical structure. In this global space, the developed countries, European countries, the US, and some newly uprising developing countries, create a space where race and racism contextualize with colonialism and global inequality. Cultural difference is the product of this asymmetrical power structure and history. I, like all other students and teachers, am not excluded from this global situation in my classroom.

Then, how can I create equality and dissensus in class by deconstructing my position in global context? All my experience as a teacher convolutes around the problems of worldviews. As Bobbi described, worldviews and value systems in textbooks, media, and our mindsets turn classrooms into arenas of oppressions and discriminations. Assigning biased readings and writings, ignoring different writing styles and arguments, or putting racial difference into judgments about students in my classes (as I did) are common mistakes instructors make. Not a single space can be a racism-free safe zone not only in the US, but also in the world. Our classes are global classes since we are connected to other spaces in the world where a more pandemic global, differential racism works regardless of our race or national origins. What is going on in Korea, Tibet, France, and Africa are connected to seemingly insular classrooms where teachers are teaching with the presence of international students, second or third generation students from immigrant families, first or second generation refugees, or from an international body like me. Global racism is equally prevalent as much as each of us and our ontological, linguistic, and cultural positions are equally different. Global racism is a trans-spatial phenomenon. Thus, "being equally different" opens a possibility to create dissensus and unlearning to prepare for true learning. But how can Bobbi and I manage to create a classroom where learning and unlearning happen simultaneously and cope with these unstable spaces of constant improvisations and deconstructions? What can be pedagogical strategies for the globalized classroom?

Hereafter, I will suggest a couple of steps to create equal difference and dissensus in class to teach and learn in the globalized classroom.

1) Teachers need to self-reflect possible otherness as Bobbi and I have tried to do here. That is a way to turn the binary structure of "we" and "they" into the polemic and individually differential, but radically equal space of Others. Only in this creation of space of Others, does emergence of a classroom as a differential space where everyone can participate without feeling discriminated against be possible. Before starting to teach, I speculated on my own prejudices: fear against skin-deep difference of colors and their cultural differences; feeling intimidated when two African American males, sitting on a couch on their porch, gazed at me; having prejudices against white males because I was suspicious that those white people were always pretending to look nice, and I could be deceived by their kindness—I am a racist more or less.

However, this is not religious confession or repentance. Neither Bobbi nor I believe we must express those prejudices in front of students, which obviously can be another form of harassment to some students. Self-victimization is not ethical, and explicit honesty without regarding others' different structure of emotion does not guarantee truth; in many cases, honesty can be an excuse for intended discriminations. What I tried to do is to speculate and explore possibilities and realize how complex my position in class is and how easily I can turn into a racist. This speculation helps me go through unlearning, creating dissensus, and possible shape-shifting resilience of my identities to create a learning community where I engage with all those disturbing issues with students arguing, laughing, disagreeing with each other's position and preconceptions, and constantly finding that we are in the same humanity in which whiteliness is meaningless, though it has real implications for individuals' lived experiences. This also happened during all of my conversations with Bobbi in person and electronically. Indeed, virtual admittance of my potentiality of racism and hatred against someone who is different might maim my authority as a teacher, but this act helps me—a stuttering foreign-faced Asian male—reflect honestly on the ethical meaning of transitions of my identities as a border-crosser and virtual encounters with Others. However, these encounters with Others in (virtual or actual) global spaces are not utopian but always polemic and full of struggles. The dichotomy of "they" and "we" which Bobbi experienced is always already prevalent and ineradicable. Furthermore, I do not have power to change whole dynamics of racism in this postmodern world where race becomes not a topic of serious issue but a quip for political joke. In this sense, the teacher's role in globalized classroom must start from speculative, virtual admittance of complexity and colonial, post-colonial, and asymmetrical geopolitics where the first world has exploited the third world for their wealth and consumerism. These are not paradoxical denials of our responsibilities but the first stage we can stand for further discussion of how to get over these and what we have to do on this limbo between "we" and "they."

2) If teachers stop at this speculative mapping of our positions in global, racial contexts, the production of space of dissensus and equal difference cannot lead to a democratic space of learning. Teachers need to develop their own strategies to cope with the class as an open global space.[28] It is obvious that more and more global experience will come into a classroom with increasing influx of national and racial Others in traditionally homogeneous classrooms. Teachers should be open-minded to different cultures and backgrounds, but this does not mean that we can accept those differences easily to create a unity. Rather, we have to produce more salient, honest, and contextual inquiries in class. Writings about students' trans-spatial experiences and discussions on global contexts of these experiences helped bring about dissensus in my case.

Conclusion

Our conversation ends here, but it will never actually end because our presences in the world and its affiliation to whiteliness as well as our constant struggle to deconstruct ourselves to engage with the amplifying effects of global racism cannot stop as long as we teach, unlearn, and learn. Antiracist work is such that these ideas are something we will—we must—continually come back to in order to disrupt the racist structures that are present in the globalized classroom. And while we know that simply attempting to unlearn our own whiteliness is not enough—"we cannot simply unlearn privilege when the cultures in which learning take place are shaped by privilege" (Ahmed, 2004, n.p.)—we believe such an act is a critical start toward reshaping the structures in which racism is entrenched. In addition to there being no closure to this process, we also cannot say that our cases were successful if "success" means unity and harmony in the classroom; rather, we look for dissensus in the classroom in relation to race in the globalized classroom, for it is in the dissensus that there is space to unlearn and recreate. Our classes have taught us that we and our students are Others, but we have the power to create new space in the global classroom. This new space is not utopia but a differential space where our "bodily presences" communicate with Others. In addition to our bodily presences, there too are the behaviors rooted in a whitely epistemology we have to be cognizant of, as our narratives of instructors' (including our own) whitely ways of being's effects on students demonstrate. As teachers in roles of perceived authority, our whitely ways need to be examined. Though Frye is talking about the role of white feminists in the quote that follows, we believe her ideas are of particular importance for instructors more broadly to keep in mind as well. She wrote that:

> We have to avoid, or be extremely alert in, environments in which whiteliness is particularly required or rewarded (e.g., academia). We know we have to practice new ways of being in environments which nurture different habits of feeling, perception, and thought, and that we will have to make these environments for ourselves since the world will not offer them to us. We know that the process will be collective and that this collectivity does not mean we will blend seamlessly with the others into a colorless mass; women unlearning femininity together have not become clones of each other or of those who have been valuable models. (2001, p. 100)

When as instructors we realize "another way of being is possible," and reconsider how we make room for those other ways of being in our classrooms, we are helping to "transform consciousness" (Frye, 2001 p. 100). In unlearning our own whiteliness and subsequent unearned authority, there is still space for difference, for radical equality.

This work is not easy, obviously, and it can be difficult, disconcerting, and troubling. Yet, "To the extent that we try, we will be called to lean into that trouble rather than to corral, contain, or legislate it; because to be troubled is a necessary condition for learning and change" (Condon, 2011, p. 7). The classrooms in American universities have already changed and are changing at this moment with shifting global situations; instructors, too, must adapt as well if we are to most ethically teach within a globalized classroom, where race, nationality, linguistic identity, and several other identity markers intersect. With purposeful reflection, we can disrupt the structures that disadvantage so-called Others in the classroom. We have been "troubled" as we have begun the work represented here, but rather than run away, we have tried to engage with each other to hear each other's perspective in order to unlock our own. Our investment in Justice, especially racial justice, does not exist only as a fancy catchphrase hung on the wall of the average classroom, nor is it a product of consensus; rather it is a bridge over troubled water filled with racial and national borders. Setting a journey over this water demands the courage to enjoy the turmoil of disagreements, intellectual savvy to map our constantly changing positions, and face-to-face conversations with Others in this zone of learning—the globalized classroom.

Notes

1. As Homi Bhabha claims in the introduction of *Nation and Narration*, "The other is never outside or beyond us; it emerges forcefully, within cultural discourse, when we think we speak most intimately and indigenously 'between ourselves'" (1990, p.4). The "other" in my discussion does not refer to someone outside or beyond "me," "us," or "them." Rather, Bhabha's "others" are ontological otherizations happening in-between ourselves. In my sections of this chapter, I am using Other instead of "other" to indicate and emphasize the ideological status of Others in global racism in contrast to the ontological presences of "others." My rhetorical choices implicate ontological others veiled under Others in discourses.

2. Here, main meaning of "discourse" originates from Enestro Laclau's theoretical context. According to Laclau (1985), discourse is ontological because it is both ideological and material. Like Derrida, there is nothing outside discourse. Within discourse, hegemonic articulations happen and bring forth various hegemonic positions. Hegemonic articulations in the social are radically equivalent in radical democracy; everyone can articulate to gain their hegemonic positions because there is no center and the chain of signifiers has nodal points of an empty signifier. Within these discourses, my ontological presence is discursively determined by various ideological and material conditions. In this sense, in this chapter, I will explore how my ontological presence as a non-native-English-speaker teacher's position in global discourses achieves hegemonic articulation and how this articulation and practice create radical equality or equivalence.

3. In fact, some writings I find about international teachers teaching courses in the U.S. academy are mostly comprised of success stories or "How I could get over cultural differences." For instance, in the collective essay "Lessons From the Culturally Diverse Classroom: Intellectual Challenges and Opportunities for Teaching in the American University" (2010), three authors (Schwieger, Gros, and Barberan), who are international teachers and teach composition classes in Georgia State University, narrate their experiences as international composition teachers in a multicultural classroom and describe their classes as multicultural utopian spaces; they even compare the American educational system with Medici during the Renaissance. Except for a teacher from France, most of these authors just praise cultural difference and cultural diversity they have experienced in the classroom without theoretically analyzing the hidden institutional and ideological aspects. Their narratives, at most, are full of superficial appreciations of a differential American educational system. Their description of the American university where a TA can work as a part-time professor hides the institutional apparatus in U.S. universities that entraps instructors' differential identities and lowers their

academic positions under the name of multiculturalism. In fact, the spaces in modern academic institutions are not colorblind, democratic, nor equally power-distributed utopian spaces; rather the spaces are locations where differences unfold interstices or fissures in those modern pedagogical ideologies such as ideal communications, democratic collaborations, and pedagogical unity.

4. Here I am using Other not as a cultural Other or the general word but as the product of Otherization such as alienation, discrimination, and racial formation on the state and global levels. Everyone is susceptible to Otherization; this ontological commonality opens a new way to deconstruct the general belief on consensus based on heuristic purpose of education—transforming students into those who are as intelligent and duteous as teachers.

5. I am using this movie because it avoids any easy generalization of the globalized classroom. Unlike many previous movies about teachers' struggles with uncommunicable students and their final breakthroughs, this movie, in mock-documentary style, exposes a lot of issues that demystify the general view of the globalized classroom.

6. In South Korea, interests and debates on racial and multicultural discourses are sharply rising because 1) more and more laborers from mostly South Asia are coming in and the ratio of biracial families is spiking; and 2) more North Korean refugees are coming into Korea. Though South Korea and North Korea were one nation before the Korean War, the social antagonism against these North Koreans is getting ferocious.

7. This is related to white students' reverse discrimination in various cases in first year composition classes at various universities, as Catherine Prendergast exemplifies and discusses in *Literacy and Racial Justice* (2003, p. 99–100).

8. According to Balibar, in the contemporary Anglo-Saxon countries, "[i]deologically, current racism . . . centers upon the immigration complex, fits into a framework of 'racism without races'. . . . whose dominant theme is . . . the insurmountability of cultural differences, a racism which, [postulates] 'only' the harmfulness of abolishing frontiers, the incompatibility of life-styles and traditions; in short, . . . differential racism"(1991, p. 21).

9. Whiteness as a property is an idea Cheryl I. Harris explored in a paper published in *Harvard Law Review*. In this paper, Harris claims that "Whiteness as property has taken on more subtle forms, but retains its core characteristic—the legal legitimation of expectations, power, and control that enshrine the status quo as a neutral baseline, while making the maintenance of white privilege and domination" (1993, p. 1715). Given Harris' argument that "According whiteness actual legal status converted an aspect of identity into an external object of property" (1993, p. 1725), whiteness as property builds the representational system in the US. In the US, other ethnic identities, especially unstable, unidentifiable identities of immigrants, become alienable, while whiteness as property and the inalienable right remains as an absent cause of hegemonic positions that whites hold in the economic and political hierarchy. Here I use whiteness

and whiteliness on the same context not ignoring their differences, but pointing out their sharing the commonality of their traits as properties.

10. I include my status as "citizen" because of the current emphasis in the US on the legal status of individuals and the relegating of non-citizens as "less than." In this context, authority and legitimacy are accorded to me by virtue of my legal status, which I was born into (and nobody questions in the first place due to how my race is read).

11. While I acknowledge the reality that a white person can be multilingual, the great majority of multilingual students in U.S. universities currently are not white. I use the term "multilingual" to refer to students whose first language is not English and who are not read as white. For those who I know to be international multilingual students, I designate them accordingly.

12. Unless I state otherwise, when using examples from my classroom, I am talking about the class I taught that was only for international multilingual students.

13. While I acknowledge that linguistic identity and racial identity are complexly interwoven in these cases, my main point here is to bring to light the way multilingual students are raced and how the lack of recognition of their race adds to their Othering in the U.S. university.

14. We use the term "racism" in this chapter due to the racial structure of the US and by extension, the U.S. classroom, where we draw our experiences from. "Xenophobia" we take to mean a more global form of racism in terms of hating those deemed Others. Etymologically speaking, xenophobia means hostility against strangers. In this sense, xenophobia is a broader term of people's universal fear against strangers; however, race and racism is more systematic and the product of history and discourses. For this reason, xenophobia as hatred against those who have different nationalities is in affinity to global racism, but the global racism is a more systematic, geopolitical discrimination against people who are not whitely.

15. Pseudonym.

16. Available in part at https://www.deanza.edu/faculty/lewisjulie/White%20Privi ledge%20Unpacking%20the%20Invisible%20Knapsack.pdf

17. It is important to note that some of these are not always true for me at times, particularly as I am a *female* teacher, and authority is not as often freely ascribed to female teachers, especially young ones. When I started teaching composition, I was not much older than some of my students; some of the instances I name in this list were definitely less true at that time. Race, however, and in turn, whiteliness, still seems to me to be one of the strongest indicators of who "earns" authority and who does not.

18. There are exceptions to this, of course—for example, people who use American Southern pronunciations of words are often judged by those from other parts of the US as less intelligent.

19. Philosophically speaking, the idea of unity originates from Plato's "One" in which multiples lose their differences. Hegel's dialectics aiming for an absolute unity also subsumes exclusion of others through teleological development of history. Traditional Marxists could not get over this ideal unity which also made possible exclusions of different identities from unified ideas of the nation, the state, the proletariat, etc. Recently, Negri's multitude, though this also emphasizes singularities and their differences, also can be criticized as a part of this dialectical understanding of the world. I personally believe that utopian desire and hope should be kept, while constant deconstruction of any unification on the level of practice and theory has to be predetermined.

20. Steven Corcorna's introductory explanation of Rancière's terms in *Dissensus: On Politics and Aesthetics*, states that "Consensus . . . is defined by 'the idea of the proper' and the distribution of places of the proper and improper it implies . . . By contrast, the logic of dissensus consists in the demonstration of a certain *impropriety* which disrupts the identity . . ." (2010, p. 2).

21. Rancière's idea is simple but powerful. He claims that politics in itself is *dissensus* or disagreement against wrongs. Consensus which founds the idea of consensus democracy is a state apparatus which Rancière calls *police*. Rancière claims that modern politics is meta-politics that perpetually creates radical equality in political spaces. This effort to create equalities entails acts to make unsaid to be said, unseen to be seen, unheard to be hard, etc. See Rancière's *Disagreement* (1999).

22. Pseudonym.

23. My readings of the Conference on College Composition and Communication's (CCCC) resolution, *Students' Right to Their Own Language* (1975) and its significance via Prendergast's *Literacy and Racial Justice* (2003, pp. 95–102) helped me acknowledge this issue and the significance of it.

24. Pseudonym.

25. Pseudonym.

26. Though the writing center is a different pedagogical space than the classroom, Matak's narrative shows the ways in which assignments with good intentions might still Otherize students who are commonly viewed as Others. I use his experience as a concrete example—and reminder to myself—that whiteliness permeates our teaching and has real disadvantages for students.

27. Available at http://www.youtube.com/watch?v=x0JKb_Cn1qc.

28. For example, in my class, with hands-on practice, via integrating diverse visual/audio media into PowerPoint presentations, I have introduced global aspects of issues such as migration, immigration, multinational corporation, eating disorders in global space, etc. I started telling my own position and my own stories. I also had fish bowl debates on immigration and racism or panel discussions on who the students think they are in the global space. Sometimes, students responded to these various perspectives of global issues listlessly; however, as the class progressed, more and more students

started responding that they had learned a lot from these presentations. For example, reading and discussing together Gloria Anzaldua's "How to Tame a Wild Tongue" and Amy Tan's "Mother Tongue" in *50 Essays* (2006) I compared and analyzed similar phenomena of oppression on women and immigrants in different locations; plus, I showed various news on YouTube and contentious blogs on websites to bring up disagreeable discussions. Reading students' response papers about these two essays after the class, I noticed how much students could improve their understanding of meaning of "immigration," "bilingualism," and "globalization." My pedagogical aim of "difference" played a positive role to elicit more thoughtful responses from the students. As my case proves, a pedagogical idea of difference is not just a concept but a joint discourse that is able to incorporate various different modes of practices into a praxis which forms differential theories for the future.

References

Ahmed, S. (2004). Declarations of whiteness: The non-performativity of anti-racism. *Borderlands, 3*(2). Retrieved from http://www.borderlands.net.au/vol3no2_2004/ahmed_declarations.htm.

Anzaldúa, G. (1987). *Borderlands/La Frontera: The new mestiza.* San Francisco, CA: Spinsters/Aunt Lute.

Balibar, É. & Wallerstein, I. (1991). *Race, nation, class: Ambiguous identities* (C. Turner, Trans.). London: Verso.

Bell, D. (1992). *Faces at the bottom of the well: The permanence of racism.* New York: Basic Books.

Bhabha, H. K. (1990). DissemiNation: Time, narrative, and the margins of the modern nation. In H. K. Bhabba (Ed.), *Nation and narration* (pp. 291–322). London: Routeldge.

Bonilla-Silva, E. (2010). *Racism without racists: Color-blind racism & racial inequality in contemporary America* (3rd ed.). Lanham, MD: Rowman & Littlefield.

Cantet, Laurent. (2008). *Entre les Murs* (*The Class*). Paris, FR: Haut et Court.

Cohen, S. (Ed.) (2006). *50 essays: A portable anthology* (2nd ed.). Boston: Bedford St. Martin.

Committee on CCCC Language Statement. (1975). Students' Right to their own language. *College English, 36*(6), 709–726.

Condon, F. (2011). A place where there isn't any trouble. In V. A. Young & A. Y. Martinez (Eds.), *Code-meshing as world English* (pp. 1–8). Urbana, IL: National Council of Teachers of English.

Condon, F. (2012). *I hope I join the band: Narrative, affiliation, and antiracist rhetoric.* Logan, UT: Utah University Press.

creasian444. (2011). *Asians in the library—UCLA girl (Alexandra Wallace) going wild on Asians ORIGINAL version* [Video file]. Retrieved from http://www.youtube.com/watch?v=x0JKb_Cn1qc.

Denny, H. C. (2010). *Facing the center: Toward an identity politics of one-to-one mentoring.* Logan, UT: Utah State University Press.

Frye, M. (2001). White woman feminist 1983–1992. In B. Boxill (Ed.), *Race and racism* (pp. 83–100). New York: Oxford University Press.

Geller, A. E., Eodice, M., Condon, F., Carroll, M. & Boquet, E. H. (2007). *The everyday writing center: A community of practice.* Logan, UT: Utah State University Press.

Grant, R. A. & Lee, I. (2009). The ideal English speaker: A juxtaposition of globalization and language policy in South Korea and racialized language attitudes in the United States. In R. Kubota & A. Lin (Eds.), *Race, culture, and identities in second language acquisition: Exploring critically engaged practice* (pp. 44–63). New York: Routledge.

Hardt, M. & Negri, A. (2000). *Empire.* Cambridge, MA: Harvard University Press.

Harris, C. I. (1993) Whiteness as property. *Harvard Law Review, 106*(8), 1710–1791.

Karr, M. (2009). *Lit: A memoir.* New York: HarperCollins.

Laclau, E. & Mouffe, C. (1985). *Hegemony and socialist strategy: Towards a radical democratic politics.* London: Verso.

McIntosh, P. (1989). White privilege: Unpacking the invisible knapsack. *Peace and Freedom Magazine*, July-August, 10–12.

Omi, M. & Winant, H. (1994). *Racial formation in the United States* (2nd ed.). New York: Routledge.

Parmar, P. & Steinberg, S. (2008). Locating yourself for your students. In M. Pollock (Ed.), *Everday anti-racism: Getting real about race in school* (pp. 283–286). New York: the New Press.

Prendergast, C. (2003). *Literacy and racial justice: The politics of learning after Brown v. Board of Education.* Carbondale, IL: Southern Illinois University Press.

Rancière, J. (1999). *Disagreement: Politics and philosophy.* Trans. Julie Rose. Minneapolis, MN: University of Minnesota Press.

Rancière, J. (2010). *Dissensus: On politics and aesthetics* (S. Corcoran, Trans.). London: Continuum.

Rothenberg, P. (2000). *Invisible privilege: A memoir about race, class, and gender.* Lawrence, KS: University Press of Kansas.

Schwieger, F., Gros, E. & Barberan, L. (2010). Lessons from the culturally diverse classroom: Intellectual challenges and opportunities of teaching in the American university. *College Teaching, 58*(4), 148–155.

Why Am I So Damaged?

Deatra Sullivan-Morgan

I've always loved the song I'm Every Woman . . . if African American women had an anthem this would be it! The lyrics: . . . I'm every woman . . . it's all in me . . . speak to my heart and soul. In my mind's eye I am fearless. Reality finds me more of a "wannabe." A quick dictionary.com check reveals when the word fear is used as a noun the denotative definition is: a distressing emotion aroused by impending danger, evil, pain, etc., whether the threat is real or imagined; the feeling of or condition of being afraid. The etcetera and the possibility of this thing defined as fear being "imagined" are more than a bit problematic. Growing to womanhood while Black left me unsure, tentative and burdened with the proclamation that hung over every person of color and every member of a minority group's head—you have to be better than the best to compete with "them." You must always remain one step ahead (even better if it is two or three steps ahead), be "more" and achieve "more" to claim a mountaintop spot and look over at the next mountain into "their" eyes. I was always questioning myself as to whether or not I measured up to this "them" whose authority and superiority grew every time I read an article or a book, wrote a paper or merely stepped outside my door. Who exactly is this group sometimes called "them," sometimes called "they," but never called me or we? "They/Them" are my Others—the not "me" or the "we" people, rather the majority to my minority, the power to my powerlessness, the Eurocentric worldview to my Afrocentric paradigm, the right to my wrong and the reason I often feel doomed to be a "wannabe" and never an "I Am." All of the aforementioned issues result in my theme song often being relegated to merely my dream song. Too often I allow the weight of the fear associated with not measuring up to hold me in a grip that keeps me bound and stagnant. If dictionary.com resorts to the inclusion of "imagined" in a definition of fear, then I am forced to ask myself if being an Every Woman/Ph. Diva is a real state or merely an imagined one.

The need to not only ace the test, but also to be the best of the rest began at my parent's knees. I heard again and again how I must prepare and be ready to face battle and conquer "them." I learned the lesson well and always exceled, however a curious thing happened along the way. With every achievement, every honor, every award and each degree the fear that has always served as a motivating factor, moving me from one level to the next, onward and upward to higher heights began to take on another more sinister role. The fear that had always been there to tease me on to and through the next challenge turned from teasing to taunting. The fear no longer spurred me along my way ever climbing; instead it began to nurture and water those seeds of self-doubt planted by my Others yet tended by me. The fears grew in voices that sang in a chorus reaching a crescendo replacing my mantra of standing, courage, growth and analysis with charges of down for the count, wimp, wannabe, stymied, paralysis. What a mess!

I continue to navigate the shark-infested waters surrounding the Ivory Tower, that place where I've decided there is a space at the table for me. I move from dream to theme to reality on a daily basis. A place where fear motivated me to move to and claim MY SPOT! A place even though when fear said "I could not," I responded with "Yes I can, I will, and I did!" I've decided that my personal definition of fear is a rhetorical construct. Like rhetoric it is exaggerated, pompous often pretentious and all the while seducing me with persuasive prowess to succumb to the belief that if I/We need an anthem, then fear most likely isn't the only problem! The realization that this place where fear smirks while whispering and sometimes shouting that I should not teach that class or reach for that promotion settles over me as if I am shrouded. The question I am left asking is: "When will fear leave me?" Perhaps the better question is: "If fear leaves me what will take its place?" The rhetoric of fear continues its seductive dance lulling me into that void where I am neither the Every Woman or the Ph. Diva, caught between the state of wannabe and I am, between everywhere and nowhere. However, it is what it is and I am what I am . . . I created, prepped and taught that new class. The promotion has also been checked off my "To Do" list. Ivory Tower culture always has another hoop to jump, another mountain to scale. I'll continue to replay my theme/dream song's lyrics stating I'm Every Woman over and over in my mind . . . But is it ever, will it ever, can it ever be ALL in Me?

References

Ashford, N. & Simpson, V. (1978). I'm every woman. [Recorded by Chaka Khan.] On *Chaka.* Retrieved from http://www.azlyrics.com/lyrics/chakakhan/imevery woman.html.

Fear. (n.d.). In *Dictionary.com.* Retrieved from http://dictionary.reference.com /browse/fear?s=t.

Section Three
In the Classroom

"Whiteboys": Contact Zone, Pedagogy, Internalized Racism, and Composition at the University's Gateway

Sophie Bell

This chapter addresses my struggles to understand the ways in which two male students of color wrote about whiteness in my first year composition course, a core curriculum "gateway" course at a large urban Catholic university. These students both attended largely white secondary schools after primary school experiences with other children of color. Through their use of language, and their thinking about race and class, I argue that these students are using their own life narratives to complicate constructions of whiteness in two educational spaces where Mary Louise Pratt's "pedagogical arts of the contact zone" are at work—the secondary schools they write about, and the college composition classroom in which they produce that writing. This chapter describes the writing they produced, my responses to that writing, and the implications for teaching race in composition.

Storytelling in a Composition Contact Zone

This chapter addresses my struggles to understand the ways in which two male students of color wrote about whiteness in my first year composition course, a core curriculum "gateway" course at a large urban Catholic university. The chapter is not a full-scale endorsement of these students' writing on race. In fact, I found their writing disturbing at times, and questioned myself about how to respond to it during the semester. Neither is this chapter a critique of their views on race, accompanied by my ideas about how to "fix" them. Instead, I want to look hard at the work they produced and the views they articulated in a classroom that became—in part by design and in part by circumstance—a place where whiteness became an enduring theme in the writing, reading, and discussion of several students. I am deeply invested in understanding the texts they produced in my class, which offer insight into the racist and antiracist dynamics at work in a class like mine. Further,

I believe their texts offer insight into the lives of college students of color who have attended largely white secondary schools.

These particular students were part of a course that I taught in the spring of 2011. They used whiteness as a complex term for narrating their families' aspirations toward upward mobility—through attending "white" schools, moving to "white" neighborhoods, and using "white" language. The central assignment of the semester was to write an extended personal narrative "book" on an event that was crucial to determining their current identities (Blitz & Hurlbert, 1998). The class read each student's narrative and offered feedback in whole-class writing workshops. I asked them to read previous students' narratives—and each other's—as the course "texts." Students also conducted fieldwork on their own uses of language as they composed their narratives. I met with each student individually three times to discuss their writing. In their final portfolio reflections, they described their experiences writing, reading, and revising these narratives, and then described themselves as writers. I taught this extended narrative project in an effort to increase student engagement in their own writing, to build classroom community, and to shake up students' assumptions about "college English." Throughout the fieldwork, conferencing, and workshops that occurred along the way, I hoped to promote an ethos of ownership and idiosyncratic energy in student writing, so that students would leave my class invested in the idea of themselves as writers able to respond to a range of writing challenges. I further hoped—though this hope was less well-developed at this point in my teaching of composition—that students would interrogate the larger social patterns and issues that formed the context for the stories they narrated.

Rhetorical risk-taking became something of a norm in this particular section of the course, where students praised each other's texts for their "honesty" and "rawness," and for going "all in" in workshop discussions. As issues of language, class, sexuality, and race emerged in writing and discussions, conversations sometimes became confrontational or loaded, although my other sections of the course would sail through similar texts and topics in fairly placid order. Early in the semester, after reading a narrative by my former student about coming out of the closet to herself and her mother, three students chose to use their writing workshops to come out as either gay or bisexual to the entire class. At a Catholic university where recent efforts to start a Gay-Straight Alliance had been publicly rebuffed by the administration, these coming-out narratives represented a move into uncertain territory, a particularly bold act of self-identifying against institutional sanction. (The university has since recognized a campus group for GLBTQ students and allies.)

The class of 26 students was among my most heterogeneous in terms of race and ethnicity. Nine students identified as white, six as African American or Afro-Caribbean, three as Latin@, two as Arab American, two as Asian American, two as Indian American, one as Chinese, and one simply as "brown." The ethnic diversity of this class at first belies the segregation of the university's five colleges along race and class lines: five of the white students and one Latina student were enrolled in the liberal arts college; five Asian and Southeast Asian students and two white students were enrolled in the health careers college; two white students, one Asian student, and my self-identified "brown" student were enrolled in the business college; six African American or Afro-Caribbean students, two Arab American students, and one Latina student came from the college of professional studies. Of the nine students in the college of professional studies, five were enrolled in this college's "Liberal Studies" program, to which students are admitted contingently to the university when their applications do not qualify them for admission into the programs to which they initially applied. All the non-Asian male students of color in the class were part of the Liberal Studies group. I do not know the extent to which students were aware of each other's program of study, though I do know they tended to sit with, and seemed to already know, other students from their own colleges. In some other sections of the course, a majority of students come from the same college or a particular program within a college, and those sections tend to look much more homogeneous.

Students wrote about a wide range of topics in their narrative projects, from the death of a friend to a car accident to experiences with bullying. The most common topic in that section of the course—more common than the three coming-out narratives—was that of being a student of color at a majority-white high school. The five students writing on this topic were all male. They included two African American and one Latino student from the Liberal Studies program, an Indian American student from the physician assistant program, and the self-identified "brown" student, who was a finance major in the business school. They were from New York City, California, New Jersey, Long Island, and South Carolina, and had grown up and attended school in suburban and urban areas. They attended Catholic, Christian, and public high schools. Most of them had attended primary school with majorities of students of color, but one had attended majority-white schools in elementary school. Although they were all somewhat familiar with each other's writing, and some requested each other as writing partners, this cohort did not agree on much of anything having to do with the racial politics of language: Freddie hated "correct grammar"; Lamar claimed he avoided "slang"; Dante wrote in what he called "Black English." Nor did they have much common ground on the racial politics of identity: Chris and Dante defined themselves as part of non-white subcultures; Lamar imagined people considering him a "whiteboy"; Freddie occasionally passed for white; and Syed ranted about how much easier his life would be if he were white like all his friends.

I will write about two members of this group whose work was particularly troubling to me, Freddie and Lamar. These two students had been deemed "white" by their high school peers and they both appeared to desire distance from the disadvantages of being people of color. Their discourse about their experiences and about writing itself appeared to me to voice a great deal of internalized racism, or acceptance of negative views about people of color. At the same time, their writing and discussion also became places to interrogate and challenge racism, and to look for rhetorical strategies that fit their purposes in narrating their experiences in majority-white schools. In what follows I will introduce the scholars I have found most useful as guides for navigating the contested terrain onto which I believe we stumbled as a class, and then focus on Freddie and Lamar in two separate, but related, case studies of students of color narrating their relationship with "whiteness." Finally, I will reflect on my struggles to read and respond to their writing, and how it has impacted my approach to teaching about race.

Marc Lamont Hill, education scholar, public figure, and antiracist activist, articulates my hopes for creating a space of shared storytelling that can offer insight into oppressive social structures evident in students' lives. Asking educators to "reimagine the classroom as a space in which teachers and students can 'risk the self' through individual and collective storytelling," Hill calls for more practitioner research into storytelling's role in critical antiracist pedagogy:

> Although scholarship in fields such as composition theory and critical race theory advocate the use of storytelling, there remains a need to develop educational theory and practice that prepare us for the benefits, challenges, and consequences of enabling personal disclosures within the classroom. . . . [T]he failure to take such considerations seriously severely undermines our ability to transform the classroom into a more safe, democratic, productive, and culturally responsive space. (2009, p. 97)

I offer my account as a contribution to the larger educational project of developing the theory and practice needed to support the kind of work called for by Hill.

On a similar note, Beverly Daniel Tatum, scholar, administrator, and race relations expert, calls for a practice of "creating identity stories" in her vision of effective interracial education in a post-Brown era (2007, p. 32). She suggests these identity stories require teachers' curiosity and an open-minded stance toward student texts: "Affirming identity is about asking who [students] are, and where they want to go, and conveying a fundamental belief that they can get there—through the development of their intellect and their critical capacity to think" (2007, p. 32). I saw particular potential in my diverse classroom for a productive sharing of identities and experiences across my students' re-segregated secondary schooling experiences post–Brown v. Board of Education. The act of narrating stories from their segregated schooling experiences as part of their entrance into college seemed calculated to deepen their self-awareness and cultural competence, as well as to raise uncomfortable questions.

Tatum cautions, "We cannot control the stories others are telling—but we must take responsibility for the identity stories we tell" (2007, p. 32). Hoping to begin the semester with my own identity story, I asked the class to workshop a piece I'd written before we started discussing their own. I wrote about my challenges as a young, white middle school teacher in a majority white school, confronting my early adolescent students' ideas about race and sexuality in my first years in charge of a classroom. I hoped my narrative would model the visibility of whiteness in all of our educational experiences, and dispel the idea that there are no "racial issues" in classrooms where most students are white. I hoped it would encourage students to look at the racial landscape of their own schooling and adolescence more generally. That semester, the students who took me up on this invitation to interrogate whiteness were all students of color who had spent time in white-dominated educational spaces.

In addition to Hill and Tatum's calls to engage students in critical antiracist storytelling, I have been helped in my attempts to interpret and respond to student narratives by antiracist scholars from a range of disciplines. The first group includes scholars in composition and rhetoric who are building on Mary Louise Pratt's 1991 call for a "pedagogical arts of the contact zone" (p. 40). Pratt's vision of classrooms as contact zones, that is "social spaces where cultures meet, clash, and grapple with each other, often in contexts of highly asymmetrical relations of power, such as colonialism, slavery, or their aftermaths" (1991, p. 34, allows me to see my students' texts as speaking to and speaking through "acting white," a trope for upward mobility through deracination. Narrating complex stories of their experiences with allegations of "acting white," my students at times affirm and at other times challenge the oppressive equation of class and race hierarchies built into this trope.

Pratt's particular term for texts produced by culturally marginalized writers in contact zones is "autoethnography." An autoethnographic text is one

> in which people undertake to describe themselves in ways that engage with representations others have made of them. Thus if ethnographic texts are those in which European metropolitan subjects represent to themselves their others (usually their conquered others), autoethnographic texts are representations that the so-defined others construct *in response to* or in dialogue with those texts. (1991, p. 35)

Pratt's conception of autoethnographic texts is particularly useful to me in understanding the potential and limitations of asking student writers to navigate intricate rhetorical power dynamics about "risking the self" in the "highly asymmetrical power relations" of the university gateway. The course's extremely mixed crowd faces a white Ph.D.-wielding female instructor who casts all kinds of shadows across that gateway. Just a glance at my ratemyprofessor.com page offers a giddy range of readings of my teaching persona, my pedagogical agenda, and its execution. In such loaded contexts, Pratt describes autoethnographic texts as "a selective collaboration with and appropriation of idioms of the metropolis or the conqueror . . . merged or infiltrated to varying degrees with indigenous idioms to create self-representations intended to intervene in metropolitan modes of understanding" (1991, p. 35). My difficulties reading and responding to my students' narratives make much more sense when I acknowledge the complexity of the tasks they undertook as autoethnographers, and the uncertainty of my role in its reception, implicated as I am in "metropolitan modes of understanding." Viewing my students' troubling and contradictory texts as autoethnographic has been immensely helpful to me, since those troubles are precisely where they may offer a map to the biologically fictional, yet socially real racial identities they engage.

The second group of scholars who have helped me think through these student texts work in Critical Race Theory (CRT), sociolinguistics, and ethnolinguistics. These scholars map radical linguistic reorientations toward capitalist, racist, sexist and homophobic doxa embedded in academic literacies. Their body of work demands attention to and analysis of the multiple emergent literacies of writers in pedagogical—among other—cultural arenas (Alim, 2006; Campbell, 2007; Gilyard, 2011; Guerra, 2004; Martinez, 2014; Smitherman, 1977; Young, 2009). As a part of their methodology, many of these scholars move between social analysis and personal narrative in their own writing. Their attention to lived experiences of race is inextricable from their broader analysis. Their work has encouraged me to challenge my students to produce a kind of explicitly critical autoethnography. Critical Race Theory's concept of "counterstory" is related to that of autoethnography, using experiences with micro- and macroaggressions to illuminate the daily intricacies of racist logic, as well as to formulate antiracist analytic responses grounded in lived experience (Gilyard, 2011; Guerra, 2004; Kynard, 2010; Villanueva, 1993; Young, 2009). The deployment of multiple genres and literacies in CRT resonates with Pratt's call for a "literate arts of the contact zone," including but not limited to "autoethnography, transculturation, critique, collaboration, bilingualism, mediation, parody, denunciation, imaginary dialogue, vernacular expression" (1991, p. 37). My students' writing over the course of a semester—to me, to each other, to imagined and real audiences outside our class—showcases a stunning range of formality and informality, use of languages, wit, inspiration, and strategy. They appear to be writing in a contact zone, and in modes that lend themselves to CRT practice and analysis, and I use tools from CRT in my efforts to respond productively to this highly uneven body of writing.

Finally, I am influenced by composition scholars engaging with whiteness studies (Ratcliffe, 2005; Ryden & Marshall, 2012). Heavily influenced by Critical Race Theory, such scholars propose their stake in antiracist scholarship as follows: "[r]ather than turn the gaze outward to the constellation of 'othered' racialized subjectivities, the study of whiteness intends to focus on the pernicious, unnamed source of that othering" (Ryden & Marshall, 2012, p. 14). The project they embark on—that of a "mapping of whiteness" (2012, p. 9)—offers a provocative model for what my students set out to do. Ryden critiques personal narratives as a way for white people to "come out" about their whiteness, to discern their silent privileging and then somehow atone through the narrative itself. And my students' narratives certainly articulate an investment in whiteness. However, my students come at whiteness from a profoundly different angle, as people of color for whom whiteness has always been visible, and tied up with ideas about upward mobility. A potential benefit of their writing in the contact zone of our college composition classroom is the rhetorical opportunity they created to undo the monolithic nature of "whiteness" itself.

In what follows, I will look at how my students' texts engage the notion of "going white" as they attempt to get ahead. As I tell their stories, I will also narrate my own responses to their writing. Vulnerable to what Pratt calls "the perils of writing in the contact zone"—"[m]iscomprehension, incomprehension, dead letters, unread masterpieces, absolute heterogeneity of meaning" (1991, p 37)—these texts require careful reading. I struggled to respond quickly and creatively to these students' writing, especially when they appeared to articulate internalized racism and a positive investment in white privilege, or "whiteness" more generally. I will speculate on the implications of our interactions for a deeper understanding of the allegations, assets, and attributes of "whiteness" in a composition class invested in the liberatory potential of writing. In my conclusion, I will discuss changes in the ways I use racial narrative writing in my classes, in part resulting from my struggle to read these texts.

Freddie: "Whiteboy"

> Whiteboy was my nickname—not because of my skin tone
> but because of who I was. I am a Puerto Rican and Spanish kid
> who was born and raised till about 13 in Bushwick, Brooklyn.
> Coming from Bushwick I was expected to be ghetto. My parents
> weren't like other parents. They molded me to live in a way that
> earned me the name of Whiteboy.

Freddie's dogged rhetorical embrace of whiteness posed a puzzle to me in reading his autoethnographic project. Solving this puzzle requires understanding how he read the rhetorical situation of our class, and how this class became the occasion for his articulation of a complex, contested depiction of himself as a "whiteboy."

"Whiteness" serves many rhetorical purposes for Freddie. Throughout his narrative, Freddie depicts race as an incredibly fluid aspect of identity, one that is highly interchangeable with class and language. Whiteness, for Freddie, is first and foremost a sign of wealth: his parents give him an "expensive" high school education at a "white school." It is an asset: his father "proves [Freddie's] nickname" by buying him a fancy car. Whiteness is also a way of speaking or writing: his "mad proper" way of talking, learned at that expensive private school. It is a way of not speaking or writing: his inability to speak Spanish. It is a jab: an outsider stance in Bushwick and Washington Heights, an accusation of community betrayal by "going white."

Skin color rarely comes up in Freddie's descriptions of whiteness. Instead, whiteness is a trope for privilege of all kinds, a way to signal an allegiance to affluence. He uses the term to represent race and class mobility as something inscribed on his body and in his speech, "not because of my skin tone but because of who I was." Here, he seems to agree with Vershawn Ashanti Young, who asserts that "passing today involves not looking white but acting white" (2009, p. 46). Young further lays out the dilemmas for people of color—he speaks of African Americans but I think the point applies to Freddie as well—when upward class mobility becomes equated with deracination. Young locates "blacks in the impossible position of either having to try to be white or forever struggling to prove we're black enough" (2009, p. 6). Freddie's take on whiteness as a form of privilege, as I read it through Young, is thus significantly different from the white privilege of white people, who are notoriously unaware of their racial privilege. Rather than experiencing the notorious invisibility of whiteness, Freddie sees whiteness everywhere.

Freddie frames his racial narrative as one of relentless assimilation into "whiteness." He describes his family leaving a poor, largely Latino Brooklyn neighborhood for upward mobility in a middle- and working-class Italian American Queens neighborhood through Catholic school, new affluence, and new language. In places, Freddie's narrative endorses his father's encouragement to "pass" as Italian in order to receive the benefits of being perceived as "white." However, Freddie's assimilation narrative—and his end-of-semester reflective letter to me about his writing—also contain moments of critique of his family's movement "out of the ghetto" and into a "whiteness" he depicts as geographic, economic and linguistic.

Language in Freddie's texts consistently marks a place where assimilation into whiteness won't "take." He inserts Latino voices throughout this piece—largely voices from Bushwick, Brooklyn and Washington Heights, Manhattan despite his move to Howard Beach, Queens, and all of them critical of his increasing "whiteness." In languages that resemble the "indigenous idioms" of autoethnographic texts, Freddie articulates a pull toward hip-hop literacy and Spanish in passages in which his assimilation into whiteness is not as totalizing as elsewhere. In Freddie's multiple deployments of whiteness, I read what Pratt calls "selective collaboration with and appropriation of" a range of languages, including the "white" English associated with Freddie's Catholic high school, the Spanish he does not speak, and what H. Sami Alim calls "Hip Hop Nation Language."

"People treat you a little better when they think you're white."

> My father always told me our last name was an advantage to us because it was very closely related to an Italian name. Plus my looks were more of an Italian-white looks than the hood looks. I couldn't complain. I would enjoy the boost from my last name in life.

When Freddie's father takes him to a car dealer to buy him a BMW, the salesman treats them in a way that Freddie describes as luxurious and highly respectful, offering them coffee and calling his father "Mr." The salesman, who Freddie takes to be Arab, also refers to them flying their "Italian flag" when he sees their address in Howard Beach. Freddie notices his father does not correct the assumption that they are Italian. Here is the conversation that follows:

> "Dad, how come you didn't say we're Spanish when the guy called us Italian?"
>
> "I always learned people treat you a little better when they think you're white. You always get a little more and further than Spanish or black people may. And because of our last name a lot of people think we are Italian because it just sounds Italian. And you and me look it. So why not take the perks that an Italian man would receive."
>
> I understood the reasoning he had between it, and I really agreed to it. Like I felt yea they do get better treatment and if I can pull it off why not. It was better to be considered to be Italian. At least when you're considered white most of the time in common situations there is no questioning. So that statement from my dad is how my life has been lived in since. If my appearance gives me a step ahead in life then I'll take it, it can only help me.

This scene endorses literal "passing" for Italian—an immigrant group that has been launched more deeply into the realm of "whiteness" than Latin@s (Lipsitz,

1998; Roediger, 2006). In a way, Freddie's father simply accelerates the historical "whitening" of Puerto Ricans along this route toward whiteness, in the same way he does by referring to himself as "Spanish" rather than "Latino." I had a tough time responding to this aspect of Freddie's narrative. I am deeply opposed to the racial labeling of selected ethnic groups as "white" in order to offer them the privileges of citizenship, while withholding citizenship from other groups labeled as "non-white." Freddie's endorsement of his father's erasure of his "Spanish" culture reads to me like a blatant moment of internalized racism in Freddie's text, one that feeds into a history of white supremacy, anti-immigrant politics, and anti-Blackness. However, a vision of my class as a contact zone precludes my explicitly shutting down such views. Further, as a beneficiary of white privilege myself, I am not in a strong position to encourage others to turn their backs on such privilege. By encouraging Freddie to critique his father's adoption of the perks of whiteness, would I be suggesting that those perks should be reserved for "real" white people like myself? Of course my desired target is white privilege, but no one in the room has a clean relationship with that privilege. Reading this text, and deciding how to respond in a public workshop, I found myself in a deeply uncomfortable, absurd position as a white teacher hoping to create space for students—especially students of color—to explore their racial identities in writing. By not responding, I was concerned about appearing to endorse the narrative of assimilation Freddie laid out. By responding, I was concerned about coopting the interpretation of his experience. This would violate my aspirations to create space for him to engage dominant narratives of racial identity with his own. Holding back seemed necessary in a classroom I conceived of as a contact zone, but I was highly dubious about leaving his words out there uncontested.

As it turned out, Freddie's text eventually addressed some of the tensions I experienced as a reader. Into his occasionally triumphal narrative of assimilation into middle-class "whiteness," Freddie intersperses several choruses of critical voices from Bushwick. When he imagines the neighbors talking about his family's move to Howard Beach, he suspends their imagined comments on the page. These disembodied communal critiques endorse his assertions elsewhere that "whiteness" is about moving out and selling out, geographically, culturally and economically:

> "They think they better they live in a white neighborhood"
>
> "They don't even consider themselves Spanish anymore"
>
> "That's what happens when you get a little money they leave the hood and live up somewhere else and don't share the wealth"

Freddie doesn't comment on these voices, which sharply contradict his embrace elsewhere of his father's pursuit of passing for white. Instead, he simply inserts these critical voices into the text. Almost dialectically, he offers multiple stances on assimilation, or what he calls "going white." This also happens elsewhere in his text, in a scene that appears to parallel the "neighborhood" quotations above. Freddie narrates a scene of dialogue with another voice from the neighborhood.

> "Yo fred, that school you going to turning you into a whiteboy huh?"
>
> "I don't get what you mean, I'm the same person," I'd say.
>
> "Well you probably cant tell but the way you speak and act aint the same you mad proper and shit."

Freddie puts the awareness of his newly-"white" language in his old friend's mouth, rather than his own. His questioner's assertion—"you probably cant tell"—appears accurate, since Freddie responds to the initial allegation of being a whiteboy with an essentialized "I'm the same person," requiring further explanation of the changes in "the way you speak and act." Here, Freddie assumes a colorblind stance, often associated with whiteness's invisibility (usually to white people). He portrays his own failure to recognize his racially-marked language. On the surface, its recognition comes from a disembodied voice from his old neighborhood.

However, belying this naïve posture, Freddie's transcription of the conversation replicates the racialization of language that his interlocutor asserts. On the page, Freddie actually transcribes his own words differently than he does the other speaker's. In the two framing lines of the passage above, he employs traditional means of rendering "Black English"—omitting the verb to be ("that school . . . turning you into a white boy"; "you mad proper"). Such omissions in Black and white English are discussed in depth by Smitherman (1977). In his own speech, however, he uses standard contractions of verbs ("I don't get"; "I'm the same person"). Similarly, he does not use a capital letter on the proper noun "fred" in his friend's speech, or end punctuation ("the way you speak and act aint the same you mad proper and shit"), whereas his own speech is capitalized (two "I"s), and he places a comma between his two spoken phrases to punctuate them more formally ("I don't know what you mean, I'm the same person"). Freddie employs two different sets of punctuation rules in this paragraph, creating tension in his avowed lack of awareness of the linguistic difference his friend describes. It also raises the possibility that—consciously or unconsciously—he presents his own voice differently in a text written for school than he does the voices from his old neighborhood.

Freddie's fluid moves back and forth between "proper" and "improper" grammar strike me as a form of what Juan Guerra calls "transcultural repositioning," a blending of rhetorical strategies and codes to navigate multiple identities and writing contexts (2004, p. 8). On the surface of his narrative, Freddie endorses a trajectory of passing into whiteness to achieve a level of educational and economic privilege. Yet in scenes like the one quoted above, this Latino writer demonstrates a nuanced sense of both the "Black" and "white" linguistic codes he has been engaging, and—through the voice of his friend—a tacit critique of passing. This blending of two systems of punctuation and capitalization also looks like what Vershawn Ashanti Young calls "code-meshing," which "allows black people to play both the black and white keys on the piano at the very same time, creating beautiful linguistic performances that will hopefully help relieve double consciousness" (2009, p. 60). Freddie may be working out the different ways of thinking about race and language in this passage through his use of "white" and "Black" syntax.

If so, I believe this juxtaposition of opposed views on whiteness points to what Jeffrey Maxson calls "the most compelling insight of Pratt's work: that language users write (or talk) themselves into and through unfriendly language environments by combinations of assimilation and resistance" (2005, p. 25). If we take my English composition class as an "unfriendly language environment"—and I will soon get to Freddie's clear statement that he found English class to be so—then transcultural repositioning is one of his tools for surviving the task of narrating his racial identity in hostile terrain. In Freddie's autoethnographic text, endorsements of assimilation into whiteness and critical resistance to that assimilation exist side by side, in his wielding of words and syntax.

Freddie's final Bushwick critic is the harshest. When Freddie visits his old neighborhood in his new BMW, an acquaintance he does not know well challenges him with this analysis of his social mobility. (In this passage "this shit" refers to Freddie's car.)

> "You left the hood to go white? White boy school, now got this shit. Why do you even come back to the neighborhood to show off. You aint like us. You don't even talk like us anymore . . ."

Freddie uses this hostile criticism as a turning point in his narrative, constructing a "return" to his heritage along two lines. First, he narrates a return to the urban geography he had left behind for a white ethnic enclave on the edge of the city. Second, he describes returning to Spanish and urban vernacular language communities he had left behind to join an English-only, "white" language community.

Freddie's assimilation received another sharp critique during the class's workshop of some early pages of his narrative. One Latina student in particular, upon reading that his parents failed to teach him Spanish as a child, became incensed. Her take was a very definitive echo of the Bushwick voices in Freddie's piece. She said by cutting him off from his language, they had created a problem for all

Latin@s. The whole class became very animated, with many students weighing in about whether or not their parents had taught them a "home language" other than English, with a decided lack of consensus in the room. Both the voices in Freddie's text and the voices in our room reinforced to me that he was writing in a contact zone, a space he and other students might have initially read as one supportive of assimilation, a space for students of color to "act white," but where the reception of texts turned out to be "highly indeterminate" because it is "addressed to both a metropolitan audience and the speaker's own community" (Pratt, 1991, p 35).

Spanish: "Now I was the Spanish white boy working in the Spanish ghetto with no idea of how to speak Spanish."

Freddie's narrative ends with a double return—back to his home language and back to a "ghetto," though this time a new one. Although Freddie describes his critic as off-base, proposing to "let the hate sizzle in him," he doesn't want to "give people reason to talk shit" like this. So he gets a summer job as a Washington Heights lifeguard as a "cover up"—something to make it look like he earns his own way. He spends his last summer before college working with largely Dominican lifeguards, and—according to his personal narrative—learning Spanish.

> They started teaching me the ways of their neighborhood and learning how to speak Spanish. . . . [T]hey would include me in conversations with them, pushing me to use the little Spanish I knew in order to learn. We grew close as friends, but they also grew close to me as my teachers. My car, my neighborhood I grew up in, my look, none of that mattered anymore. They were opening the doors for me to learn about my ethnicity that I wasn't able to pick up myself in the past. We went to parties, I was able to pick up girls now at the pool since I was learning Spanish speaker. And the girls even found it cute that I had such broken Spanish. I told them I was learning and that the lifeguards were teaching me. . . . I grew a bond with people who thought of me as a white boy but not only that, they saw I had the potential in me.

Freddie's narrative constructs a resolution to his dilemma as a Spanish whiteboy that allows him to keep his car while learning Spanish in a new ghetto, one where he is not judged as a sell-out. His happy ending returns him to a "home language" away from home.

Attachment to Error

Freddie's narrative and his end-of-semester reflection invest a lot of energy in talking about "proper" language—the first sign of his "whiteness." While it marks him as "white" in Bushwick and Washington Heights, the pursuit of proper language—which I take to mean more or less "standard English"—oppresses him at school and as a reader and writer. In his final reflective letter to me, Freddie mentions frequently that he "hates English." While marked as different from his old friends in Bushwick by his "proper" language, Freddie's reflections on his writing expressed active distaste for "proper" language. He failed English in his junior year of high school and went to summer school, possibly because his own language was marked as non-white. He mentions many times the oppressive sensation of struggling to express himself in writing. If "proper" writing is "white," Freddie is not white at his new school. The remediation of his non-"white" language is marked at school as a failing point, and may contribute to his marginalization there, as he depicts it.

More than once, Freddie claims incorrect grammar as an essential part of his writing voice: "Though it may be very grammatically incorrect I enjoy using my voice and technique of getting the situation across. . . . I feel when pieces of writing are too correct or grammatically correct it bores me as a reader." Either he has taken my class's emphasis on holding off on attention to mechanics until late in the revision process to an absurd point, or Freddie is actually arguing for incorrect grammar as a rhetorical tool. He never defines exactly what he means, but he values editors who let him keep his "mistakes." He explains this in fieldnotes from a conference in the university's writing center: "I had many mistakes that needed help but he kept it cool with me . . . he didn't fight me about it." Freddie explicitly links his voice with his errors again in his notes here: "I told him I don't mind correcting my wrongs but at the end I still wanted my voice to be in the piece still so he understood that. He said my flows and topics were good ones."

I am tempted to read Freddie's attachment to error as a response to the emphasis on eradicating error in much secondary English instruction. Quite conceivably, Freddie could have encountered a writing curriculum focused on conforming to assimilated forms and rules, as modeled by largely white writers, when he arrived at his Catholic high school. Indeed, a brief look at the English Department curriculum of his high school's website reveals that no writers of color and only one female writer are included in the syllabi of English courses in grades 9 through 11. Further, the writing curriculum for all three of those years consists of "formal instruction in essay writing," beginning with "the five paragraph essay" in ninth grade. Two years after his experience failing English in eleventh grade and going through remediation in summer school, he describes English as a space where his voice has been taken away.

Hip-Hop: "I get lost in the music and find myself in the writing."

Freddie's articulation of resistance to correction occurred as he reflected on writing at the end of the semester. His reflections coincided with a new assertion that hip-hop music was a central influence on his writing, both as lyrical inspiration and as impetus to create original, resistant prose. At the end of the semester, I asked students to read H. Samy Alim's "'Bring it to the Cipher': Hip Hop Nation Language," and to help me evaluate it as a tool for teaching future composition students about language. Responding to this piece, Freddie's writing took an unusual turn to poetic enthusiasm: "I'm not one to enjoy English, but I read this piece like it was a menu at the restaurant with interest and hunger to learn more." Freddie's end-of-semester reflection ultimately asserted: "Only voices that help me when I write is voices that sing." Citing Kanye West as his strongest influence, Freddie explains Kanye "gets my creative juices flowing from writing, to my memoir cover, to even my thoughts that occur before I write that help it to flow. He is known for his taking of chances in the public eye, and his unique sense of fashion and art."

Unlike his personal narrative, Freddie's reflections on his writing never refer directly to race. However, by making hip-hop music his inspiration, he may be referring to what Cecelia Cutler calls "the normativity of Blackness in Hip Hop . . . as a discourse that privileges the Black body and the Black urban street experience" (2009, p. 80). In fact, Cutler intriguingly suggests that DuBois's "double consciousness conceivably plays a role in Hip Hop culture, but in the opposite direction" (2009, p. 79). If something like this is going on, Freddie is finding writing inspiration in a place where whiteness is marginalized, in sharp contrast to the kind of linguistic whiteness he was supposed to be seeking through his journey out of Bushwick.

Although Freddie cites hip-hop as a major influence on his writing, and his narrative explicitly raises the topic of altering his racial identity to obtain greater cultural capital, Freddie does not directly discuss the racial politics of his use of language, beyond his early invocation of his "white" speech. He uses the term "Black English" only when quoting another student who described his own writing using those words. Despite opportunities in course readings and discussions, Freddie is fairly muted on the racial dimension of hip-hop's influence on him. He never gets more explicit than to say hip-hop is "about change in a society which claims to change everyday meanwhile there is standstills in so many different aspects out there." Perhaps Freddie's interest in this cultural form is no different than numerous white fans of hip-hop. His final engagement with language in his personal narrative offers a cryptic investment in linguistic innovation. He speculates that "the best quote . . . from my own words may be 'If the world isn't changing; at least language does.'"

In his personal narrative, Freddie's collage of assimilation and resistance can make him seem lost, easily co-opted, what Min-Zhan Lu calls a "discursive schizophrenic" (quoted in Guerra, 2004, p. 20). At the very least, he seems susceptible to influence as his narrative repeatedly repositions him vis-a-vis his critics and inspirations. On the other hand, his engagement with outside voices and influences creates a dialogic, multi-perspectival quality in his writing, as he experiments with language itself to work out his questions about identity and assimilation through the semester. Freddie's refusal to invest in error-free writing, his influence by hip-hop, and his recent interest in learning Spanish suggest that his pursuit of "whiteness" as a site of rhetorical privilege is multi-dimensional. The dialogic dynamic he creates enables him to voice conflicting views on whiteness throughout his narrative. In fact, Freddie puts almost all beliefs about the meaning of his "whiteness" in the mouths of other people, including a critique of his father's upward mobility and deracination. The range of these voices suggests to me that he is working something out here, constructing a racialized self out of materials that offer contradictory takes on class, race, language, and identity.

In a composition class where I asked students to identify what "language they speak" on the first day of the semester, and got answers ranging from "Spanglish" to "Flushing Chinese American" to "Brooklyn English" to "Black English" to "18 year old girl English" to "just normal English, I guess," Freddie was markedly on the terrain of a linguistic contact zone. His uneven, sometimes experimental textual response signaled to me that he registered the uncertainty of that terrain. Freddie's story, at least on the surface, privileges a narrative of racial whiteness, cultural assimilation and upward mobility. However, other aspects—including his eleventh-hour pursuit of Spanish, his reliance on hip-hop, and his voicing of friends' sentiments critical of his move to whiteness—resist the assimilationist thrust. To some extent, his uneven narrative is itself a contact zone for the perspectives and forces that bear on his journey of upward mobility and racial assimilation—an amalgam of conflicting cultures, discourses, and what Pratt would call "highly asymmetrical relations of power." As such, it is an instructive text for me as an aspiring antiracist teacher in a course often considered the gateway to upward mobility and linguistic assimilation.

What the Hell is a Lamar?

> Now my voice I think is just an ordinary voice . . . of a black kid from the inner city, with the private school background in a suburban community, with both sides telling him he talks "dif-

> ferent," with finding out that both sides say some stupid things about each other, while he finds out that what people say about another group of people aren't always true. There you have it the voice and definition of a Lamar, an "ordinary" teenager.
>
> —Lamar, final portfolio, "What the Hell is a Lamar?"

Lamar used his personal narrative essay—"Not-So Ghetto Boy"—to tell the story of a year in his life when he was caught between a poor neighborhood in Paterson, New Jersey and its neighboring wealthy suburban county; between his urban Catholic elementary school, where "I never even had a class that I could remember . . . that had a white kid in it," and his predominantly white Catholic high school; and between his two parents, who split up that year, then got back together. Like Freddie, he wrote about his ambivalence at being perceived as a "whiteboy." Unlike Freddie, although his texts expressed distance from other African American young people, ultimately he appeared to value community with other young men of color in his secondary school and in our class. Freddie's ambivalence toward whiteness appeared to verge on "discursive schizophrenia," as he voiced multiple conflicting attitudes toward language and other attributes of "whiteness." In contrast, Lamar's ambivalence toward whiteness seemed to place a value on hidden safe spaces for communication among African Americans in a predominately-white institution—what Carmen Kynard calls "hush harbors," after Nunley (2010).

Lamar chose to write about this year of his life when he was suspended across urban/suburban, race, and class fault lines. As a result of his parent's break-up, Lamar wrote that he, his mother, and his brother moved into his aunt's apartment in an urban neighborhood and building where he was scared to spend time outside. At the same time, he went to his first year of high school—leaving the city by bus to attend a suburban Catholic school. He argued that the contrasts he experienced during this year made him a stronger person, able to overcome hardship.

As I did with Freddie, I struggled to respond to Lamar's writing about both race and language early in the semester. In retrospect, I can see that as a progressive white writing teacher, I had two goals for Lamar—one conscious, the other less so—during the semester he was my student. My first goal was about writing. I wanted him to elaborate in his writing, to render his experience in vivid, compelling terms. Second, and much less consciously, I wanted him to experience positive racial identity development. At this point in my teaching, I had a sense that a university gateway class could harm African American male students in particular by offering assimilationist politics and ideas about writing that would interfere with their happiness, sense of self, and success. These ideas were not fully evident to me, except in my discomfort when his writing appeared to buy into many stereotypes about young Black people, and to endorse "acting white" as a strategy for Black male success. Internalized racism is not something I would address directly, as I would writing with "details"—constantly demanding more in the margins, writing workshops and conferences—but I could, however, unconsciously and/or with good intention, treat him remedially as an African American student with defective consciousness, happier in the white suburban throng than among his own people. Jeffrey Maxson reports that "several studies demonstrate how contact zone approaches may open up clashes between teacher and student cultures, as students challenge that instructor's commitment to such progressive values as cultural diversity and gender equity" (2005, p. 26). What looked like internalized racism in his personal narrative initially challenged my ability to listen to his story. Krista Ratcliffe would find this inability to listen a serious pedagogical block, since she argues effective "rhetorical listening" can operate as "interpretive invention," forming a "code of cross-cultural conduct" between writers of color and white audiences (2005, p. 17). So while my story of Freddie's semester is largely about how he repositioned his writing in relation to language and race, my story of Lamar's semester is about how I tried to reposition myself as an audience for his writing about language and race.

My inability to read a student's personal narrative whose politics struck me as problematic threatened to become an encounter in which a student was obliged to mimic what he perceives as my politics around identity and access to opportunity in order to do well in a college gateway class. This would have been one more case of Lu's "discursive schizophrenia" (Guerra, 2004), which I think Lamar successfully avoided by the deliberate construction of rhetorical and interpersonal in-between spaces, and which he ultimately did describe to me in his final portfolio.

Stereotypes: "I'm too hood for the kids not from Paterson and not hood enough for the kids from Paterson."

A lifelong urban Catholic school student, Lamar carried heavy stereotypes about the hardened, uncaring schools, buildings, and young people of Paterson, New Jersey's public schools. He writes about these schools in the language of an outsider, accepting stereotypes of an unfamiliar place: "my local high schools . . . were really bad, filled with teachers and students who just don't care. The schools had low test scores, high drop out rates, and a reputation for having a majority of the town's gangs." In my early readings of his writing, this description read like a list of stereotypes about urban public education. However, it is also important to acknowledge that he is describing real and difficult learning conditions in under-resourced schools.

Arriving at his wealthy suburban high school, his initial hope was to find a cohort of like-minded students from Paterson: "Maybe there will be more like me, maybe even some from the same city, people I could relate to." He bristled at the thought that white, suburban, middle-class students would pre-judge students of color from Paterson: "It kind of got on my nerves a little bit because of the stereotype. If you're from Paterson you were probably poor, Black or Spanish, in a gang, smoked weed, or you were an athlete. That is what most people thought. I guess it was because they did not know what it was like there so they were misguided."

Although more students from Paterson attended the school than he originally expected, Lamar was unexpectedly alienated from them. After initially puncturing white stereotypes about urban students of color, Lamar found himself agreeing with them: "Many of the people [from Paterson] were ghetto, hood, and people noticed it." He described feeling distant from other students of color, and concerned that they were responsible for any bad treatment he received: "There were many more than I had imagined would be there and many of them acted the same, like assholes. I knew kids that made our city look shitty. No wonder when I told people where I was from they would be surprised as if no one with even an ounce of intelligence could come from there." Lamar separated himself from this group of students: "I guess I could not really fit the description. I was a smart kid. I talked differently than most of the kids from my city. . . . I was in all honors, except Spanish." To avoid being stereotyped as an urban Black student, in his logic, it seems Lamar has to avoid other urban Black students. In my early readings of his narrative essay, I was concerned that these passages reflected negative racial identity, rejection of Blackness, and internalized racism. I struggled to respond to this aspect of his writing. Fortunately, this kept me quiet, so that Lamar could keep writing.

Like the monolithic specter of "ghetto, hood, city" students of color he depicts, Lamar initially stereotyped the wealthy white suburban students he encountered at school as hopelessly different from him:

> Most kids were from one of the richest counties in the country, and even when they weren't wealthy, lets say they were middle class; I rarely had much in common with them at first. I mean it goes beyond skin color when I say something in common. Whether they were black, white, or Spanish it did not matter. The kids from this county were different.

However, his sense of their alterity did not last. Even in the passage above, he begins to break down the idea that the school is all white, or all wealthy. Stuck in a homeroom with no one from home, he slowly began to "be cool" with white suburban kids, commenting, "I noticed they weren't too different from me after all. I came in with the idea that everyone was rich and stuck up but most people were middle class and very chill." After this passage, the other students began to seem neither exclusively white nor exclusively rich.

While at school, Lamar describes his stereotypes against rich white people beginning to break down. At home it is the opposite. He depicts minimal contact with urban Black people. Alone in his aunt's cramped apartment, he feels isolated and claustrophobic. The building itself sounds straight out of a movie about urban squalor: "The hallways were dirty; the elevators smelled like piss and were broken half the time as I found out the first day. The staircase was a place for pot smoking drug dealers to meet and chill as I walked up inhaling the aroma that was the foulest thing I've ever smelled." Lamar felt oppressed by his surroundings: "All I thought about how bad it was. The look, the people, the attitude was just awful to me." Lamar does what I've been asking here—he describes in clear, vivid detail the impact of poverty on his building and the feeling it created.

The main impact he focuses on is how these conditions isolate him from other people of color in the city where he lives. Although he has little contact with people outside his family, he imagines how they might have responded to him. He called himself "quite the outcast at that building. I felt as though I was not as 'hood' as the other people my age I would encounter." He imagined stereotypes the people in his building might have about him: "The people themselves frighten me, as I was not used to them. There was hardly anyone my age in the building, and if they were I doubt they wanted to befriend this little fat kid who goes to the white school." He could not imagine connection with the other people there: "I could not really get to know anyone there, even if I wanted to I mean. It was too hard to make friends with complete strangers; I was one of the shyest kids ever and still am. How would I talk to them? Why would they talk back?" His isolation in the building, and the stereotypes that help reinforce it, echo his hopeless take on the city's public schools.

The turning point in Lamar's isolation from other young people at home and in school comes from what he describes as distinctly hopeful contact within and across color and class in his new school. Importantly, this contact rarely occurred within the school day and never within the formal instructional frame of a class. At first the lack of a cohort is what drives him to connect with his classmates. He describes one classmate in particular:

> I would learn to fit in a little bit more because of the kid who sat in front of me. His name was Mike and he was different. He made me comfortable talking to white kids well because he wasn't what I expected. He talked about smoking weed, rap music, and just had the funniest stories to tell me. He was that person that everyone knew and no one could hate.

Strangely, Lamar seems drawn to Mike for the same reason he is repulsed by other kids of color from Paterson—Mike is "acting Black," as defined by Lamar. Although Lamar describes himself as strongly interested in rap music, he negatively associated smoking weed and joking around as something other Black people do in other places in his narrative. However, these qualities in Mike helped form Lamar's first bond with a white student. Were the rules different for Mike? It seemed he could afford to engage in the oppositional drugs, music and humor that are off limits to Lamar.

While my initial reading of this passage foregrounded the possibility of Lamar's internalized racism, a more open stance toward his text as autoethnography might have lent me insight into his placement of value at the margins of the school day, and the power of the class clown when the class is a contact zone. "[M]ore powerful than a goody-two-shoes with respect to his peers," (2005, p. 29) Maxson writes, the class clown is in a position of power not allied with the teacher's authority. Lamar's attraction to this kind of in-school-but-not-of-school power illuminates how Mike connects diverse groups and violates the boundaries that Lamar has depicted as so rigid. He made it possible to be "someone everyone knew and no one could hate." Mike offers cross-cultural contact at the margins of Lamar's new school.

Don't Mess with Mr. In-Between

Lamar depicted "being cool" with middle-class white students in the informal space of his homeroom as a watershed moment in acclimating to his new school. Homeroom takes place inside school, with members of the school community, but is not part of the formal academic program. Similarly, Lamar described himself as fully comfortable only after he developed his own cohort of Black friends, which occurred as they navigated the routes in and out of the city together. In the interstitial space of the bus ride, with other kids making the same journey he's making, he described exchanging rap music and words of caution, debriefing culture clashes, and analyzing social spaces. One friend always shared "this new song or that new mixtape or this freestyle" while another "helped me understand much more about our city, the good places, the bad, and the gangs. He helped me know a little bit about the area in which I now lived in, and he just confirmed my nightmares about this place." Lamar's text gestures to a space of shared cultural understanding and expression connected to, but not part of, both their suburban school and their homes in the city.

Lamar articulated the values of in-between spaces rhetorically in other texts as well, titling his portfolio and its contents according to lyrics and song titles by Jay-Z, a hip-hop artist who benefits from an in-between identity, a parallel "businessman" identity between his drug-dealing past and his music industry giant corporate success. For Jay-Z, success in self-expression, success in the music industry, and success as a drug-dealer weave in and out of his writing to create a rich series of contradictions and connections, particularly in his own memoir *Decoded*. Marc Lamont Hill calls Jay-Z a "trickster" figure—a drug dealer and commercial success who got away with it all, came out on top, maneuvered around the rules in white and Black worlds (2009, 45). While Lamar presents himself as anything but a trickster figure, such a figure capitalizes on the same logic of juxtaposition, irony, and connection that holds sway in in-between spaces like those that Lamar occupies.

Despite alluding to these "decoding" conversations in the in-between space of the bus ride, Lamar was singularly unrevealing about them. If these are the spaces where his "decoding" takes place, these young peoples' code-breaking practices remained hidden. I was disappointed in Lamar's revisions of his narrative, which never developed the scenes in which he apparently fulfilled "the developmental need to explore the meaning of one's identity with others who are engaged in a similar process," according to Beverly Daniel Tatum's research on Black adolescents attending majority-white schools (2007, p. 71). This seemed like a failure in both of my initial goals for his narrative. Lamar neither shared with an audience the visceral immediacy of his thoughts and feelings, nor expressed an unequivocally positive racial identity. Reading from my playbook as an aspiring antiracist white teacher, I felt that we had both failed.

Lamar's refusal to spill the beans on his experience extended from the content to the style of his writing. The rough draft of his final reflective letter to me voiced a determination to use "proper language" in a class where most students were experimenting with their own voices, from "Brooklyn English" to "Black English." His rough draft contained a passage describing how he "waters down" his language in school: "I do try to limit the slang terms when I am speaking to a teacher, you for instance, a parent, or an older person." Because "I do not want people to stereotype me as an idiot," he wrote, "subconsciously . . . I write very proper. I feel like I try to speak so it makes the person that I am speaking to more comfortable." Tellingly, this articulation of his fear of being feared as a Black man, did not make it into the final draft of his reflective writing. His revision "watered down" even that allusion to racial fear directed at him.

I ended the semester torn between the story Lamar told and the larger story he seemed not to have told, as well as frustrated by his buttoned-up prose and behavior in class. Lamar clung to a cluster of rhetorical and social practices that looked to me like they reflected an investment in "acting white." His avoidance of slang in his speech; his choice of a seat directly next to me in class (an unusual choice—in the circle of desks in my classroom, the seats directly next to me generally remained empty); his reticence in class discussion—all made it seem that he was keeping a tight lid on self-expression, even as he made a point of narrating his experiences negotiating his identity across class and race differences. I felt the class had failed to reach him, despite the fact that he had something important to say about negotiating multiple worlds. Stuck in my inability to remediate my students' prose or his politics, I eventually returned to contact zone pedagogy for help navigating the challenges Lamar's texts presented to me.

First, I needed to abandon my goal that Lamar act like he felt safe in my classroom as a sign of his readiness for "college success." This class was not Kynard and Nunley's hush harbor, nor was it Pratt's "safe house." The classroom where we met was part of another private Catholic school, one far less segregated than either his all-Black elementary school or his predominately-white high school. I suspect Lamar was developing his own hush harbors to deal with this new social challenge, in which he sat around the table with African American, white, Indian, Latino/a, Caribbean, Arab, suburban, urban, and rural students from a range of economic backgrounds. He may or may not have been aware of the ways in which he was considered a contingent member of that class by the university. As a member of the "Liberal Studies" program and, as a Black male college student, he was considered more "at risk" of not completing his college degree than students in other ethnic groups and other majors (St. John's University Office of Institutional Research, 2010). His rhetorical caution suggested a high degree of awareness, however.

I believe now that his investment in "proper" English and "white" learning spaces was a lot more complex than I initially gave Lamar credit for, and that he was in the process of forming—or attracting—a cohort in his college composition class, under my radar. Articulating what happened in this space to me, his teacher, would have been either beside the point, or actually counterproductive.

Kynard adapts the term hush harbors from Nunley, and calls them "literal and metaphorical meetings and gathering points . . . unauthorized by the white gaze and its hegemonic centers" (2010, p. 34). Hush harbors "enact African American rhetoric, as opposed to merely providing utopian safe havens or survival strategies, and . . . do the important work of disrupting the social reproduction of bourgeois whiteness that the majority of classrooms and college faculty maintain" (Kynard, 2010, p. 34). I tried very hard not to inflict the "racialized policing of language and being in schools" (Kynard, 2010, p. 35) on my students that Kynard argues hush harbors resist and respond to, but I am not in a position to judge the extent to which I succeeded. In fact, it would be unrealistic to imagine this particular high-stakes gateway course—with its association with academic language and its caste-like composition of "diverse" college students, all positioned in excruciatingly intricate relations of proximity and distance to the privilege the university proposed to bestow on them—could operate as anything like Pratt's "safe house" within the contact zone. Instead, I needed to come to terms with my class as a contact zone, and to expect that students would create their own safe spaces within the class to navigate their ways through it. Recognizing the uneven power relations in the room, and Lamar's strategies for navigating the class, has lent me an appreciation of what Maxson calls "the most compelling insight of Pratt's work: that language users write (or talk) themselves into and through unfriendly language environments by combinations of assimilation and resistance" (2005, p. 25).

Both Freddie and Lamar combined such volatile combinations of rhetorical and racial "assimilation and resistance." Because of the shifting institutional and cultural positions they inhabit (between classes, moving up through educational zones and in heterogeneous classrooms), they both (albeit in different ways and to different degrees) embrace and critique white, assimilationist discourses. Only once I began to discern this could I understand the ways Lamar represented his rhetorical relationship with hegemonic whiteness, the task he undertook all semester. I could notice that whenever he wrote about allegations of "acting white" based on his speech and attendance at a "white school," he consistently rejected the idea of being a "whiteboy." Whenever he addressed these allegations, which happened several times, Lamar described how calling him "white" misses the point of his story. He imagined that people in his aunt's building "would probably think I was rich and that I was a whiteboy . . . [b]ecause of the school I went to. . . . Kind of weird because would I live here if I were rich is what I would be thinking about. I had no luck in that building." He ironized allegations of both his wealth and whiteness here. His epilogue concluded with a sense of freedom from racial stereotyping, a sense of exploration: "I wanted to find out more of what I am. I felt like people did not know who I really was. I did not want them to think of me as a little ghetto kid[,] this black kid that is really white inside." Here, he rejected both the externalized racism that dismisses him as a "little ghetto kid" and the internalized racism that would call him "the black kid that is really white inside." Lamar's take on this was quite different from Freddie's, whose embrace of the label "whiteboy" appeared less ambivalent.

I want to read a final autoethnographic scene in Lamar's narrative, one in which he illustrates his cautious rhetorical strategies of racial self-representation. The scene comes late in the narrative and stands out for a number of reasons. First, it took place on the street in Paterson, a place where he had been both terrified and forbidden to set foot for most of the previous pages. Second, it contains dialogue, physical description, and is more fleshed out and developed than the rest of his narrative—in short, it adhered more clearly to the qualities of "effective" narrative prose that we discussed all semester. Third, it described a crucial miscalculation in racial self-representation.

Toward the end of his difficult year, Lamar finally began to leave his aunt's apartment and venture out to visit friends. On his first trip, he had to walk 40 minutes across town to get to his friend's house, and he was "scared as hell." He recalled his father's advice about walking in the street in Paterson:

> He said, "Keep your head up. Don't look down at your feet when you walk. It makes you look scared. You do not want to look scared or weak or like you don't know where you are. Those are the first people that get messed with. Be aware of your surroundings, if something does not look right avoid it."

> I walked for what seemed to be forever that hot summer day. I remember messing up my Air Jordans that day, I scuffed the side and got a little dirt on them. I stopped and wiped it off. They were white with red on the side and a little black at the back. I had on the white shirt with a bunch of red skulls on it to match. I looked up continued walking and then I see two guys sitting in front of the store I was walking by.
>
> One of them asked me, "You blood?"
>
> I did not know how to respond. With the colors I had on I thought someone could ask me, I was just hoping they wouldn't.
>
> I replied, "Nah."
>
> And just kept walking.
>
> Then I heard the other one looking at him and saying, "Chill n[__], that's a kid."
>
> I guess that one had enough sense to know I was a bit young for that and knew that was a dumb question. The guy was probably high as he had the same smell as the staircase, that skunk-like odor that I was not a fan of. I thought to myself that maybe this outfit might be a bit much with the red and the skulls. I also thought wow that guy was fucking stupid. . . . I told [my friend] what had happened earlier and he laughed. He thought it was funny someone would ask me that. I was a "goodie goodie" in the eyes of most people so him laughing did not surprise me.

Lamar appears to lampoon a stereotype he also fears. To be labeled himself as a gang member is "fucking stupid," and perhaps anticlimactic, given the reservoir of fear of Black gangsters he had built up after a year cooped up in an apartment. For someone who portrays himself as so disconnected from the people around him in a poor Black neighborhood, Lamar now takes DuBois's African American "double consciousness" to the point of incoherence, showing its absolute foundation in erroneous fear. Lamar's curious lapse in self-policing—wearing gang colors on his first walk through what he feels to be gang territory—demonstrates the extreme care required for young Black men to present themselves as non-threats. In this scene, he both makes fun of, and shows the dangers of, walking while Black.

I sense a parallel here to Lamar's explanation of "watering down" his prose for adults to avoid trouble when he writes while Black. Lamar might be nodding along with Homi Bhabha singing Johnny Mercer's lyric, "Don't Mess with Mr. In-Between" at this point in his text. If, as Bhabha argues, the racial stereotypes with which Lamar's text is preoccupied are a prime tool in the belt of "colonial discourse," Lamar's descriptions of himself and other young Black people are riddled with racial stereotyping. However, Bhabha believes these stereotypes are slippery, "a form of knowledge and identification that vacillates between what is always 'in place,' already known, and something that must be anxiously repeated. . . . [A]mbivalence . . . [is] central to the stereotype" (1994, p. 66) and makes them thus unsettle the hierarchies they are meant to cement. Lamar, in upending the stereotype of a Black gangster—one of several stereotypes of Black men that had haunted him all year—managed to undo that very stereotype, staging a scene in which he entered the urban street, "scared as hell," and was mistaken for the very threat he fears, "a blood." He displayed the arbitrariness of this label, the Emperor-has-no-clothes element of his fear.

On the other hand, he does the opposite. He shows how easy it is for him to inspire fear in others, demonstrating the wisdom of surviving by refusing to show his "Blackness"—the specter of threatening male Blackness that he accidentally assumed in this moment. Paired up with the "idiots" and "assholes" he describes as the mass of his peers from the city who've come out to suburban high school with him, Lamar articulates the necessity of keeping a lid on his rhetorical Blackness. Like Bhabha, Lamar knows the complexity of living as Mr. In-Between. He is articulating a similar space to Bhabha, but it looks "different," as Lamar has called himself numerous times. In his narrative, that space is both more urgent and more reserved.

"My Voice Is a Very Different Voice"

> Honestly I think that my voice is the voice of multiple groups. It comes from me being around different groups of people throughout my life especially high school. I think it is hard to describe my voice in words, but it is sort of like that gray area where the labels of black and white meet, but I wouldn't call myself a "black kid that acts white." It's a little more complex than that. Rather than being focused on one group of people and how they talk, like the people I grew up around, my voice is drawn from everything I have learned and been through.

By "gray," I don't take Lamar to mean a "postracial" identity, but rather a highly limited expression of identity in the uncertain terrain of a mixed-race school. Lamar doesn't believe what any particular group says about itself or its others. What he does demonstrate in my classroom is participation in what looks like a cohort that is neither in-school nor exactly out-of-school: a cohort of other male students of color who also began writing about their experiences as racial minorities in mostly white schools, and found other ways to connect throughout the semester. Most of this took place in texts or places that I could not monitor easily, such as peer review groups and side conversations.

The first sign was a seating change in the middle of the semester. Lamar, as I mentioned before, always sat next to me in the circular seating arrangement of our class. It seemed to pain him, since he often had to speak directly to me, or after me, in whole class workshops and he spoke as little as possible in class. But he stayed there. Midway through the semester, another member of the cohort—an African American male student who had sat in the back of the room and gotten laughs for his comments from day one—got frustrated. In the middle of a conversation, he made a comment about another students' writing, and his whole corner of the room erupted in laughter. It had not been a particularly funny comment. "Why does everybody laugh after everything I say?" he asked rhetorically. At the next class meeting, this student moved his seat next to Lamar so that the three of us made up the front row of the class. This student worked especially hard on his writing in the later part of the semester, which he was choosing to write in a much more pronounced version of "Black English" than Lamar's. But he wasn't doing it for laughs. He wanted to qualify as a walk-on for the university's Division 1 basketball team. His grades were the obstacle. He took care of this by the end of the year, when he pulled up his grades and got a spot on the team.

This was not the only student who gravitated to Lamar as the semester wore on. Another student who wrote about transferring to a majority white Catholic high school requested Lamar as a writing partner, describing how he felt their narratives were closely connected. This was a student who kept his cards perhaps even closer to his chest than Lamar, never revealing his ethnic identity beyond "brown." He named his writing portfolio "Ciphertext," and described inscrutability and encryption as central qualities of his rhetorical style. He and Lamar met a few times to discuss their narratives, and though I had access to some of the material that they wrote to each other, most of what passed between them happened at the margins of my ability to monitor them—in-between.

What I now believe Lamar was doing—in his narrative, his reflections on his writing, and in my class—was carving out rhetorical and literal spaces for connecting with other young men of color in a volatile integrated gateway course in his new university. These spaces afforded them opportunities to devise critiques and strategies for navigating the complex institutional cultures of writing at a university like mine.

Lamar's work didn't conform to my expectations, and I believe I learned from him about the lens I brought to bear on his situation. I assumed that because his texts voiced negative depictions of other urban Black people, and because he became comfortable at his predominantly white institution, that Lamar was suffering from internalized racism. That may or may not have been the case, but I gradually came to appreciate how he consistently rejected allegations of "acting white," despite his articulations of stereotypes about Black people that seem to create distance between himself and other African Americans. Further, I began to see and value his work building relationships with other male students of color in my class.

I believe that deeper understanding of the ways in which men of color in college support each other would repay further investigation in the contemporary contact zone of college composition. Shaun Harper's important recent study of highly successful Black male college students suggests there is no current evidence to support the widely-held belief that academically successful Black college students are ostracized by peers and accused of "acting white." Even John Ogbu, who initially asserted the "Acting White Hypothesis" with Signithia Fordham in 1986, suggested in 2004 that critical discourse surrounding that hypothesis may have drifted from the original intent of it authors. In fact, the Black male college students Harper interviewed identified the support of their Black peers on campus as crucial to their success. While Harper's demographic population is not one that Lamar fits into, Lamar's status is one Harper points to in "lingering questions" at the conclusion of his study, Harper wonders about the support received by students who are less high-achieving, less drawn toward leadership, and "whose racial identities are not as well developed" (2006, p. 354) as the highly successful students he spoke with. I hope my teaching account can contribute to a better understanding of the meaning of "acting white" for more marginalized Black and Latino male college students.

Lamar's rhetorical and social moves in the classroom yielded fresh insights for me about the intensity and subtlety of student writing in the "contact zone" of a college composition classroom. Ultimately, I began to see Lamar as part of a quiet cohort of male students of color who make spaces for themselves outside the direct awareness of their white female professor, who is, after all, liable to do things like publish their words in the academic street as I am now, however well-meaning my intent.

Conclusion: Composition Pedagogy "Acts White" in the Contact Zone

If Lamar's texts articulate the value of in-between spaces for negotiating the whiteness of the academy or composition pedagogy, Freddie's text may simply be such a space. His acts of "transcultural repositioning" are so multiple as to create a blur where his own take on "whiteness" might be found. Freddie and Lamar, and to some extent the three other male students of color in my class who wrote about attending "white schools," interrogate what Kermit Campbell calls "the hegemony of whiteness and middle-classness in the academy and in composition" (2007, p. 330). I believe the highly indeterminate receptions of their texts by this class made a dent in this hegemonic whiteness for all of us. Keith Gilyard has argued that "in most classrooms . . . 'race' simply inscribes another othering discourse. It is an unproblematized matter of the non-White, the other" (2011, p. 82). With these writers at work in the class, the invisibility of whiteness simply could not be maintained.

My open-ended narrative assignment and whole class workshops were motivated by something like contact zone pedagogy, a practice of de-centered authority in discussions of autoethnographic writing. In this pedagogical space, these students' texts articulated nuggets of what appear to be internalized racism against themselves and other people of color. Having elicited such writing, I hesitated to "correct" this internalized racism, while I remained concerned about seeming to validate these negative ideas about people of color through silence. Ultimately, neither student seemed entirely comfortable making capitulation to class and race hierarchies the last word and produced what I read as their own nuanced takes on allegations of rhetorical "whiteness" aimed at them. For both of them, school seemed a central place for personal and social transformation in ways that go beyond transformation into a "whiteboy."

As far as I could tell, Freddie was not trying to "pass" at college. He was playing up his "street" identity, almost acting more like a kid from Washington Heights or Bushwick than one from Howard Beach. Or perhaps a kid from Howard Beach who affiliates with hip-hop music. And Lamar, who trumpeted his watering-down of slang, actually used a range of rhetorical styles in his texts. Both students used personal narratives of "acting white" to chart a course of ongoing thinking and writing for themselves, and subsequently for me and the rest of the class, too.

There is a danger that these narratives could function like what Wendy Ryden calls "whiteness narratives"—written by white people to make their whiteness visible to themselves and others. Ryden identifies "a rhetorical tradition of 'confessing' whiteness . . . a kind of 'truth and reconciliation' strategy of responsible owning of experience from which one can then move forward to become a member of the new group of antiracist workers" (Ryden & Marshall, 2012, p. 15). These students' relationships to whiteness and its privileges are much more complex than this kind of whiteness narrative. They offered our class opportunities to perceive and analyze whiteness as a force in the lives of people of color, from which we all benefitted. But I may have expected them to also confess on some level, to disavow internalized racism and its allegiances to whiteness; I know that I struggled to respond where they failed to do so. It is useful to notice my somewhat unconscious impulse to guide student narratives into performing a rejection of whiteness and assimilation. My goal to give my students the opportunity to discern the role of race in their personal lives, and to articulate that role, is well-served by personal narrative. However, my goal of promoting awareness of systemic racism and racial injustice in both historical and contemporary contexts is not particularly well-suited to these means.

Since Freddie and Lamar were my students, I have altered my use of narrative as a tool for teaching about race in composition. My courses have gone from "happening" to involve a lot of writing about race, to explicitly addressing race as a core theme. I am undertaking another writing project reflecting on these new developments in my course and the writing that students have produced in the course of this new focus. I am grateful to Freddie, Lamar, and my other students for helping me learn to ask better questions and offer feedback that tries to help them articulate the role of race in their daily lives, and the larger systemic forces that lie behind those daily experiences. I hope my students and I can continue to learn from each other, and to use our understandings of the role of race in our lives to motivate us in reaching for ever-clearer racial analysis and more immediate action toward racial justice.

References

Alim, H. S. (2009). Intro: Straight outta Compton, straight aus Munchen: Global linguistic flows, identities, and the politics of language in a global hip hop nation. In H. S. Alim, A. Ibrahim & A. Pennycook (Eds.), *Global linguistic flows: Hip hop cultures, youth identities, and the politics of language* (pp. 1–24). New York: Routledge.

Bhabha, H. (1994). *The location of culture.* New York: Routledge.

Blitz, M. & Hurlbert, C. M. (1998). *Letters for the living: Teaching writing in a violent age. Refiguring English studies.* Urbana, IL: National Council of Teachers of English.

Campbell, K. (2007). There goes the neighborhood: Hip hop creepin' on a come up at the U. *College Composition and Communication, 58*(3), 325–344.

Cutler, C. (2009). You shouldn't be rappin', you should be skateboardin' the X-games: The coconstruction of whiteness in an MC battle. In H. S. Alim, A. Ibrahim & A. Pennycook (Eds.), *Global linguistic flows: Hip hop cultures, youth identities, and the politics of language* (pp. 79–94). New York: Routledge.

Fordham, S. & Ogbu, J. (1986). Black students' school success: Coping with the "burden of 'acting white.'" *The Urban Review, 18*(3), 176–206.

Gilyard, K. (2011). *True to the language game: African American discourse, cultural politics, and pedagogy.* New York: Routledge.

Guerra, J. C. (2004). Emerging representations, situated literacies, and the practice of transcultural repositioning. In M. N. Kells, V. Balester & V. Villanueva (Eds.),

Latino/a discourses: On language, identity & literacy education. Portsmouth, NH: Boynton Cook Publishers.

Harper, S. R. (2006). Peer support for African American male college achievement: beyond internalized racism and the burden of "acting white." *Journal of Men's Studies, 14*(3), 337–358.

Harper, S. R. & Quaye, S. J. (2007). Student organizations as venues for black identity expression and development among African American male student leaders. *Journal of College Student Development, 48*(20), 127–144.

Hill, M. L. (2009). *Beats, rhymes and classroom life: Hip-hop pedagogy and the politics of identity.* New York: Teachers College Press.

Jay-Z. (2010). *Decoded.* New York: Spiegel & Grau.

Kells, M. H. (2002). Linguistic contact zones in the college writing classroom: An examination of ethnolinguistic identity and language attitudes. *Written Communication, 19*(1), 5–43.

Kells, M. N., Balester, V. & Villanueva, V. (Eds.). (2004). *Latino/a discourses: On language, identity & literacy education.* Portsmouth, NH: Boynton Cook Publishers.

Kynard, C. (2010). From candy girls to cyber sista-cypher: Narrating black females' color-consciousness and counterstories in *and* out of school. *Harvard Educational Review, 80*(1), 30–52.

Lipsitz, G. (2006). *The possessive investment in whiteness: How white people profit from identity politics.* Philadelphia: Temple University Press.

Martinez, A. (2014). Critical race theory: Its origins, history, and importance to the discourses and rhetorics of race. *Frame 27*(2), 9–27.

Maxson, J. (2005). "Government of da peeps, for the peeps, and by the peeps": Revisiting the contact zone. *Journal of Basic Writing, 24*(1), 24–47.

Ogbu, J. (2004). Collective identity and the burden of "acting white" in black history, community, and education. *The Urban Review, 36*(1), 1–35.

Overall trend retention by various demographic characteristics. (October 14, 2014). *Graduation and Retention Rate Reports.* St. John's University Office of Institutional Research. Retrieved from http://www.stjohns.edu/sites/default/files /overall_trend_retention_by_vaious_demo_chara.pdf.

Pratt, M. L. (1991). Arts of the contact zone. *Profession, 91*, 33–40.

Ratcliffe, K. (2005). *Rhetorical listening: Identification, gender, whiteness.* Carbondale, IL: Southern Illinois University Press.

Roediger, D. (2006). *Working toward whiteness: How America's immigrants became white. The strange journey from Ellis Island to the suburbs.* New York: Basic Books.

Romney, A. (2011). Guaman Poma's contact with the rhetorical tradition. *College composition and communication, 63*(1), 12–34.

Ryden, W. & Marshall, I. (2012). *Reading, writing, and the rhetorics of whiteness.* New York: Routledge.

Shaughnessy, K. (1979). *Errors and expectations: a guide for the teacher of basic writing*. New York: Oxford University Press.

Smitherman, G. (1977). *Talkin and testifiyin: The language of black America*. Detroit, MI: Wayne State University Press.

Tatum, B. D. (1992). Talking about race, learning about racism: The application of racial identity development in the classroom. *Harvard Educational Review, 62*(1), 1–24.

Tatum, B. D. (1997). "Why are all the black kids sitting together in the cafeteria?": And other conversations about race. New York: Basic Books.

Tatum, B. D. (2007). *Can we talk about race?: And other conversations in an era of school desegregation*. Boston: Beacon Press.

Villanueva, V., Jr. (1993). *Bootstraps: From an American academic of color*. Urbana, IL: National Council of Teachers of English.

Young, V. A. (2009). "Nah we straight": An argument against code switching. *JAC, 29*(1–2), 49–76.

Young, V. A. (2007). *Your average nigga: Performing race, literacy, and masculinity*. Detroit, MI: Wayne State University Press.

Writing and Unwriting Race: Using Hip-Hop in Writing and Literature Classrooms

Jessica Parker

While I was a voracious reader as a child, I had no exposure to African American literature until I was late into my teens and read Ralph Ellison's Invisible Man. This was a book I felt was life changing; however, I did not consider becoming a scholar of African American literature until I was embarking on my doctoral studies. Like many of my own students now, as an undergraduate student, I believed that to be an "authentic" scholar of the African American tradition I needed to have been raised in it; I needed to be African American myself. Despite my relatively late exposure to canonical African American texts, I was quite familiar with hip-hop. Hip-hop CDs were a normal part of the rotation on my Walkman, but as a teen and young adult, I didn't see hip-hop as a part of the literary tradition. This also mimics the way many of my own students now feel. They often have more exposure to hip-hop than to other types of African American texts, but they tend to see it as "only" pop culture and not as a topic for academic exploration. When I made the decision to focus my doctoral studies and my dissertation in the African American literary tradition, specifically hip-hop, I was forced to strongly consider my own position in the culture and in the academy as a white person and white scholar. The time I have spent contemplating that position has led me to recognize the necessity of asking students, both white students and students of color, to reflect on and acknowledge their own identities and how these identities inform their readings of and writing about African American texts in an African American literature class or a composition course. Hip-hop is my frame for these reflections in both writing and literature classrooms.

As a white scholar of African American literature, I try to remain highly conscious of how my own position of authority and privilege in the classroom—based both in white privilege and in academic credentials—influences how my students regard the texts, cultural issues, and historical information that are discussed in the various classes in which I teach African American texts. At the institutions where I have taught classes focused on the African American tradition, the majority of the students on the campus, and in the classes, have been white. This makes the recognition of the potential for othering of African Americans and of the texts a practical as well as an ethical concern. The classroom must be a safe and comfortable environment for all students, and the courses and discussions must be structured and facilitated to avoid African American students being made to feel that they are expected by the rest of the students (or by me) to represent African Americans as a whole, to have an intrinsic understanding of the texts, or to feel marginalized or dismissed in the discussions. Students need guidance in addressing the form and content of African American texts and in understanding how the texts work inside the broader American context and literary traditions, including the contexts of institutional racism and of the stereotypes and negative assumptions about African American English (AAE) and Black discourse. In the process of textual analysis of hip-hop lyrics and analysis of the aesthetics of the form, my students and I are traveling through and writing about the uncomfortable issues of race and class and the current inequities and issues implicated in these topics. This chapter gives a snapshot of what those journeys have been like for me and for my students, from the foundational ideas of the approach to a typical first-day discussion to an example assignment.

Discussing and writing about racial issues and characterizations are a necessary part of any examination of the African American literary tradition. However, due to the somewhat taboo and certainly difficult nature of discussions about race in American culture, I have found it vital to begin the class (or the discussion of hip-hop within a composition course) with an examination of our positions, both conscious and unconscious, about race. This has been particularly true since the idea of a "post-racial" society has gained currency. Most of my students have not given much thought to how racial privilege or lack thereof (actually privilege in general) affects the ways they read and interpret texts and the ways they approach writing, academic writing in particular. My students have made decisions to take the African American literature or writing course with a hip-hop theme based on interest; the institutions where I have taught courses focused in the African American literary tradition have not required these courses for a degree or major. That they have an interest in the material is often the only thought that students have given to signing up for the course. In fact, many students have come into the classes without the vocabulary to discuss their own positions. Many students are unfamiliar with or only partly understand terms like white privilege, benevolent racism, and essentialism. This lack of conscious reflection or the vocabulary to discuss the issues has often meant that students have to resort to other strategies to ask questions or to read and write about the texts. One of the ways to provide students with the strategies to effectively understand their own positionality and to engage with the texts and with the difficult issues about race, race relations, and our country's racial and racialized history is to ground the courses in something many of the students are already familiar, and often comfortable, with: hip-hop.

There are hip-hop classrooms across the country, and many scholars such as Elaine Richardson and Kermit E. Campbell have made explicit hip-hop's value in the college classroom. The National Council of Teachers of English has recognized this value as well and so have done "what any responsible educator should—that is, tapping into the cultural interests of students instead of, as is usually the case, putting school culture at complete odds with the popular culture" (Campbell, 2005, p. 78). Other scholars, notably Geneva Smitherman in books like Word from the Mother (2006), and Arnetha Ball and Ted Lardner, in African American Literacies Unleashed: Vernacular English and the Composition Classroom (2005), have made the necessity for the recognition and study of AAVE and Black discourse in composition and literature classrooms clear. These scholars have laid the groundwork for teachers such as myself—and point out the ways in which teachers and students can explore the hip-hop nation together to enrich their reading and writing practices. As Smitherman puts it in Word from the Mother, "Language makes the impossible possible" (2006, p. 78); the seemingly impossible unpacking of race and class in the classroom is made possible through the power of the words and works of hip-hop and through the work of these scholars who blazed the trails.

In "Diaspora" (1999), the Speaking Seeds' hip-hop ode to their roots and the roots of hip-hop as a genre, they repeatedly tell us "It was the traveling that mattered." This describes hip-hop in the writing or literature classroom—the reading/writing is a journey through the genre, across avenues of appropriation and appreciation, through the 'hoods of race and class, in search of authentic voices. We truly live in a hip-hop nation. Hip-hop consistently is one of the best-selling genres. It is the soundtrack of films, dance clubs, and advertisements. For many of the young people in America, it is the soundtrack to their lives; it is their music. For many college students, it is a familiar gateway into the unfamiliar territory of a critical assessment of the roles of race and class in our society.

Hip-hop is an important addition to the curriculum of writing or African American literature classes. It provides another type of text to use as the basis of writing exercises, a type of text many students are interested in and feel that they have more access to and understanding of than more traditional or historical texts dealing with issues of race, like Martin Luther King Jr.'s "Letter from a Birmingham Jail." Students also often feel that the hip-hop texts are more relevant to their lives and experiences. It is very effective when hip-hop is the framework for the writing classroom's curriculum or is a framework for entering into a survey of canonical African American literature. When I have taught classes using hip-hop in these ways, my students have been willing to engage deeply with difficult issues that they often are reluctant to discuss in the context of more traditional texts or of simply "real life." They might admit as one student did that he was "an ignorant white boy" or point out the rhetorical differences in how students approach other students in their own racial groups and those in other racial groups—employing "Black speech—of the 'yo, what up variety'" as one African American student characterized how her white peers spoke to her. Hip-hop opens new dialogues, new roads that student readers and writers can travel.

The road map of Hip-hop makes explicit the issues of race and class that traditional models of the "American dream" and our own discomfort with race, our history, and our social practices have worked so hard to make invisible. Yet this is also a hip-hop nation where one of the top-selling and most recognized hip-hoppers is Eminem—a white rapper. The issues of race and class that confront the larger society can be approached through the microcosm of the hip-hop nation. Although hip-hop is the cultural creation of socioeconomically underprivileged, urban African Americans and Latinos, its audience is now comprised not only of other African Americans and Latinos but also of white youth, many of whom are suburban and middle-class. The dichotomy between many of the artists and large parts of the audience allows for discussions about how we try to both write and unwrite race and class: what is the line between appreciation and appropriation? Can artists and audiences "keep it real" yet bridge boundaries of class and race? Can race and class be unmarked without changing the art form? These are the questions that center the hip-hop classroom. Students often feel uncomfortable discussing or writing about these issues in a general sense or based in canonical texts. They may feel they lack the authority to address issues as large as race and class because they believe they are too inexperienced or uneducated about the issues. Hip-hop provides a familiar foundation from which to explore these issues, in the hip-hop nation and in the wider culture.

Students' initial reactions to the issues of race and class in the classroom framed in discussions of hip-hop are much the same as in many classrooms and in many other forums: "things are better than they used to be"; "racism doesn't really exist anymore"; "we're post-racial now, so that stuff doesn't matter"; "hip-hop has moved beyond all that—all that matters are your skills." The students exhibit the signs of having succumbed to what Julia Kristeva describes, in The Sense and Nonsense of Revolt, as "the failure of rebellious ideologies on the one hand, and the surge of consumer culture on the other" (2000, p. 7). Everything must be okay because people of all cultures can make and sell records and books and we can all buy and consume them. Many students seem most comfortable when they are submerged in what Kristeva calls our "culture of entertainment, the culture of performance, the culture of the show" (2000, p. 7) in which nothing carries more significance than its price tag or brand name. They often start from the premise that as long as people of all cultures can dance to the same music, watch the same movies and TV shows, read the same books, or even just be in the same classroom, all must be right with the world. As Richardson points out in Hip-hop Literacies, students work from "their structural positions which offer them certain views of reality, deny or offer them access to adequate social goods, deny or offer them certain discourses" (2006, p. 43). My job as a teacher is not to tell them that their ideas are reductive, that they should engage more deeply rather than simply accepting the "show." My job is to journey with them below the surface spectacle—to take more than a one-hour tour of the hip-hop nation.

Hip-hop refuses to be simply the spectacle, the culture of the show. It is not a comfortable, quiet, non-revolutionary entertainment. It keeps up the insistent beating and bass thumping of its revolutionary heart and roots. Hip-hop is not spectacle, not merely consumable product; it is, in the words of KRS-One (2002), "what we live." It is the art of the street demanding appreciation and actively rejecting appropriation. Geneva Smitherman describes African American Language (AAL) as a "resistance discourse" (2006, p. 3), and hip-hop functions as this same type of discourse in the classroom. It provides the context in which students can resist the unwriting of race and class issues that pervades the broader culture (and too often happens in the classroom as well). While many students—Black, white, and brown; rich, middle class, and poor—feel they lack the lived experience or educational background or simply the comfort or confidence level to actually write about socioeconomic class and race outside of the fairly fixed and specific framework of historical events (e.g., the Civil War or the Civil Rights movement), hip-hop authorizes the examination of race and racism, class and classism. It creates a contemporary framework and unearths contemporary and historical issues—bringing them defiantly and loudly (think of Public Enemy's soundscape of police sirens and street noise) to the forefront of any discussion of the genre. Furthermore, many students feel that it is a framework that they already have access to. While it takes them down unfamiliar streets and into new 'hoods, it is a vehicle they feel they know how to drive.

This familiarity with hip-hop provides one of the first street signs for students seeking direction in their reading and writing to explore the nature of race and class relations in America. If their initial reactions to the importance, or even existence, of race and racism are indeed based in fact, if race and class issues have become irrelevant, why does so much of hip-hop explicitly reference the fact that the genre is the creation of "ghetto" dwelling Black and Latino youth? It is hard to find a respected emcee who doesn't celebrate his or her roots—whether it's De La Soul (1993) celebrating the area codes of their members' neighborhoods in "Area" and telling the "fake ass frauds" to "clear my area" or KRS-One and BDP (2002) celebrating the birth of hip-hop in their native South Bronx or NWA (1988) announcing that they are straight outta Compton. Even white emcees like Eminem reference their roots (in Eight Mile, for instance). Hip-hop insistently locates itself in the economically deprived areas that have populations that are largely African American or Latino. Hip-hop is the vehicle that takes students to the issues of race and class, even when the students are aiming at a location where these issues have been unwritten by the leveling power of the green—if people have the money they can consume the culture.

Before they can effectively engage with the question of whether their first reactions that we are "post-racial" or that race has become irrelevant in their generation if not in the society more broadly are well-founded, they must examine their own assumptions about African American texts. This can be achieved through a relatively simple, but often illuminating, exercise. On the first day of class (or at the beginning of a hip-hop unit), before we have examined any texts, hip-hop or otherwise, I ask students to tell me what first comes to mind when they think about texts by African American writers. I do this either as a free writing exercise or as a discussion where I will list what they say on the board. A typical list generated by this activity looks like this: race, racism, oppression, slavery, Civil Rights, violence, abolition, history, religion, culture, family, names of famous African American figures (usually Martin Luther King, Jr., or Rosa Parks), and music. Less frequently, matriarchy or mothers and family make the list. We then have a class discussion about what this list suggests about the assumptions we are bringing to the texts, to our own reading of and writing about the African American tradition and/or racial issues, and how these assumptions affect how we see connections between the textual tradition (both oral and written) and racial issues. Elaine Richardson points out that the "social location of performer and audience determine how meaning is interpreted" (2006, p. 6). The exercise helps students see their social positions (and mine) and see how the nature of their assumptions and their own positionality might affect the way they read and write.

This discussion tends to center on three things that are common to the lists:

1. the list is more historical or sociological than literary or rhetorical;
2. the list focuses a great deal on the negative; and
3. many of the elements of the list imply but do not explicitly state that African American texts (and by extension African Americans themselves) exist and have meaning most in their relation to white people and white culture.

We then try to unpack each of these areas. I am careful to frame the discussion as non-evaluative; students are not graded on their contributions and they are not judged for the cultural capital they bring to the table, whatever that capital or knowledge may be. I do not want to "dislocate" my students from their positions and relocate them to mine; I want to help them "intervene in [their] own context" in a way analogous to the way that Richardson describes African American students' literacy education (2003, p. 116). The hip-hop classroom is a way of intervening in our own context in understanding race and racism, privilege and position. The discussion of our unconscious assumptions about African American texts helps us formulate central questions for our journey: Why, in approaching African American texts, do we focus so heavily on the content and not on the literary or rhetorical devices, techniques, and innovations? Why haven't things like love or overcoming adversity, incredibly common themes in literature generally, made the list? Do we expect that the texts will always have white characters or address white concerns, even if those concerns are addressed only in opposition to racism?

While this discussion is often somewhat, or very, uncomfortable (one student admitted in a later writing assignment that she had been embarrassed by her own subconscious assumptions that the exercise brought forth), it helps students begin to understand their own unacknowledged approaches as readers and to be more proactive in how they position themselves as writers taking on explorations, interpretations, and analyses of texts by African Americans and issues of race. The exercise also helps students understand my position as a white scholar whose work focuses on the African American tradition. While my approach includes historical aspects, it also focuses on the literary techniques and rhetorical devices that weave throughout and connect various elements of the tradition. What also becomes clear through this discussion (and through my syllabi) is the importance I place on challenging my own and my students' culturally inherited ideas and biases and the need for us to recognize difference without dismissing or othering texts, authors, or each other based on these differences. These "cultural politics" must be made explicit early on in the course because of the responsibility I have as a teacher to "make certain that all the positions as represented by different members of the class are articulated and critiqued" (Richardson, 2003, p. 26). By making my own position clear, and recognizing I am on the journey with the students, I help students allow themselves to question and challenge and recognize the factors in their own rhetorical positions and in the texts and the cultural issues they raise.

The recognition of difference and of our own ethos as students of the African American tradition is first addressed through a statement about language on my syllabi for any course in African American literature or any writing course centered on hip-hop. The final statement on these syllabi is:

> **A Note on Language:** Because many of the texts deal with race and racism, there is some use of offensive terms. There is also use of terms that were acceptable at the time some texts were written but that we may now find offensive (Negro for instance). The presence of derogatory terms in the texts does not mean that general use of derogatory terms is acceptable in the class. Certainly in quoting from or referring to the texts (offensive terms are in some titles), the use of the terms is allowable, but please think carefully about your use of these terms. Also,

> some of the texts use African American Vernacular English (AAVE), which at some points was referred to simply as "dialect." AAVE is a recognized variant of English, as is Standard American English (SAE), and we will discuss it as such. It is important to understand that AAVE is not improper SAE; it is a variant with its own rules.

This note, the final thing we look at before embarking on the exercise discussed above, explicitly introduces the importance of language in not only conveying our ideas but also in shaping them. I deeply believe in the power of words to not only express ideas but also to shape them. Because words shape our worlds, we must pay special attention to language and its ability to be oppressive or liberatory in the hip-hop classroom. The note on language is one of the few parts of the syllabus that I devote significant class time and discussion to. This helps us to understand from the first day of class the importance of our own rhetorical choices and positions as we discuss the texts, language uses, and issues of race. Our language is our power, and it is vital in any class that aims to address racial myths and stereotypes and to engage in serious discussions and analyses of texts in the African American tradition to frame those texts, and the language we use to discuss them, in a way that acknowledges the power of racial slurs and the ease with which the quality of a text can be dismissed by the simple application of descriptions of "improper" or "uneducated" language use rather than recognition of linguistic variation. This discussion of language use also lays the foundations for discussions of appropriation and discussions of discourse communities and their function in academic writing. It allows us as a classroom community to have the tools to think about, discuss, and challenge ideas of linguistic hierarchies, who "owns" particular discourses and who may (or should) participate in them, and how understanding points of connection and disjunction between various discourse communities impacts our thinking and our own rhetorical choices and impact on our audiences. It opens the door to ideas about how our language shapes our ideas and worldviews.

These issues of language use are embedded in hip-hop itself and in many of the mainstream discussions about hip-hop that often center around the use of "the N word" or of terms like bitches and hos, for instance. In particular, the question of language "ownership" and the related right to identity creation and self-representation can be unpacked through analysis of hip-hop texts. The issue of whose voice is native, of what tongue is the mother tongue of hip-hop or of Americans is illustrated by the prevalence of the idiom of "keepin' it real" in the hip-hop culture. Audiences (the students for instance) and artists (both rappers and the students as writers in the context of these classes) passionately engage in this discussion across the hip-hop culture. De La Soul's "I Am I Be" (1993), explicitly addresses the idea of whose voice is authentic:

> Or some tongues who lied
> and said "we'll be natives to the end"
> nowadays we don't even speak . . .
> This is not a bunch of Bradys
> but a bunch of black man's pride.

This is not the sanitized television world of the Brady Bunch—it is a world where speech is most privileged when it is that of a "native son, speaking in the native tongue" as Mos Def (1999) does in his rap simply titled "Hip-hop." These texts and discussions of language use "flip the script" that most students enter the classroom with—the expectation that SAE, because it is a Language of Wider Communication, is superior to other variants and the expectation that the most privileged speaker is the "native" speaker of SAE—most often implicitly seen as white, male, formally educated, and older (relative to the students).

These language issues start the traveling—the part that matters—for students and teachers, like myself, seeking to understand and write about African American texts or race and racial issues more generally. When using hip-hop as a vehicle to explore race and class and whose voice gets to represent, students are forced to confront whether or not they are in their own 'hoods; race and class can no longer be glossed over. Many of my students, white, African American, Asian American, or Latina/o, enter my classes with little knowledge about AAVE as a language system (although students who have taken linguistics courses on our campus have do often have this exposure). Many of them hold the idea, consciously or unconsciously, that SAE is "better" or "more proper" than other variants. Because the majority of them are white, it is easy for them, as Campbell compellingly describes, to "be color blind when you don't see yourself as having any color to be blind to, when you don't see yourself as anything but an authentic American existing perpetually in a state of natural entitlement, when you own the American language or voice that is, of course, naturally good, naturally right" (2005, p. 12). But to take the journey, to understand, we have to remove the blinders we may not even know we have. In the hip-hop nation, your area code, neighborhood, your geography (and the connotations these have of race and class) are central to an understanding of the genre, and as Christopher Holmes Smith points out, the use of these identifying markers of place has been an "agent of unprecedented transformation for the visual intelligibility of race and class throughout America" (1997, p. 346). Hip-hop, through helping address negative attitudes about language variants, helps remove the blinders of our (teachers' and students') own "insecurities and prejudices" and helps us move toward "self-efficacy and reflective optimism" (Ball & Lardner, 2005, p. 149) Hence Mos Def (1999) can establish his right to speak because he is "blacker than midnight on Broadway and Myrtle/hip-hop past all your tall social hurdles" while a rapper like Vanilla Ice lost all credibility not only because he was white but because he came from an upper-middle-class area.

In this context, students come face-to-face with the idea that in the hip-hop nation the typically privileged speakers and audiences (whites, often males, of high socioeconomic status) are an afterthought, as in Mos Def's "Mathematics" (1999) in which he says he has "beats by Su-Primo for all of my peoples, Negroes and Latinos" and only after a pause and offhandedly does he acknowledge that it is for "even the gringos." Whiteness also may be a marker of frontin' or being in-authentic—as in some of the reception of white rappers such as Vanilla Ice, House of Pain, Whitey Ford, the Beastie Boys, and even Eminem to some extent—although he is deemed acceptable by his class (he lacked economic privilege) and because he is supported by important Black members of the hip-hop community. At best, it is cause for some skepticism about whether the person in question can participate with understanding in the discourse, and if they can, whether they should. White audiences have a vested interest in the elision of the importance of race in this question of authenticity because blindness to the issue allows them to maintain that they are authentic rather than sucker emcees who should "clear the area" (De La Soul, 1993).

But that elision is not sustainable for students or teachers if they are going to read African American texts closely and effectively and write about them productively.

Students must consider whether they can "keep it real" or "drop science" in their own writing. They must confront the issue of their own positionality, what privilege they possess or lack, whether they are appropriating techniques or themes, and how they are allying themselves with or distancing themselves from the tradition and writers and people of color. Part of the journey is learning how we have negotiated and how we will negotiate our reality. Will we take the highway of appropriation and privilege, or will we take a road of resistance to privilege and acknowledge the value of multiple discourses and languages? Mos Def (1999) deals explicitly with the idea of appropriation in his rap "Rock N Roll" in one of the variations of the chorus:

> Elvis Presley aint got no sooull (hell naw)
> Little Richard is Rock and Roll (damn right)
> You may dig on the rolling stones
> But they aint come up with that shit on they own (nah-ah)

Students have to decipher their own voices and their rhetorical positions: Are they Elvis or Chuck Berry? Can they rock like Nina Simone, or are they only the Rolling Stones and hence cultural thieves who are trying to take over yet another space carved out by those historically marginalized by the mainstream culture? Part of a responsible pedagogy is helping students in this navigation. Awareness of the history of appropriation (e.g., in rock and roll) is a starting point in helping students in this navigation and negotiation of their context. Smitherman quotes a young African American, Jamal, who said, "White folk kill me tryin to talk and be like us. They just want the good part. But it don't go like that. You got to take the bitter with the sweet" (2006, p. 118). In classrooms that uncover and make explicit the "bitter," students learn to navigate their privilege and to question their entitlement. Their ethos in their interpretations of African American texts or essays about hip-hop and culture depends on it. Faced with the complex and nuanced verbal agility and arguments of emcees, they cannot help but confront the dominant idea that posits "literacy and literacy education [I would add literature itself] as a white thang" (Campbell, 2005, p. 133).[1]

Furthermore, hip-hop makes students (through its insistence on the role of the audience—in the shout out, call and response, etc.) confront the realities of the social inequities and stereotypes predicated on race and class. De La Soul's "I Am I Be" (1993) declares that Posdnuos (the rapper), and by implication other young African Americans, "be the new generation of slaves" and that despite hard work they don't get ahead: "I am an early bird but the feathers are black/so the apples that I catch are usually all worms." The Coup's Boots Riley (2001) raps that "the world ain't no fairy tale/it's run by some rich white scary males . . . and we still get paid barely enough to eat" ("Wear Clean Draws") and "this ghetto is a cage/they only give you two choices be a rebel or a slave" ("Get Up"). KRS-One, Nas, Public Enemy, Mos Def, and many, many other emcees and hip-hop acts consistently reference the deprivations of life at the bottom of the socioeconomic ladder. The Coup (2001) explicitly raps about those who try to move up legitimately but face resistance from the social or legal institutions:

> I'm a young black heterosexual male
> Don't drink drank
> Don't smoke
> Don't sell
> That's the real reason that they want me up in jail
> They want me to fail ("Pork and Beef")

Faced with lyrics like these, students have to consider their own role in the system. Can middle class students authentically speak/act/dress in the guise of the hip-hopper (a guise often associated with the "gangsta" pose by the suburban middle class audience)? How can they address the intertwined issued of race and class and stereotypes of criminality when they don't (and sometimes feel that they can't) understand the economic desperation that pushes the poor to be "thug[s] selling drugs" (De La Soul, 1993) to "keep they belly filled" (Mos Def, 1999)? How can they authentically write about these texts and issues at all if they are white? How can their white teacher? While these are incredibly challenging questions to address in a culture that desperately wants to be "post-racial," that wants to believe that racial issues, racial inequalities, and racism are things of the past, they are also fruitful areas for examination. In this context, even the "bling bling" rappers are calling attention to stark inequities in the socioeconomic system. They have achieved socioeconomic success despite all odds. They have achieved despite the fact that most mainstream institutions and traditions send messages that young men (and women) from the inner city, from impoverished backgrounds, from non-European and non-white heritages, are not supposed to achieve material success. They have achieved where those who do achieve that success are often perceived as criminals who can achieve only through breaking the law. The constant references to money and the lack of it make it impossible for the student of hip-hop to ignore the socioeconomic system that we all participate in or to ignore how race is tangled up in that system.

Hip-hop also makes it impossible to ignore that we still live in a society plagued by racial and ethnic divisions. Hip-hop is deeply concerned with its roots, with "the old school" and what happened "back in the day." Can those who are the oppressors in the history of African Americans and Latinos in this country authentically speak about these issues when their "great-granmomma was[n't] raised on a plantation" (Mos Def, 1999)? The history of hip-hop goes back to the African American and Latino experience where the songs were for "inspiration . . . relaxation . . . to take their minds off that fucked up situation" (Mos Def, 1999). Those who want to participate in the discussion must at least begin to understand that history—and their relation to and position in it—especially when they cannot claim that history as their own. The rhetorical and literary analysis of hip-hop lyrics and analysis of hip-hop aesthetics starts students on the journey through reading and writing about the American taboos of race and class in history and in our current life. Ball and Lardner point out how this type of explicit examination of race is an opportunity as it allows teachers and students "to construe 'difference' as a strategic category of meaning that may be foregrounded or relegated to the background for purposes that are determined by the agents involved" (2005, p. 150). This is key in not only reading the wide variety of texts by African Americans as not all "foreground" difference, but also in our writing because understanding that resistance to owning our own social positions is what allows the unwriting and erasures of race and class that are so culturally and historically pervasive.

Hip-hop allows us to see how strong the impulse to unwrite race and class is (an impulse made explicit in a sample on De La Soul's Buhloone Mind State (1993)—"why we always crossing over; they can accept our music as long as they can't see our faces?") Students see how strongly we attempt to erase race and class or at least their significance even from a genre that is predicated on the experience of, a genre that is the creation of, African Americans and Latinos from the lower socioeconomic classes. Hip-hop also allows students to actively engage in writing race and class in reactions to texts (particularly those by Afrocentric hip-hop acts), in the connections between hip-hop texts and more canonical African American texts, and in critical analyses of the media and social reactions to these texts (for instance the hysteria around gangsta rap despite the fact that it existed side by side with "conscious" rap and rap that was mostly party music), and of critical analysis of their own assumptions and reactions as well. An example of a classroom exercise that connects hip-hop texts and more canonical works follows:

> Hip-hop Aesthetics
>
> Propaganda Exercise
>
> Thus all Art is propaganda and ever must be . . . I stand in utter shamelessness and say that whatever art I have for writing has been used always for propaganda for the right of black folk to love and enjoy.
> —W. E. B. DuBois, Criteria for Negro Art, 1926
>
> More than mere weakness, it [beat] implies the feeling of having been used, of being raw. It involves a sort of nakedness of mind, and, ultimately, of soul; a feeling of being reduced to the bedrock of consciousness.
> —John Clellon Holmes, "This Is the Beat Generation," 1952
>
> The Black Artist's role in America is to aid in the destruction of America as he knows it.
> —Amiri Baraka, "State/ment," p. 169, 1965
>
> The dicta we arrived at 1. To create a true Afro-American Art 2. To create a mass art 3. To create a revolutionary art
> —Amiri Baraka, "The Black Arts Movement," p. 503, 1994

Focusing on Hughes' and Baraka's work and on one hip-hop piece, answer the following questions. Use specific details in answering.

1. Do you think Baraka's early work fits Holmes' definition of beat? Why? Does Hughes? Why? Does the hip-hop piece? Why?
2. How does Baraka's work, Hughes' work, and/or the hip-hop piece either support or reject DuBois's position that art is propaganda? If the pieces are propaganda, what are they propaganda for? Why is it propaganda and not just entertainment?
3. Does Baraka's poetry meet his own dicta? How? Does the hip-hop piece? How? How do Baraka, Hughes, the hip-hop piece, or all three "aid in the destruction of America"?

4. How does form (how the poetry/music is put together, language use, etc.) contribute to the poem's/song's use as propaganda/destructive agent/revolution? Or is this a question of lyrical content only? Why?
5. What effect do the words propaganda, destruction, and revolutionary have on the audience (us)? How do they affect our perception of the author's ethos?

This type of exercise gives students an opportunity to reflect not only on how their assumptions might affect their readings of texts, but also on how those reactions are based in perceptions of the rhetorical positioning of authors and potentially in racialized ideas. Further, these types of exercises provide a gateway into discussing junctions and disjunctions in the African American and broader American traditions, literary and cultural. They allow students to prepare themselves to write about race, to understand the importance of rhetorical positioning (the authors' and their own as writers and students), and to challenge culturally inherited ideas about race in America. Richardson's examination of how "hip-hoppers continue to flip the public script on undervalued Black life by making their aesthetics the overwhelming standard" (2003, p. 71) undergirds this type of exercise—the aesthetics of hip-hop and the African American tradition become the center of the discussion on their own terms. It is a re-visioning of hip-hop, African American literature, our writing, and ourselves.

In the Sense and Nonsense of Revolt, Kristeva points out that art can be revolutionary, that it can allow us to work out and work through displacements (like the unwritten race and class issues in our society) and that art can allow us to transgress prohibitions (like fully addressing and writing about these issues) (2000, Ch. 1). Hip-hop is this kind of revolutionary art. Christopher Holmes Smith's "Method in the Madness" claims rap "promotes symbolic forms of travel that are often denied to the physical bodies" (1997, p. 350). This traveling opens new vistas for students in literature and writing classrooms. And while hip-hop is not the solution to our social ills and inequalities, it does allow for important academic and personal explorations of these ills and inequities. Mos Def's 1999 rap "Hip-hop" summarizes hip-hop's powers and limitations:

> Hip-hop will simply amaze you
> craze you, pay you
> do whatever you say do
> but black, it can't save you.

We should be aware that hip-hop can't change the social structures based on race and class. But as Elaine Richardson calls for in Hip-hop Literacies, "our critical pedagogies must guide students beyond challenging to changing of systems that tolerate inequality, sexism, and racism" (2006, p. 55). The hip-hop classroom is one road on this journey of change. In the class that utilizes hip-hop, it can take us, students and teachers, into new territory, away from our comfortable 'hoods, down new streets and avenues. My journey, and my students', continues. And in writing, as in much else, it is often the traveling that matters.

Note

1. Campbell discusses this from the perspective of African American and Latina/o students. However, I believe this idea is also quite current among white students (particularly middle or upper class) who see high school graduation and attending college as the natural path.

References

Ball, A. F. & Lardner, T. (2005). *African American literacies unleashed: Vernacular English and the composition classroom.* Carbondale, IL: Southern Illinois University Press.

Campbell, K. E. (2005). *Gettin' our groove on: Rhetoric, language, and literacy for the hip-hop generation.* Detroit, MI: Wayne State University Press.

The Coup. (2001). *Party Music.* [CD.] New York: 75ARK.

De La Soul. (1993). *Buhloone Mind State.* [CD.] New York: Tommy Boy.

Kristeva, J. (2000). *The sense and nonsense of revolt: The powers and limits of psychoanalysis.* New York: Columbia University Press.

KRS-One & BDP. (2002). *Retrospective.* [CD.] New York: Zomba Recording Corporation.

Mos Def. (1999). *Black on Both Sides.* [CD.] Los Angeles: Rawkus Records.

Richardson, E. (2003). *African American literacies.* New York: Routledge.

Richardson, E. (2006). *Hip-hop literacies.* New York: Routledge.

Smith, C. H. (1997). Method in the madness: Exploring the boundaries of identity in hip-hop performativity. *Social Identities, 3*(3), 345–375.

Smitherman, G. (2006). *Word from the mother: Language and African Americans.* New York: Routledge

Speaking Seeds. (1999). Diaspora. In *Eargasms: Crucial Poetics, Vol 1.* [CD.] New York: Oxone Music.

Dangerous Play: Race and Bakhtin in a Graduate Classroom

Timothy Lensmire, Nathan Snaza, Rebecca Nathan,
Susan Leigh Brooks, and Chiara Bacigalupa

The Players (in order of appearance)

Tim, an old but laughing professor of education

Nathan, a graduate student who really is from South Dakota

Rebecca, whose graduate studies don't always go swimmingly

Susan, a graduate student who is *not* a bureaucrat in real life

Chiara, who actually believes in risk-taking in the classroom, even as a graduate student

As the curtain rises, the players are seated on stools arranged in a semicircle. Tim is immediately recognizable as the old professor because he has long grey hair and, in general, looks old. Rebecca, seated in the middle of the semicircle, is immediately recognizable as the only person of color in the group, which, as we shall see, is a normal part of her experience in graduate school—you know, "normal" as how things are in our schools and society, given historical and ongoing oppressive systems and practices.

Tim: The work of progressive and radical educators is often grounded in a storyline that goes like this—

Nathan: Traditional schooling is bad because it silences student voices and controls student bodies.

Rebecca: Something better would liberate voices and bodies—

Susan: Let them sound, move around.

Chiara: So . . . Once upon a time—

Tim: There were three small groups of Ph.D. students at work creating skits in my graduate seminar on race and Bakhtin. The first group chose to work with an example brought in by Mary. Mary had heard her small son appropriate and use words and phrases from Harry Potter books, as he tried to impress a more popular classmate who was playing video games with him in Mary's home. Mary's small group created a performance styled after sports programs featuring video-playback and analysis. They re-created the conversation of Mary's son and his classmate, and analyzed what was going on. The rest of us in the classroom smiled, nodded, maybe remembering what it was like to be a little kid, looking out of the side of our eyes to see if our words were helping us make friends.

The second small group made everything bigger—the conflict embedded in the example, the volume of the presentation. The smiles of the audience grew into loud laughter. The second group performed and theorized classroom discourse between a floundering beginning high school teacher and a tough, too-smart, resistant high school student.

Do you know Conan O'Brien's "In the Year 2000" bit? With the darkened stage, the band singing like Monty-Python-making-believe-they-are-Eleanor-Roosevelt, and O'Brien and Mr. T.'s faces illuminated with flashlights as they make ridiculous predictions of future events? In the second small group's performance, the two group members playing at teacher and student were interrupted repeatedly by two other group members who were standing over in the corner. These two offered interpretations of what had just happened in the teacher-student talk—but they offered these interpretations by first flashing the light of an overhead projector that they were holding onto their faces, like O'Brien and Mr. T. with their flashlights, and then singing their interpretations, like Eleanor Roosevelt. The class was rolling.

The third small group . . . the third small group (Tim gestures to the others on the stage)—they worked with a word. Two words, actually. Or one word, that became two: Nigger. Niggah.

Nathan: Freud understood that "the essence of a group lies in the libidinal ties existing in it" (1922/1959, p. 35). That is, unless each person's own desires enter the work of the group, we won't have much of a "group" to speak of. My attempt here will be to sketch out my own needful attachments to this small group during the construction stage of the skit. First I will briefly lay out a framework for making sense of my experience.

The basic unit of speech for Bakhtin is the utterance, a "concrete unit . . . preceded by the utterances of others, and . . . followed by the responsive utterances of others" (1986, p. 71). It is the built-in necessity of a response that characterizes the utterance. The referent of the utterance is less important than the active reception by the listener: "It is not the object that serves as the arena for the encounter, but rather the subjective belief system of the listener" (Bakhtin, 1981, p. 282). This is to say that each listener's response is conditioned and colored by desire. Our being-in-language is determined by our concrete lived experience, and the desires that pulse through our daily lives condition our relations to language and communication no less than they help construct our identities.

Bakhtin understands identity as an ongoing internal dialogue between all the discourses we have heard and incorporated into our own worldviews during the process of verbal-ideological becoming. The questions of power and desire are intimately linked with these linguistic/developmental questions, for as Bakhtin says, "there can be no such thing as an absolutely neutral utterance" (1986, p. 84). Put differently, "world views, trends, viewpoints, and opinions always have verbal expression" (Bakhtin, 1986, p. 94) which we then integrate into our dialogic identities.

Tim: The graduate seminar I was offering, in my Department of Curriculum and Instruction, was entitled, "Race, Bakhtin, and Literacy." The politics of language, representation, and humor, especially as these figure in Black-white relations in the United States, were central concerns. I hoped to put scholarship on race into dialogue with the writings of Russian literary theorist and philosopher, Mikhail Bakhtin.

By the third night of the seminar, students had read Bakhtin's "Discourse in the Novel," his essay on speech genres, and had begun reading his work on Rabelais and carnival (Bakhtin, 1984). We hadn't yet read anything specifically about race.

Across my years as a professor, I've learned that a class usually needs a few sessions to get used to the intense reading and the rhythm of small group and large group work that characterize my courses. And then, as that gets familiar, I need to shake things up again, in order to continue the development of a different sort of classroom community. I learned this mostly in experimenting with an undergraduate philosophy of education class that I taught for many years at Washington University in St. Louis. There, I usually shook things up in the third or fourth week with a debate in which teams would argue for and against Plato and Rousseau. In my seminar on race and Bakhtin, the readings on Bakhtin didn't lend themselves to a debate—so I came up with what I called the "Show Off Your Bakhtin Contest" in which (and I'm quoting from the written directions I gave to students):

> In which you dazzle your friends and best your enemies by making believe that you understand Bakhtin and can apply his ideas to that which you apply them. To be pursued in four groups. In three stages. No prizes for winning, except that satisfaction that comes when there are no other rewards and you are desperate to feel that it was worth it anyway. (See Appendix)

Students had written short papers in preparation for the class—in these papers, they had used Bakhtin's ideas to interpret an example of language in use that they had experienced or found. Mary had written about her son playing video games with a classmate; another student, Tom, had written about the beginning teacher and the resistant student. Rebecca had written about her response to hearing her son say, "Niggah please." These examples were the jumping-off points for the three small groups, who had 25 minutes to prepare a five-minute presentation and performance. A fourth small group served as judges and questioners—they prepared questions about language and Bakhtin that they would ask of the other three groups, after their performances.

In trying to make sense of what was at stake in the "Show Off Your Bakhtin Contest," Chiara, Susan, Rebecca, Nathan, and I met a number of times as a group, we wrote dozens of emails, and we generated various accounts of different aspects of that evening's work. We also asked three other students in the class (Mark, Mary, and Cassie)—one from each of the other three small groups—to write an account for us, from their perspectives, of what happened that night.

You need to know (Tim again gestures to the other players) that this group's presentation and performance, their skit, was brilliant. It had three parts. In each, an applicant approached a bureaucrat, played by Susan. This bureaucrat had the power to decide whether or not any particular applicant could use a particular word or utterance. That is, Susan worked in the Utterance Permission Office, and if people wanted to use a particular word or phrase, they had to petition her to use it.

The skit began with Nathan approaching Susan and saying he needed to be able to use the word "nigger" because, as a high school teacher, he wanted to teach Twain's *Huck Finn*. After asking him a series of questions that referenced Bakhtin's ideas on utterance and appropriation, Susan denied Nathan's request. Then, Chiara came in—she was angry that there even was such an office, and argued that words came from dictionaries, were neutral, and that therefore anyone could use them whenever they wanted. Susan, as harried bureaucrat, drew on Bakhtin's arguments in the speech genre essay to talk back to Chiara, who eventually stormed out. Finally, Rebecca entered and requested permission to use the word "niggah." She answered Susan's questions and was granted her request.

Nathan: In our small group, as we planned the skit we would present, I had an internal dialogue with all the utterances that came before this evening and that formed the background for my external dialogue with my fellow group members. It is worth dwelling for a moment on this interplay between my internal dialogue and the external, seemingly "academic," dialogue.

As we talked together, later, about the process leading up to the performance of the skit, where the word "nigger" became a magnet, attracting all our fears and hopes about language as well as all our fears and hopes about racial politics, it became clear that I had been pushing the group toward engaging this word. Once I heard Rebecca's scenario I jumped on the idea. The reasons I did this have to be reconstructed in order to make sense of what the skit meant to me as I attempted to steer the group toward this topic.

First, Rebecca's story was simply the best one in our small group. Second, her story was the only one that directly addressed the problems signaled in the title of the course and it seemed like building a skit around it would try to take the pedagogical context of our skit seriously.

Additionally, Rebecca's story resonated with a range of experiences where my own understandings of race and language came into focus for me, often in uncomfortable and problematic ways. These included, on the one hand, a whole series of engagements with people, texts, and ideas that left me desiring to engage and learn from Black cultural forms. On the other, I recalled reading bell hooks's "Eating the Other" (1992) for the first time, which sent me reeling into a diagnosis of all my past engagement with "Black" texts and left me feeling a need to uncover my motives for and ways of understanding these texts in relation to my own identity. This investigation was intensified a great deal during a class in the department of American Studies on "Soul." We read Ralph Ellison's writings about culture and hybridity along with LeRoi Jones' *Blues People* (1963), creating heated discussions about the ties between discourse and the concrete lived experience of people, about capitalism and culture, and about "authenticity." I found that during the class we were often going to great lengths to position ourselves relative to each other along axes of theoretical knowledge, familiarity with jazz, blues and hip-hop, and access to self-reflexive engagement with texts. In that classroom space, it became crucially important for us to both know about Black cultural forms and to recognize the conflicted and uncertain ways we engaged with texts.

I brought all of this into our small group: a strong desire to argue about "authenticity," to position myself as willing to talk about the most difficult issues of language, culture and power, as someone who knew about discussions of "nigger"/"nigga" from Black sources (hip-hop music, call-in shows on Minneapolis' KMOJ radio station, etc.), and as someone who was willing to examine my own relationship to this word through our class discussions. Stated differently, my own desiring investments in knowledge, culture, power and language drove my participation with the small group. The external conversation about skit construction grew from a need to work through an internal dialogue.

The results of my desiring attachment to this activity were complicated. On the one hand, it may have spurred me to be more driving in my assertions of power—that is, I have to wonder if I wasn't, in some way, bullying the group into something that would suit my own internal desires and conflicts. On another hand, the libidinal investments caused things I wouldn't have predicted (as is common): I thoughtlessly revealed my South Dakota origins (which I usually avoid) and I "played" at being the nerdy, naïve teacher, so uncomfortable in his whiteness that it hurts to watch. The trouble arises when I need to admit that my character is fairly close to what I fear I am in the classroom. The desire to pursue a difficult topic led me to expose a range of fears and uncertainties I would not have otherwise admitted.

The realization that my internal and external dialogues cannot be kept separate, that my desires will always outpace my conscious control of what I'm doing, and that the classroom is, for better or worse, a site where my own identity struggles constantly play out has been slow in coming. While I have, for obvious reasons I suppose, focused on my own desiring attachments, I have no reason to think that I'm alone in this. If Bakhtin and Freud are correct—and I think they are—we are always using groups in order to pursue our own desires. Moreover, without those desires pulsing through the groups we participate in (in the classroom, home, city, culture, world), the group ties would dissolve and we would end up alone and silent. I therefore draw the following insight from an examination of my needful attachment to this activity: that we cannot possibly avoid the libidinal nature of group work—we couldn't construct identity without it—but we must recognize that this energy has the potential for an enormous range of consequences (from bullying and domination to submission and self-negation).

Rebecca: There were many interesting things that I learned from this classroom experience, but the part of this activity that surprised me and opened up a whole new area of personal learning was role playing. When Nathan, Chiara, Susan, and I planned our skit during our small group time we all agreed and were excited to demonstrate how Bakhtin's ideas worked out through racially charged language. Nathan and Chiara were going to "play" white people who wanted to obtain permission to use the word, but could not. I was to "play" a Black person who was able to obtain permission to use the word. Through this skit I anticipated that we would demonstrate many things that are true in our society—that different people can have a different history with and emotions toward the same word, that history can make the same sounding words two totally different utterances, and so on. It wasn't until long after the skit was over that I considered what truths in society exist about role playing.

See, the process of having to act "Black" in class was very strange and uncomfortable. This surprised me, I think, because often times in class I consciously bring a Black perspective to a mostly white group of scholars. Often this includes exposing information specific to African Americans that is new to others in the class. And I think I thought along those lines as I anticipated doing this performance—I figured I would just simulate the times when I use a variation of the "n" word with my friends or family and show my peers that there are times when this word is used in a different way than they're used to. There was just one problem: the scenery in which it is acceptable to use this word was not there to support me or my actions. Instead I was surrounded by twenty of my white peers who rarely or never use this word and felt uncomfortable with it. The entire acting process felt very, very strange.

I tried to ditch my classroom dialect and switch to a dialect that I might use with close Black friends or family. As I went through the motions of my "role," my subconscious immediately began to wonder what role I was having in enforcing negative stereotypes about Black people. It seemed like I sounded insincere and ignorant in this setting, when normally this same language was comforting and brilliant in its connecting power and transfer of ideas.

Historically, white society has consistently tried to create and control the role that African Americans would have in America (Watkins, 2001). The Jim Crow system was created to "keep Blacks in their place." We can see the roles traditionally ascribed to Blacks in society play out in the media, even today. There is the maid, the jokester or buffoon, the uneducated, the lazy, etc. (Boskin, 1986; Brown, 1933; Collins, 1991; Delgado & Stefancic, 1997; Ellison, 1953/1995; Kelley, 1997). Overwhelmingly, Black societal roles are negative. All of this suddenly became relevant as I tried to act out "my part" in the skit. White people have always had the freedom to be who they wanted to be—the roles for whites are arrayed over a wide spectrum. What does it mean to play a role in a society that has maintained a stronghold on the role that your people will play? Regardless of your good intentions or creative energy, what does it take to overcome the stench of the roles that have been created for us?

Recently I saw a presentation on Blacks in Hollywood for the last one hundred plus years. Hattie McDaniel, who repeatedly played the Mammy role, said that she'd rather play a maid than be a maid, as she had been before becoming an actress. For African Americans a tension—between the good that might result from a performance, in terms of physical and financial survival, and the potential damage, in terms of culture and society—has and continues to exist. These thoughts along with my reflection on my "performance" add another dimension to Du Bois' (1903/1997) concept of double-consciousness. For African Americans, there seems to be a heightened responsibility factor inherent in playing a role.

Bakhtin says that words or utterances are all connected to the words and utterances that came before them, as well as those that will follow. Clearly, this applies to my performance—as the only African American in the class, my role playing was steeped in knowledge of white people in the past creating and controlling the role of Black folks. But it was also connected to my present and future desires to be creative, interesting, and informative.

Controlling role and role playing is important because the role of one group or individual is always shaped by the role of another. Many children spend more time deliberating on who can be what role, than they do actually engaging in the role that they've either selected or been stuck with. How can a good guy be good, if there is no bad guy for him to overcome? How can white be known to be light without something darker to compare it to? So the attempt to control a role or societal position requires that one define and shape the role of others around them.

Today I see many white liberal people mandate, for Black people, roles different from Jim Crow ones. For example, some of our classmates were uncomfortable and upset that we chose to use this word—even though it was a class about race and language. Furthermore, I've had many conversations in which white people express anger, confusion, and resentment toward the fact that Black people still use the "n" utterance. In order to feel not guilty about America's racial past and present, some white people have created and defined Black America's societal role as "friend." Using the "n" word violates the boundaries of the Black person in the racially uncharged friend role. I think this accounts for a lot of the resistance from my peers to my role playing.

I have used the phrase "role playing"—in terms of acting out—very similarly to the way that I have used the phrase "role playing"—in terms of the roles we live out or are expected to live out every day. That's because I'm suggesting that these terms are not very separate or different, but rather that they're very similar cousin-like ideas existing close together on one continuum. The roles that we take on in real life are often the roles that we take on even when we "play."

Susan: When our presentation began, the class, having enjoyed two very light-hearted and entertaining presentations, was ready to laugh and "play along." The group, too, anticipated laughter as it entertained the class with exaggerated characters and the ridiculous setting of the Utterance Permission Office. However, the atmosphere of the class and the audience response was transformed instantly when the "n" word was stated. Mark, who had held the overhead projector and sang like Eleanor Roosevelt in an earlier performance, recalled:

> I found myself becoming more and more engaged, laughing as the officer and the South Dakotan bantered back and forth until the officer asked the South Dakotan what word he wanted to apply to use. The moment the word "nigger" was uttered, the entire feel of the room changed. It was like nothing I had ever experienced in the classroom. Suddenly, there was this serious, contemplative feeling in the room. I don't even remember looking at another student in the classroom, but I was positive everyone collectively created this serious feeling. No longer was there playfulness in the air.

This impression was similar to Mary's, whose group had explored her son's appropriations of Harry Potter discourse:

> Everyone was having a great time, and then . . . the utterance. It felt like everything just froze up. The once jovial mood of the class vanished in a split second. I think my jaw dropped. I was actually kind of upset with this group for "ruining" the festive mood of the evening.

Cassie, who was a member of the judging/questioning group, recounted:

> During the last presentation, the atmosphere in the class instantly changed. It became serious and charged with unstated—questions? Un-comfort? I remember watching this presentation and getting nervous, but I did not know why.

Even though this was a course on race and language, which puts the word "nigger" immediately in the crux, students clearly were not prepared for its use in this setting.

There had been many permissions already given that evening that normally aren't granted in the graduate classroom. Certainly, the permission to play had been granted, and the permission to use humor. Tim stated later that he "wanted to break the frame of the class" with the Bakhtin assignment. Permission had been given not to know everything about Bakhtin and to learn from each other. Permission was granted, even, to be less than polite and to play at being overt about judging others.

However, the use of the "n" word was clearly a transgression. Cassie thought that:

> The word "nigger" was loaded for me with history, guilt, and negative connotations. I do not think the class knew how to initially respond to the skit—it covered unmarked and unclear territory. And as a member of the judging group, how could I judge the skit? I remember feeling not "qualified" to extend my judgment.

Students were expected to make immediate and public responses to this transgression, responses that very well may have defined their roles in the class for the rest of the term. What if, instead, the instructor had given an assignment like "Explore the use of the word 'nigger' in the American Literature class and write a one-page, double-spaced summary of your thoughts on this topic"? Students would have been able to read and think at home—to find out what experts had to say, think about new ideas, and formulate a response. They would have been able not only to spend extended time on a response, but they could think about how much of it they would have felt comfortable sharing and how their responses might have positioned them with the rest of the class. Such an approach would offer some protection from shock and discomfort, or at least allow people to experience shock and discomfort individually, process it, and bring it to class in a nice neat package.

This activity brought the audience to a place where they had to deal with these important ideas whether they wanted to or not. And they didn't have access to much of the previous conversation that had led to our group's decision and performance. The audience members didn't know that our group had discussed other possible words, but couldn't come up with one that illustrated Bakhtin's points about language as effectively, particularly when the class was interested in how Bakhtin, race, and language intersected. They didn't know that it really wasn't the point of the skit to shock people. Our group felt that it had some very important quotes and big ideas from Bakhtin, and the point of the assignment was, after all, to "show off your Bakhtin."

The audience didn't know that this particular presentation was based on a conversation that had taken place between Rebecca and her seven-year-old son (who, as it turned out, had come to class with Rebecca that night). Mary stated that

> I still kept an eye on Rebecca's son because I guess you have this protective part of you that wants to shield children from all that is ugly and horrible in the world—stuff like this. I also got the impression from Rebecca that she wasn't all that comfortable with it either.
>
> Mark worried about whether Rebecca actually wanted to do this:
>
> I grew considerably uncomfortable for a few reasons. Here was an African-American woman actively involved in a group that was using the word nigger to demonstrate their point(s) about utterances. Whose idea was this? Was Rebecca in favor of this idea? She was in favor of it enough to allow the group to proceed. Was she even a little uncomfortable with the idea?

The group members, on the other hand, had access to that subtext (even if, as Nathan demonstrated earlier, there are always more subtexts). We also had more processing time—the element of surprise had been removed for us. The members of our group—or at least the white members of the group—may have also been able to distance ourselves from the word because we could respond to the word as characters—the harried bureaucrat or the civil libertarian. Ironically, then, those closest to the presentation—the group members—perhaps had the most opportunity to distance themselves from the word in this particular activity.

However, responses from both group and audience members indicated that, in this case, the lack of distance from the word brought people to realizations that they may not have come to otherwise. Cassie wrote that she was "grateful for the uncomfortableness I felt after the skit both as an observer and questioner. They were growing experiences for me." Chiara, in one of the texts she wrote as part of our group's attempts to make sense of our performance, said that "I was worried that I had somehow managed to behave as a typical, insensitive WHITE person—saying/doing something that was seen by others as completely inappropriate but not knowing what it was." The intense engagement that students reported in this task may have helped them realize more about their unprocessed feelings about race and language than a more "distanced" and "processed" activity would have. Nathan noted that "one of the odd ironies is that while we have all sorts of 'rules' about who can say this, the only way to find out if you've met them is to say it."

Did our attempt to suspend these rules and bring the word to immediacy in the classroom succeed? If success is defined by new realizations and personal connections, it may have. We also thought that our performance would be light and funny, even if pursuing important things—but perhaps this was expecting too much. The air leaked out of the room when the word hung there. The "n" word stole the show.

Chiara: It did. But it is worth exploring more if our presentation and the larger contest activity succeeded, if they "worked."

If we evaluate that night's activity in terms of traditional classroom goals, then I would have to say that yes, it worked. There is no doubt that people in this class worked with the Bakhtinian texts, applied what they had read, and came away with a pretty good idea of how the ideas in the text might apply to life.

This activity led to a much deeper engagement with the reading than do most other in-class assignments. Tim had started the semester by stressing the importance of reading the assigned readings closely. He noted that his reading assignments were relatively brief because he wanted us to spend our time trying to understand and think about the readings. We could have disregarded these instructions, but Tim added on the assignment to bring to class a written account of an example of language-in-use. Thus, most students came to class ready to discuss and work with Bakhtin's ideas.

It was the contest, however, that really enabled us to pull together Bakhtin's ideas. We had approximately 30 minutes to decide upon and prepare our skit. Working under time pressure as well as the pressure to provide an intelligible skit, we had to extract core ideas from the readings and apply them coherently. The fact that all three groups were able to pull together excellent skits is an illustration of how engaged all of the students were with difficult Bakhtinian concepts.

But I think we were all most impressed that a different kind of learning seemed to be happening that night. When we talked about this activity, one of the themes that we kept returning to was the idea that we all felt we were taking a risk when we decided to do this skit. Everyone in the class took a risk by standing up in front of their peers and exposing their interpretations of Bakhtin to scrutiny. But we took on an additional risk when we decided to use the word "nigger" in our skit. We weren't sure what kind of classroom and social taboos we might be breaking, and we couldn't predict how our audience might react. We were out on a limb.

Although our audience's immediate reaction was the kind of stunned silence that any performer dreads, it is clear that the risk we took was a positive one in the end. Members of our audience later reported to us that even though the skit had initially shaken them, it provoked them to think about this word and race in new ways. And they reported that that new thinking continued for some time after the class was over. Any project that encourages students to think about new ideas in new ways, and encourages them to continue thinking about those new ideas, must be, by definition, a powerful learning experience.

At a basic level, education is not possible without risk-taking. To learn anything, the learner must risk trying something she hasn't tried before and must risk exposing what she doesn't know. Taking such risks expands the student's sense of the world. Yet, many classrooms are full of students who are loathe to take such risks.

In our group, we took risks when we agreed to perform, when we exposed our specific interpretation of Bakhtin to scrutiny by our peers, and when we decided to make Rebecca's "niggah" example the focus of our skit. Other, less risky, words might have been used, but none would have worked as well. Thus, we chose to take a risk and use this word, even though we felt that it might be controversial to do so. It was the specific classroom atmosphere that had been established by Tim along with the "anything goes" feel of the contest that enabled us to take that risk.

And taking that risk paid off for us. Using that word in our skit took us into unchartered territory, where we and our classmates were forced to confront our ideas and feelings about race.

So . . . Once upon a time—

Rebecca: In a certain time and in a certain place existed a girl who was fashioned much like a mermaid. The bottom portion of her being was scaled and shaped like the tail of a giant fish, while her upper body possessed human-like characteristics—a head, arms, and shoulders.

This girl resided in a giant glass bowl. The bowl's environment was womb-like—filled with warm comforting water that allowed her to move freely and swim with ease. She could flip her tail left or right and move with speed and precision. And although other individuals like herself also existed in the enormous glass bowl, the girl would often swim up to the top of this world and perch herself at the ridge of the bowl. Her arms draped down the side of the bowl, the way a swimmer's arms hang over the side of a floating intertube.

She enjoyed this activity because outside of the bowl existed other beings who were very different from the beings in the world of her water bowl. They had no tail and in their world there was no water. The girl in the bowl found the beings outside the bowl interesting and as she popped her head above the surface and hung her arms over the top edge of the bowl, she would talk with the beings outside of the fish bowl.

And the beings outside of the bowl found the girl very interesting.

The girl became friendly with some of these beings and she learned many of their ways. She learned the conversation patterns, facial expressions, and hand gestures that the beings outside the bowl considered appropriate. The girl had many lively and interesting discussions with these beings. When she felt angry or disheartened or full of the fatigue that naturally comes from being in a constant outsider position, she would retreat back to her warm, water fish bowl world; to her own world where she didn't concern herself with the facial expressions and hand gestures of the beings that lived outside of the bowl. Instead she swam freely with movements and freedom too natural to capture with expression.

One day as the girl was visiting the beings that lived outside the bowl, something unusual happened. One of the beings suggested that she come out of the bowl. Naturally, the girl resisted—come out—all the way out of the bowl? Certainly, she was not afraid of the world outside the bowl. She had draped her arms and talked freely in that world many times, yet the thought of bringing all herself to that world was foreign to her; almost unimaginable. But the being outside the fish bowl quickly pulled out a long scroll and began reciting several persuasive arguments as to why she could come out of the bowl.

The idea flashed through the girl's mind. Her gut was reluctant, but her head, shoulders and arms envisioned the success and benefits of jumping out of the bowl. And after all she liked the beings more than she didn't.

So, like a child on the count of three she impulsively jumped out of the bowl. For the first time all of her being became exposed to the chilling air. With the beings that lived outside the bowl looking on, she tried to move her tail to the left and then to the right, but without the water she was cold and cumbersome. The shock of the moment pulled her inside of herself and caused each moment to unfold slowly and deliberately. She looked upon the faces of the beings that lived outside the bowl, but could gather up no meaning. She imagined that her fellow beings from inside the bowl were looking upon her with confusion, dismay, or even laughter.

Outside the bowl, the girl shivered. Although she was moving, her movements felt still. She went through the motions of movements she'd done effortlessly millions of times. But without the water the motions weren't the same.

And then the moment was over and the girl splashed back into her bowl. Through the glass bowl she could see that the beings outside the bowl were clapping, cheering, and praising her performance. She wondered if they were just being polite.

Today the girl is still swimming in the bowl, inspecting her tail and scales, trying to make personal sense of her moment outside the bowl.

A short pause followed Rebecca's story, and then the audience clapped politely. The auditorium was not well lit, but Tim saw a hand raised toward the back and gestured for the person to speak.

Questioner: Thank you for your presentation, but I'm troubled by the story at the end. It uses an old trope based on a model of human agency that's mired in Enlightenment individualism. This is not good, not good antiracist practice.

The players exchanged glances. They had received a similar comment from a white male professor at a previous performance and on that occasion, Nathan had first responded that the comment seemed to ignore everything else said by Rebecca and the rest. When the professor persisted, arguing that the story made it seem as if the outside could not be changed, so that the individual would just always have to choose to move out of the bowl or not, Rebecca had finally stood and spoken. The other players could tell she was angry, but in a controlled voice she reported that even though it was an allegory, the story was very much an attempt to express and make sense of her personal experiences with moving into and speaking in white-dominated spaces. She added that she was used to other people telling her what her experiences were supposed to be and mean.

This time, Nathan and the others remained silent. Eventually, Nathan and Chiara and Susan and Tim all ended up looking at Rebecca. Two times, Rebecca leaned forward as if, on the count of three, she might jump out into the dispute. Then she leaned back in her chair. Finally, she smiled at each of the other players, in turn, and shrugged.

The curtain closes.

References

Bakhtin, M. (1981). *The dialogic imagination.* Austin, TX: University of Texas.

Bakhtin, M. (1984). *Rabelais and his world.* Bloomington, IN: Indiana University.

Bakhtin, M. (1986). *Speech genres and other late essays.* Austin, TX: University of Texas.

Boskin, J. (1986). *Sambo: The rise and demise of an American jester.* New York: Oxford University Press.

Brown, S. (1933). Negro character as seen by white authors. *The Journal of Negro Education, 2*(2), 179–203.

Collins, P. H. (1991). *Black feminist thought: Knowledge, consciousness, and the politics of empowerment.* New York: Routledge.

Delgado, R. & Stefancic, J. (Eds.) (1997). *Critical white studies: Looking behind the mirror.* Philadelphia: Temple University Press.

Du Bois, W. E. B. (1997). *The souls of black folk.* Boston: Bedford Books. (Original work published 1903)

Ellison, R. (1995). *Shadow and act.* New York: Vintage International. (Original work published 1953)

Freud, S. (1959). *Group psychology and the analysis of the ego.* New York: W. W. Norton & Co. (Original work in English published 1922)

hooks, b. (1992). *Black looks: Race and representation.* Boston: South End.

Jones, L. (1963). *Blues people: Negro music in white America.* New York: William Morrow & Company.
Kelley, R. (1997). *Yo' mama's disfunktional: Fighting the culture wars in urban America.* Boston: Beacon Press.
Watkins, W. (2001). *The white architects of black education: Ideology and power in America, 1865–1954.* New York: Teachers College Press.

Appendix: The First (and probably last) SHOW OFF YOUR BAKHTIN Contest

in which you dazzle your friends and best your enemies by making believe that you understand Bakhtin and can apply his ideas to that which you apply them. To be pursued in four groups. In three stages. No prizes for winning, except that satisfaction that comes when there are no other rewards and you are desperate to feel that it was worth it anyway.

Stage One—Preparations

The three competing groups: You will have 25 minutes (no more) to prepare a five minute presentation/performance. Review the short papers you wrote for class. Choose one or two examples/samples of language-in-use from these papers to work with. Develop a deep, profound, exhaustive, bordering-on-ridiculous reading/interpretation of your example(s), drawing on everything you know from Bakhtin's "Discourse in the novel" and "The problem of speech genres." Your presentation/performance should please us by teaching us about Bakhtin's work and by providing insight into our uses of language, and, by golly, even insight into what it means to be human. Make sure to include, in your presentation/performance, at least one original couplet that rhymes.

The judging-questioners group: You will have 25 minutes (no more) to prepare a list of seven or eight questions (about Bakhtin's work and the use of his ideas) that you will ask of the three competing groups (do you like my frequent use of parentheses so far?). Review and share the short papers you wrote for class. As you read, make snide almost-audible comments to the effect that your own examples and analyses are most certainly superior to anything you are going to see from the competing groups, but, that's the way it goes when you are smarter than everyone else—you'll do your best to help others learn what they can, as little as it is. Develop your list of questions, wording them in a way that is clear to you but that will probably confuse and embarrass the competing groups when they first hear them. In the end, the questions should be sincere questions that you have about Bakhtin, questions you would like to hear someone intelligent respond to (you understand

and are resigned to the fact that this is not going to happen when you ask these questions of these groups).

Stage Two—Presentations/Performances

The three competing groups will present/perform, one after the other. The judging-questioners group will take notes and look haughty. The competing groups not in front will also take notes (said notes occasionally illustrated with silly drawings).

Stage Three—The Questioning and Judging

After a brief period in which the judging-questioners group chuckles and decides which specific questions it wants to ask each group, the competing groups will be asked questions, in turn. Competing groups will be given the opportunity to ask questions. After which, the judging-questioners group will again chuckle and share their evaluations of the presentations/performances and question-answering—ultimately declaring their own group the best. A tussle ensues.

Epilogue

Frankie Condon and Vershawn Ashanti Young

> *An analysis of F.B.I. data from 2010 to 2012 concluded that the police killed black men ages 15 to 19 at a rate 21 times greater than the statistic for white men the same age. Department of Justice numbers indicate that a black person is about four times as likely to die in custody or while being arrested than a white person is.*
>
> —Olevia Boykin, Christopher Desir and Jed Rubenfeld
> http://www.nytimes.com/2016/01/01/opinion/a-better-standard-for-the-use-of-deadly-force.html?smid=fb-share&_r=2

We speak their names (hear our voices) and honor their lives:

Tanisha Anderson
Sandra Bland
Rumain Brisbon
Michael Brown
John Crawford III
Jordon Davis
Amadou Diallo
Ezell Ford
Freddie Grey
Akai Gurley
Eric Garner
Dontre Hamilton
Eric Harris
Trayvon Martin
Donte Parker
Jerame Ried
Tamir Rice
Tony Robinson
Walter Scott
Phillip White

You too know who they are—Black individuals killed in encounters with mostly white police officers or vigilantes. We begin our last word in this book with their names because they can no longer speak, their voices taken. While there is contention that these victims were not murdered, that they must have done something that lead to their deaths, this contention depends upon the very racial logic to which we call attention—a lens that dysconsciously reproduces as it justifies the racial thinking that conditions the lived experiences of people of color, including our students. These are the very conditions that we argue we all need to see, hear, recognize, and acknowledge. It is this terrible lens—notoriously distorting our perception of ourselves, our histories, our relations—that must be torn away, dismantled, and destroyed if we are ever to realize justice, racial justice.

> We claim outright that racism is a murderous and a soul-destroying force not only in the streets, but in our classrooms, and in our revered institutions. True, our main concern in this book is antiracist activism in academic institutions and in courses associated with communication, rhetoric, and writing. But we need look no further than to the insidious trend of the Academy of Motion Picture Arts, known best for the Oscar Awards, to routinely self-justify its fierce promotion of whites, whiteness, and whiteliness, to the exclusion of peoples of color. For instance, the Academy has for many years unflinchingly unveiled an all-white slate of nominees. And in 2016, when the Black president of the Academy announced that it would increase its diversity efforts, the *New York Times* reports that the backlash was swift, shifting blame and hiding behind inanities: "The most common cri de Coeur: The changes were ageist (a possibility) and insulting to Blacks (if there's a Black academy member out there who agrees, please do get in touch). Another: 'I'm liberal, so I can't be racist,' a tautological cry that largely misses the point." (Buckly, n.p.) http://www.nytimes.com/2016/01/28/movies/the-oscars-and-race-a-stir-over-rules-to-change-the-academy.html?emc=edit_th_20160128&nl=todaysheadlines&nlid=70223966&_r=0.

The Academy's dilemma and its members' outcry against antiracist activism illustrates that institutional and everyday racism, especially in its most dysconscious forms, poisons relations between whites and people of color; it poisons our nations. So we offer our list of names above in order to remember, acknowledge and act—and we want you also to remember, acknowledge and act on behalf of those who have lost their lives as a result of white supremacist ideology. Act on behalf of those who stand together to eliminate that ideology.

We have listed a few of the more well-known victims of state-sponsored racism, but please know that these names stand in for a terrifyingly longer list: the thousands of unarmed Black men, women, and children killed by police year after year, day after day, hour after hour even as too many of us tsk tsk tsk, then return to stasis. (Mapping, n.p., http://mappingpoliceviolence.org/unarmed/; Hudson, n.p., http://www.occupy.com/article/black-man-killed-us-every-28-hours-police)

Because of the men, women, and children whose names compose these lists, and because of our own everyday experience, we are compelled to discuss, and compelled to ask you to discuss racism openly, honestly, and courageously—compelled to wake ourselves to the reality not only of the United States, but also of Canada (where we both are currently located), the European Union—all nations and regions where white supremacy continues to thrive and in thriving to shape the lived experiences (and deaths) of peoples of color. We are compelled to join and spur change that is afoot, like that noted in the New York Times article, from which our epigraph is taken, calling for different standards of policing, precisely because current standards disproportionately and negatively impact Black people.

Some—perhaps too many—may disaggregate and isolate "racial incidents," may count the numbers of those Black Americans murdered by police, for example, one by one, but the totality of white supremacy as a primary influence in both repressive and ideological state apparatuses globally refuses to be so contained.

We note with sadness, but with a still glowing hot ember of hope, that since we wrote the introduction at the start of this project (back in 2011), the dismantling of racism has become a project that some—but not enough—of our colleagues have taken up with collective discipline and dedication. In contrast, students in the U.S., Canada, and around the world show us the way, and engage antiracist activism with stunning success. Consider a few examples of what has recently taken place on the campuses where students have organized protests, demanding greater inclusion and access.

- Amherst College—hundreds of students held sit-ins to protest racial injustice on campus.
- Claremont McKenna College—student leaders demanded the firing of a high-ranked administrator considered insensitive to minorities and received promises of a more diverse faculty and staff.
- Occidental College—students occupied an administrative building on the campus, calling for President Jonathan Veitch's resignation.
- University of Missouri—members of the football team, students and faculty groups demanded that President Tim Wolfe step down because of inadequate response to racial incidents.
- University of Kansas in Lawrence—students presented university administration with a list of demands to improve campus diversity.

- Yale University—students and faculty protested discrimination. President Peter Salovey announced plans to support minority students on campus, including the establishment of an academic center for race and social identity and an increase in diverse hiring.

While we recognize the work of our colleagues across the disciplines who are active antiracist campaigners on and beyond their campuses, can we truly say that our efforts match those of our students? Have our actionable commitments kept pace? Students are modeling for us the work of antiracist activism, public intellectualism, intellectual activism, policy revision, and changes in everyday teaching and learning. Student organizations across North America are building coalitions to rise up and speak out: in the United States, the Black Liberation Collective, La Rasa, Students for the Dream, and in Canada, the Canadian Federation of Students.

Should we not answer the call of our students, to work with as well as for them? Can we be convinced to place our pens, mouths, and bodies in solidarity with them as did some 1300 Black professors across the nation in "An Open Letter of Love to Black Students?: #BlackLivesMatter" (Black Space Blog, n.p., http://blackspaceblog.com/2014/12/08/an-open-letter-of-love-to-black-students-blacklivesmatter/).

Our students' activism is predicated on their recognition and critique of the social problems they perceive outside their universities. But our students also recognize the relationship between that injustice and what they experience on their campuses. Our students understand that they are not immune to the visceral as well as implicit dangers of racism within their institutions.

We call on our readers and our disciplines to join with students in a multiracial antiracist struggle for justice. Let us demand of ourselves and encourage one another to do more than mouth our commitments: to make our actions match our words; to transform our classrooms, our departments, and our institutions as well as our communities; and to learn from one another as allies who possess the courage to effect change.

Works Cited

Black Space Blog. (December 8, 2015). An open letter of love to Black students/ #BlackLivesMatter. Retrieved from http://blackspaceblog.com/2014/12/08/an-open-letter-of-love-to-black-students-blacklivesmatter/.

Boykin, O. & C. Desir, J. Rubenfeld. (January 1, 2016). A better standard for the use of deadly force. *New York Times*. Retrieved from http://www.nytimes.com/2016/01/01/opinion/a-better-standard-for-the-use-of-deadly-force.html?smid=fb-share&_r=2.

Buckly, C. (January 27, 2016). The Oscars and race: A stir over rules to change the Academy. *New York Times*. Retrieved from http://www.nytimes.com/2016/01/28/movies/the-oscars-and-race-a-stir-over-rules-to-change-the-academy.html?emc=edit_th_20160128&nl=todaysheadlines&nlid=70223966&_r=0.

Hudson, A. (May 31, 2013). A Black man is killed in the U.S. every 28 hours by police. *Occupy.com*. http://www.occupy.com/article/black-man-killed-us-every-28-hours-police.

Livingston, K. J. (September 17, 2012). Study says a Black person killed by police every 36 hours. *The Louisiana Weekly*. Retrieved from http://www.louisianaweekly.com/study-says-a-black-person-killed-by-police-every-36-hours/.

Mapping Police Violence. (December 31, 2015). Police killed more than 100 unarmed Black people in 2015. Retrieved from http://mappingpoliceviolence.org/unarmed/.

Contributors

Chiara Bacigalupa is Professor of Early Childhood Studies at Sonoma State University. Dr. Bacigalupa's focus in recent years has been on working with her community to increase opportunities for early childhood professionals to earn advanced degrees. Her research and thinking has spanned different aspects of early childhood education, but her general orientation is to contribute to social justice efforts through helping increase our understanding of what children, families, and the professionals who work with them need most.

Sophie Bell is Associate Professor at St. John's University's Institute for Writing Studies. She teaches a first-year writing course titled "Race, Language, Writing, and Activism." Her scholarship looks at the intersections among American literature, education, race, and culture in nineteenth-century and contemporary contexts. She has published essays in *Studies in American Fiction*, the volume *The Children's Table: Childhood Studies and the Humanities*, and *Radical Teacher*. Her current project looks at her students' use of writing to increase their cultural competence in diverse classrooms.

Susan Leigh Brooks is Professor of English at Bethel University in St. Paul, Minnesota and completed her Ph.D. in Curriculum and Instruction/Literacy Education at the University of Minnesota-Twin Cities. The power of language fascinates her, and she is especially interested in exploring how literacy makes a difference for her preservice teachers and their students.

Frankie Condon is Associate Professor in the Department of English Language and Literature at the University of Waterloo in Ontario, Canada. Frankie's books include *I Hope I Join the Band: Narrative, Affiliation and Antiracist Rhetoric* and *The Everyday Writing Center: A Community of Practice* (both published by Utah State University Press). She is currently completing research for her next book, *Absolute Equality: The Radical Precedents of Post-Racial Rhetorics in the 21st Century.* This work is funded by a grant from the Social Sciences and Humanities Research Council of Canada. Frankie's articles have appeared in such journals as *College Teaching, Writing Center Journal*, and *Praxis*. In addition to her work as a teacher, scholar, and writer, Frankie frequently consults with secondary and postsecondary schools in the area of cultural competence and antiracism. She serves as an antiracism trainer and provides support for institutions seeking to develop antiracist leadership from within.

John Dean is an Adjunct Faculty Member in the Department of English at Chandler-Gilbert Community College. He graduated with his MFA from Texas State University.

Rasha Diab is Associate Professor of Rhetoric and Writing at The University of Texas at Austin. Her work focuses on the rhetoric of peacemaking and rights, comparative rhetoric, and the history of rhetoric. She has recently published a book on reconciliation titled *The Shades of Sulh: The Rhetorics of Arab-Islamic Reconciliation*. Together, with Thomas Ferrel and Beth Godbee, she has been exploring how to make commitments to racial and social justice actionable (with special attention to the role of affiliation)—the project on which this chapter and previous articles in Praxis and Across the Disciplines are based.

Thomas Ferrel is Director of the Writing Studio, Lecturer, and a Ph.D. candidate at the University of Missouri-Kansas City and is a Co-Director of the Greater Kansas City Writing Project. Thomas has published in *Composition Forum, Praxis, Across the Disciplines*, and the NWP's Projects in Action series. His research focuses on critical pedagogy in relation to institutional social justice work and writing center studies. His current projects explore how teachers carry commitments to equity and principles from their classroom pedagogy into service work for their departments, home institutions, local communities, and professional disciplines.

Beth Godbee is Assistant Professor of English at Marquette University in Milwaukee, Wisconsin. She studies how more equitable relations can arise in collaborative writing talk, which includes attention to power, relationship-building, and epistemic rights and injustice. This study highlights writing in a range of settings, including among graduate writers and in community literacy programs. Among her publications are pieces in *Research in the Teaching of English, Community Literacy Journal, Feminist Teacher, Writing Center Journal*, and the edited collections *Writing Centers and the New Racism* and *Stories of Mentoring*.

Dae-Joong Kim is Assistant Professor of English Education at Kangwon National University in South Korea. His research considers critical theory, teaching literature to English-language learner, contemporary American fiction, etc. His recent research topics include passing in the context of bio-politics in contemporary American fiction, ethico-ontological pedagogy, and post-diaspora literature. His work has appeared in various literary journals and English education journals.

Asao B. Inoue is Associate Professor of Interdisciplinary Arts and Sciences, Director of University Writing and the Writing Center, a member of the Executive Board of CWPA, and the Assistant Chair to CCCC. Among his various articles and chapters on writing assessment and race and racism studies, his article, "Theorizing Failure in U.S. Writing Assessments" in *RTE*, won the 2014 CWPA Outstanding Scholarship Award. His co-edited collection, *Race and Writing Assessment* (2012), won the 2014 CCCC Outstanding Book Award for an edited collection. More recently, his book, *Antiracist Writing Assessment Ecologies: Teaching and Assessing for a Socially Just Future* (2015) was published by WAC Clearinghouse and Parlor Press. He has guest co-edited a special issue of *College English* on writing assessment as social justice, coming out in the fall of 2016, and is currently finishing a co-edited collection on the same topic.

Timothy J. Lensmire is Associate Professor in the Department of Curriculum and Instruction, University of Minnesota, where he teaches courses in literacy, critical pedagogy, and race. His early work focused on how the teaching of writing might contribute to education for radical democracy. His current research seeks to build descriptions of, and theoretical insights about, white racial identities, as part of a larger effort to figure out better ways to work with white students and teachers on issues of race and social justice.

Calvin M. Logue is Josiah Meigs Professor Emeritus of Communication Studies at the University of Georgia (U.S.A.). He received the Ph.D. in the history and criticism of public address from Louisiana State University in 1967. He has written on initiatives of African Americans under slavery, during reconstruction, and "after freedom." The University of Georgia Research Foundation awarded Logue the Creative Research Medal for criticism of southern discourse.

Aja Y. Martinez is Assistant Professor of Writing Studies, Rhetoric, and Composition at Syracuse University. Her scholarship, published both nationally and internationally, focuses on the rhetorics of racism and its effects on marginalized peoples in institutional spaces. Her efforts as teacher-scholar strive towards increasing access, retention and participation of diverse groups in higher education.

Deatra Sullivan-Morgan is Associate Professor in the Department of Communication Arts and Sciences at Elmhurst College, Elmhurst, IL. Her research interests include the rhetorical coping strategies of marginalized communities and the subsequent identity building process. She teaches a variety of Communication classes including Interpersonal Communication, Intercultural Communication, Media Influences and Cultural Identity and Language, Identity and the Rainbow.

Rebecca Nathan is an educator and instructional designer with a focus on sharing culturally relevant research and programming with historically marginalized groups and communities. Within this work, Rebecca has developed a lens for understanding the ways in which educational systems impact children and families and often supports them in mitigating the adverse impact of such systems. Her publications include the creation of empowering spaces ripe with honest dialog, illustrious pages in adult coloring books and meaningful interruptions in oppressive systems.

Bobbi Olson is Assistant Professor of English and Director of the Writing Center at Grand View University in Des Moines, Iowa. Her research considers the politics of language teaching in both writing center and classroom contexts, and her work has appeared in *Praxis: A Writing Center Journal, Across the Disciplines*, and the edited collection *Tutoring Second Language Writers.*

Jessica Parker is Associate Professor of English at Metropolitan State University of Denver, where she directs the First Year Writing Program. Her areas of specialty include African-American literature, American literature, and hip hop studies. Her work with hip hop involves examinations of race, class, and gender, and their intersections in identity creation for emcees and hip hop fans. Her current work in MSU Denver's First Year Writing Program focuses on implementing a program-wide translingual approach and on the continued growth of alternatives to remediation in order to close the equity gap.

Charise Pimentel is Associate Professor at Texas State University in the Department of Curriculum & Instruction within the College of Education, where her areas of specialty are in race and education, bilingual education, multicultural education, and critical media literacy. The courses she teaches include such titles as, Multicultural Teaching and Learning, The Politics of Language, Bilingual Education Principles and Practices, and Literacy Education for Culturally and Linguistically Diverse Children. She has published widely in top, peer-reviewed journals and has contributed several book chapters to edited books. Her most recent work is an edited book, *From Uncle Tom's Cabin to The Help: Critical Perspectives on White Authored Narratives of Black Life.* Dr. Pimentel has been recognized for excellence in the areas of teaching and scholarship, receiving the Presidential Distinction Award for Excellence in Teaching and in Scholarly, Creative Activities. She has also been recognized with publication honors such as "Most Cited," "Most Read," "Top Article," and "Featured Article" designations as well as a nomination for the NCTE award for Best Article Reporting Historical Research or Textual Studies in technical and Scientific Writing.

Octavio Pimentel is Professor in the Masters in Rhetoric and Composition Program housed in the Department of English at Texas State University. Critically trained in rhetoric, writing, and education, Dr. Pimentel has published extensively in these fields, specifically addressing critical issues of minoritized individuals in the composition and rhetoric field. His publications include two books: *Historias de Éxito within Mexican Communities: Silenced Voices* (Palgrave Macmillan, 2015) and *Communicating Race, Ethnicity, and Identity in Technical Communication*—with Dr. Miriam F. Williams—(Baywood Press, 2014), *which* won the 2016 Technical and Scientific Communication Award for Best Original Collection of Essays in Technical or Scientific Communication. Along with Dr. Cruz Medina, Dr. Pimentel is working on his third book, *Racial Shorthand: Coded Discrimination Contested in Social Media.* Additionally, Dr. Pimentel has published nearly 20 academic journal articles as well as presented in over 50 national and international conferences. Dr. Pimentel currently serves on the Editorial Board for the *College Composition and Communication Journal* as well as a CCCC Executive Committee Member.

Mya Poe is Assistant Professor of English at Northeastern University. Her research interest focuses on how people become better writers and what we mean by "better" writing. She is especially interested in what the answers to those questions mean for culturally and linguistically diverse students. She has co-authored *Learning to Communicate in Science and Engineering: Case Studies from MIT*, which won the CCCC 2012 Advancement of Knowledge Award, and co-edited *Race* *and Writing Assessment*, which won the 2014 CCCC Outstanding Book of the Year. She also has guest-edited a special issue of *Research in the Teaching of English* on writing assessment and diversity and is guest-editing a forthcoming special issue of *College English* on writing assessment and social justice. In addition to being a series co-editor of the new Oxford Brief Guides to Writing in the Disciplines, she has two books under contract—a monograph entitled *Intended Consequences: What Students and Statistics Can tell Us About Writing Assessment* and a co-edited collection entitled *Writing Assessment and Social Justice*. Her articles have been published in *College Composition and Communication, The Journal of Writing Assessment*, and *The Journal of Business and Technical Communication.*

Nathan Snaza teaches modern English literature, educational foundations, and contemporary cultural theory at the University of Richmond. He is the co-editor of *Pedagogical Matters: New Materialisms and Curriculum Studies* (Peter Lang, 2016) and *Posthumanism and Educational Research* (Routledge, 2014). His essays have appeared in journals such as *Journal of Curriculum and Pedagogy, Journal of Curriculum Theorizing, Educational Philosophy and Theory, Educational Researcher, Symploke, Angelaki, Journal for Critical Animal Studies*, and *Critical Literacies: Theories and Practices.*

Vershawn Ashanti Young is a member of the faculty of arts at the University of Waterloo, Canada. He has also served on the faculties of the University of Iowa and the University of Kentucky. He teaches communication, English, and performance studies. He serves as a consultant to schools and organizations in the areas of cultural competency and diversity. He values collaboration and has authored or co-authored several books, including *Other People's English: Code Meshing, Code Switching, and African American Literacy* (Teachers College Press 2014). His articles have appeared in *African American Review, American Literary History, PMLA, College Communication and Composition, Journal of Advanced Composition* and *Souls*. For the past decade, he has been developing the concept of code-meshing, using multiple Englishes and dialects in formal written and oral communication in school and at work. For more on code-meshing and Vershawn, see http://dr-vay2014.wix.com/vershawn-young.